Also by Mic

Afterwards Our
a comic h

Bodies fo.
20 weird ꞇales

As editor

Tales of the Scorpion,
a 1ˢᵗ anthology by Northants Writers' Ink

While Glancing through a Window,
a 2ⁿᵈ anthology by Northants Writers' Ink

Coming soon

Speaking Man to Man,
stories about male relationships

as yet untitled,
a 3ʳᵈ anthology by Northants Writers' Ink (as editor)

to David -

Frank Peters:
his life, times and crimes

by

Michael J Richards

Published by New Generation Publishing in 2017

Copyright © Michael J Richards 2017

First Edition

www.newgeneration-publishing.com

to Sandy

Look round and round upon this bare bleak plain, and see even here, upon a winter's day, how beautiful the shadows are! Alas! it is the nature of their kind to be so. The loveliest things in life, Tom, are but shadows; and they come and go, and change and fade away, as rapidly as these!

– from Ch 12,
Martin Chuzzlewit,
Charles Dickens

Contents

Introduction

by Michael J Richards

May 2015. Maggie Allen, the Northampton-based writer, approaches me after a writers' get-together and says, "I've got a project you might be interested in. I've been offered a new ghost writing job but I'm too busy to take it on. You're the only one I would offer this to – it won't be straightforward, it's a tough story, and the client is – well, shall we say, a bit rough around the edges? It's a professional assignment. I think you can do it. Are you interested?"

Although I don't hesitate, it takes a while to get the project off the ground. I go on holiday. Someone falls ill. Frank goes on holiday. At least twice, terrible weather stops me from travelling.

October 2015. Frank Peters and I meet for the first time at his home in the South East of England.

He's a small chap, bald and wearing a permanent hangdog expression that in itself tells a story. He seems thrilled to meet me, talks non-stop in the most animated fashion for the three hours we're together. At the end of it, we know we can work together.

He accidentally lets slip that over the years he's written a diary. He's kept notes. He's collected newspaper reports of all his court hearings. He's saved photographs, postcards, official documents, all kinds of records. Invaluable for a ghost writing project like this. I am definitely interested.

I ask him why he's so keen to tell his story. He says he wants the world to know what crime is really about.

It's not, he says, about stabbings in grubby East End pubs that get made into glamorous films of cool dudes in sharp suits. Nor is it fast car chases and incompetent police. And it's never jokey heists by robbers wearing silly masks.

1

It's about mixing with people who are oddly wired, violent and ruthless. Sometimes, all three at the same time.

It's politics with muscle-bound thugs in formidable prisons. Police trying to do an impossible job in impossible circumstances and who – sometimes – bend the law to get criminals off the streets. Prison officers who don't stand a chance and have no choice but to apply rough justice in a savage, caged jungle.

It's about the survival of the fittest. And how sometimes even they come a cropper.

* * * * *

Next meeting, we sign a contract and the work begins.

For the next fourteen months, he records his story and sends it to me. Which I transcribe and try to make sense of, to find order in the chaos. As I write chapter after chapter, I develop a real empathy for Frank and the life he has led.

We meet regularly to discuss progress and issues. Sometimes, he finds it difficult to concentrate, always preferring to tell uproariously funny stories and talk about people he's known down the years, things he's done.

It's as if the past is the only thing he can relate to and he daren't let go. Even after all these years, he speaks in an underworld lingo, rhyming slang, every other word "effin' this" or "effin' that", his East End accent still as distinct as it must have been when he was a teenager.

But we get there. We always get there. Because he is tremendously likeable and, I suspect, was always so.

* * * * *

Frank Peters isn't his real name. Of course it isn't.

I have changed all names except three: Evan Phillips (the 1960s pornographer), Patrick Fraser (son of "Mad" Frankie Fraser) and Roger Insall (the *Sunday People* reporter).

2

For dramatic reasons, I have combined three characters into one. I have not invented scenes, although some are embellished for dramatic effect. I have telescoped one essential scene into two lines because it's too horrific even for this book. Two locations have been changed for dramatic convenience.

At Frank's request, one episode in his life has been left out as, even after all these years – and even though he goes under an alias in this book – he's worried the character featured will recognise himself and go after him.

In many chapters, Frank doesn't come out looking at all good. But he's relaxed about that.

"After all, Mike," he says, "it's what 'appened, ain't it? You mustn't hide the truth."

* * * * *

My thanks go to Maggie Allen for introducing me to Frank, for doing such a superb editing job, for her re-writes of my laughable attempts at Scottish brogue. Most of all, I owe her my gratitude for her unending humour, support and encouragement when the writing, at times, became difficult.

Michael J Richards
July 2017

Chapter 1. Home

It's cold, really cold, when I get in from school. Early winter's setting in, so I switch the light on. I always switch lights on and off when I go from room to room, 'cos we have to save money and, as Mum says, light costs money. Everything costs money, she says, "So remember, Frank, it's not *your* money you're wasting when you leave a light on you're not using."

She'll be home in an hour or so to make my tea, so I've got time to make up the fire and get the kettle on.

I love my mum. She works hard to give me nice meals and lovely clothes so I reckon the least I can do is make the home welcoming for when she gets in.

I go into the kitchen, take my coat off, throw it on the chair and look at the grate. I didn't have time to see to it after I got up this morning.

Mum says she'll do it but I tell her, "No, it's my job to look after the fire."

"You're such a pet," she says.

"Anything for you, Mum. You're the best."

And she is.

I fetch some newspapers and put it in front of the grate. Then I get the brush and dustpan and set to cleaning out the ashes, wrapping them up in the newspaper, and take the lot outside to the dustbin. I empty the ashes into the bin but keep the paper 'cos I can use that for the fire. I don't like wasting things.

We keep the wood with the coal in the coalhole next to the dustbin. I pick up some kindling, take it into the kitchen with the paper, get some more paper and scrunch it all up in the grate. Then I criss-cross the wood into a neat pattern on top. Take the shovel, get some coal and balance that on top of the wood. Then I light the paper and stand back. When the flames are going, I watch for a few more seconds.

Now, fill the kettle, put some PG Tips in the yellow

teapot and set out the milk, sugar, two cups, saucers and teaspoons.

That's what I do every school day. Methodical, that's me.

And before I know it, Mum's home from the glass factory, tired and ready for a cuppa. She's a good old mum, works hard she does, bless her.

"Here y'are, Mum," I say. "Give me your coat. I'll make some tea."

"Oh, thanks," she sighs, taking it off. "You're a good boy, Frank."

I hang it on the back of the door, then light the gas for the kettle.

She sits at the table. "Have you been a good boy today?"

"I'm always a good boy, Mum," I say, watching the kettle.

"Frank?"

"Well, I tried."

We sit quiet as we watch the kettle boil. I make the tea, put the pot on the table and sit down.

"Is Dad coming home on Friday?"

"I hope so, Frank," Mum says. "We've got to pay the rent this week – "

"Where does he go all week?"

"Where does he go any time?" Mum says. "Do you know, when you were born, nobody could find him to tell him he had a son."

"And where was he?"

"In the pub, I 'spect."

"That was when we lived in Wembley."

"We were always being chased for the rent then."

I pour the tea. I like to hear Mum talk about our early life.

"You know, when we lived in Wembley, we were in one room above Mr McCuthbert – "

"Who?"

"McCuthbert, Mr McCuthbert – "

I burst into giggles. "What a silly name!" I mouth the name, then say it out loud as if reciting a witch's magic spell. "Mc-Cuth-bert. Mc-Cuth-bert, Mc-Cuth-bert – "

Mum's laughing. "His first name was just as odd. Johnson. Not John or Johnny or Jonathan. Johnson."

"Johnson McCuthbert," I say, relishing the oddness. "Like someone in Dickens."

"But," she says, "he was a grumpy old man really, a nasty bit of work. Not a nice bloke at all." She takes her first sip of the tea. "And he was always chasing us for the rent. We struggled then."

"I remember," I say, wanting to say something that'll cheer her up, "being in the garden and watching the jet fighters going over above."

She chuckles. I smile. I've made her happy.

"I don't think so, love," she says. "When you were born, the war had been over nine years. There were no jet fighters then."

"I tell you," I say, "I was standing in the garden and some jet fighters flew overhead."

"Sometimes we remember things that didn't happen," she says.

I stand up, cross. Why doesn't she believe me? "I tell you, I saw some jet fighters!"

Mum drinks up her tea. "Yes, well, let's get something to eat, shall we? What would you like?"

"I saw them," I insist. "I really did!"

"Beans on toast," she says. "Build you up, that will."

* * * * *

"You were a terror even then," Mum says a couple of days later. She has this habit of carrying on conversations days later as if time hasn't passed. "We always had to keep our eyes on you. Even at that age, let's see, you couldn't've been more than three – well, couldn't leave you alone for a minute."

I smirk at her, feeling a bit proud. Pretty good.

"All we had," she says between sips of tea, "were a small kitchen and the one room. We shared the bathroom with Mr McCuthbert. Your dad, me and you ate, slept and lived in that one room. We used to keep warm round the gas-fire and we always had to have a stock of sixpences and shillings to put in the meter, otherwise you'd be screaming, 'Cold, cold, Frank is cold!'"

I'm sniggering at the thought of me, three years old, running the outfit. Some things never change.

"And you were on the bed, jumping up and down, like you loved to do. You were happy enough, so your dad and me went into the kitchen to get something or other, I don't remember what it was. And the next thing, we heard a little scream and ran in to see you laying on the floor, crying your little eyes out."

I pour Mum some more tea. She's chuckling away.

"When we'd got you comfortable and calm, Dad found that the plug on the cord hanging over the bed, you know, the one we used to switch out the light, had come undone."

"Did I do that?"

"Well," Mum says, "your Dad says you'd unscrewed the plug and you must've shoved your finger into the socket and electrocuted yourself. Sent you speeding across the room."

"Sounds right," I say, like a scientist wisely nodding after the event.

"Then there was the time when you set fire to yourself."

"What?" I say, laughing my head off, loving every minute.

"In the winter months, the only way we could get things dry was to hang them on a clothes-horse in front of the gas-fire. I'd washed the bed sheets in the bath and draped them in front of the heat. You were playing on the other side of the room, building a house with your bricks, or something like that, I don't know. So your dad and me were in the kitchen – again – we were always in the kitchen – as usual, you got up to your tricks – "

"Thought I could get away with it, I s'pose – "

"Even at that age, Frank, you thought you could get away with it. D'you know, you're going to spend the rest of your life thinking you can get away with it – "

"Mum!"

"And take it from me who's seen more than you'll ever know," she says, "you won't, you know. Sooner or later, you'll get found out. Mark my words, everyone gets found out sooner or later."

"Not me, Mum," I tell her. "Not me."

"Oh yes, Frank, you too," she says.

"The bed sheets, Mum."

"Your dad and me are in the kitchen and he says, 'Can you smell burning?' 'No,' I say. 'There's definitely burning,' he says. 'What's he up to now?'" He pops his head round the corner and there you are, standing by the fire. You'd pushed the clothes horse right up to the fire. And the sheet, it's in flames! Like a wigwam set alight by evil cowboys. 'Quick!' shouts your dad. 'I'll get the boy, you get some water!'

"He rushes in and scoops you out of harm's way. I get a basin of water, run in and throw it at the fire. Your dad does the same and we're doing that for a good quarter of an hour. And you're standing up the corner – and do you know what you're doing?"

"No," I laugh, "what was I doing?"

She looks at me. She's not laughing. "Exactly what you're doing now, Frank. Laughing your silly head off. You thought it was funny!"

"I was three, Mum," I say. "What did I know?"

* * * * *

"One day," Mum says, "well, it was late afternoon, November, dark it was. I was getting tea and your dad was reading the paper or sleeping or something, I don't know, and I suddenly realised you weren't there. 'Sid,' I said, 'where's Frank?' He said he didn't know. Couldn't've been sleeping, I s'pose, 'cos he answered straight away. He got out his chair and looked everywhere – "

I give a little giggle, thrilled to hear another story about what I was like. "Were you worried?"

"Course we were worried," she yelps. "You were only four, for heaven's sake. And Wembley wasn't like what Hertfordshire's like, even now. It was busy, there was always traffic everywhere, you could've got run over and nobody'd know who you were – or anything."

"Did you find me?"

"Well, course we found you," Mum says. "I mean, you're here, aren't you? We looked everywhere. Even got Mr McCuthbert – "

"Mr McCuthbert!"

"Yes, Frank, Mr McCuthbert," Mum says with more force than what's necessary. "He even looked with us. We were going frantic. Then your dad noticed the front door was ajar. Why it took us so long to notice that, goodness only knows. The front door went straight on to the street, you see. That was the thing. It went out on to the street. And, sure enough, there you were. On the street."

"What was I doing. Mum?"

She leans back and laughs. "You were collecting up the parking lights they put next to their cars – "

"Yeah," I say, "'cos you had to leave your car lit up – "

"Like you have to now," Mum says. "Anyway, and you were lining 'em up outside our house. There they were, little red lamps, oil burners, ordinary lamps, all standing in a row, like soldiers on parade."

By now, we're both laughing our heads off.

"Your dad wasn't best pleased, I can tell you, 'cos – "

"What did he do?"

"First of all, he picked you up and brought you in and you went straight to bed without your tea. Then he had to put the lights back by the cars. But, o' course, he didn't know which light went with which car. So he put any light against any car without any idea whether it was the right one. We didn't have a car then, of course, so it wasn't a

10

problem for us. When he came in, he swore me and Mr McCuthbert not to say a word next day. He went off early next morning, as usual. I didn't dare go out until it was light – "

"Why not?"

"Well, I didn't want to get caught up in the confusion of everyone standing there wondering what on earth had happened to their parking lights during the night, did I?"

* * * * *

"I was glad we got out of there," Mum says.

"Where?"

"Mr McCuthbert's, of course," she says, her voice going up a few notes, as if I should've known. "It wasn't right, bringing up a young boy in those surroundings. I mean – "

"Bad, was it?"

"He had a big garden behind the house," she says, "and he used to let you play there. Kind of him, I s'pose. Right at the bottom, a little stream ran by and you spent a lot of time paddling and splashing about. Anyway, one day, you were down there and I was watching you from the kitchen and I saw you pick something up and wave it around in the air – "

I pour another cup of tea. Mum's in full flow and I don't want her to stop.

"Quick as a flash," she says, nodding at the tea, "I drop everything and I'm down there in the garden – "

"Why?" I say. "What had I done this time?"

"You were swinging a dead rat around. Oh, Frank! I shudder when I think of it now." Her hand jerks up to her mouth. "Oh, it was a monster, I tell ya... And when I looked down, there was another one. Two dead rats, and you were playing with them like they were, oh, I don't know what.

"Rats!" she cries out, as if one has just run across the kitchen floor. "They were all over the place. You'd go out

11

to play with the other kids in the street and I'd catch you picking up dead rats. In the street! Oh, it was a horrible place to live, Frank. Just horrible."

I shake my shoulders too much to make sure Mum can see me shuddering.

"You fell very, very ill," she carries on, now lost in her own world. "My poor little baby. The doctors were really worried. They thought it was polio. But then they found out it was scarlet fever. We were so relieved. We thought you were going to die. It was those rats, they said. You got it off those dead rats."

* * * * *

"The first thing I can remember," I say, "is me standing on a platform somewhere and a great big train coming towards me and all the steam coming out of it."

"Oh, that must have been when we moved out of Wembley."

"When was that, Mum?"

"Oh, let's see."

She smiles, pretending to think, 'though I know she doesn't have to remember the date. I bet it's etched on her brain.

"About 1957, I think. What with one thing and another. You getting so ill and your dad not getting the work. Things were hard, Frank. Things were hard. And Mr McCuthbert, of course, he wanted his rent paid, didn't he? Only natural. After all, whatever we thought of him and Wembley and the rats, we still had to pay the rent."

"So we came here," I say.

"It seemed the natural thing to do, what with your dad's family being here already. We packed what little we had, took the tube from Wembley to Victoria Park and got the Green Line and moved in with your Nan. It was cramped, living on top of each other like that. But it was better than what we'd come from. And it was good of her to take us in. Later, of course, we got this house. A few streets away from your nan. But away from your nan – oh, your nan! I tell you, Frank, Hertfordshire's paradise compared to what we left behind. Best thing we ever did."

* * * * *

While we're washing up one Thursday evening, I say, "When's Dad coming home?"

"Tomorrow," she says, putting a plate on the draining-board.

I pick it up to dry. "He's never here. Haven't seen him for weeks."

"He's a long-distance lorry driver," she says. "He can't be here."

"No, I s'pose not. But – "

"But what?"

"Well, when he is here," I say, "he stays for a bit and then he's off again, ain't he? I mean, when he's not on the road – "

"I know."

"I wish he'd stay here with us."

She takes her hands out of the washing-up bowl and looks at me. "Your dad works hard, Frank."

"But he's never here."

Staring at the bubbles, she plunges her hands into the water and doesn't move.

"Where does he go?" I say.

"Drinking with his mates, I 'spect. Up to London – "

"London?" That's the first I've heard of it. "What's he wanna go to London for?"

She swirls the soapy water around. "Harry Whetstone."

"Him that comes round here sometimes."

"Yes, him. Your dad does a bit of work for him."

I'm waiting to dry the next thing. "I don't like him."

"Neither do I, Frank," Mum says.

We finish clearing up the tea things without saying another word. Mum's a bit upset and I'm thinking hard about Dad and Harry Whetstone.

Next day, like Mum said, Dad comes home. He's happy and laughing and says he's pleased to see us.

"Let's have a cup o' tea," he says, handing Mum the week's money. "C'm' on, Val, put the kettle on. What we having to eat?"

Mum doesn't answer. So, while she's making some tea, Dad and me go into the living-room and sit down on the settee. He lights up a fag.

"Dad," I say.

"What?"

"Can we go fishing tomorrow? I've found this smashing spot. The fish jump out at you. It's really good –"

"Sorry, Frank," he says. "Busy."

"Oh."

"'Ere," he says, looking up, smiling, "did I tell you I've been doing a bit o' work for Reggie Kray. You've heard o' Reggie Kray, haven't ya?"

"Can we go Sunday, then?" I say. "Let's go fishing and – "

"I told you, Frank," he says. "You're not listening, are ya? I'm busy."

"Just a couple of hours – "

"Where's the bloody tea?" he shouts at the top of his voice.

I back off the settee and go and sit in a chair on the opposite side of the room.

"Dad," I say.

"What?"

"Spurs are playing Leicester tomorrow – "

"I told you, didn't I," he says as Mum brings in a mug of tea. "Val," he says as he takes the mug, "did I tell you? I'm doing some work for Reg – "

"Tea'll be ready in half an hour," she says and goes out, slamming the door behind her.

"Put the telly on, eh?" Dad says.

I switch it on. Course, we have to wait a few minutes for it to warm up. Then on comes *Pinky and Perky*. I like *Pinky and Perky*.

"Go and see who that is, Frank," Dad says.

"What?"

"There's someone at the door," he says.

"I didn't hear nothing."

"Do as you're told, will ya?"

I get up and go to the front door.

A tall, fat man with black hair and a droopy moustache stands there. He's wearing a neat navy suit with trouser creases you can cut your finger on and a blue tie with bright yellow diamonds. It's Harry Whetstone.

"Hello, Frank," he says, smiling, holding a package.

"Dad!" I call out. "Someone for you."

I stand in the hallway, saying nothing, as Mr Whetstone carries on smiling.

Dad's head pops round the corner. "Oh, Harry, come on in. Frank, let Mr Whetstone in."

As I stand back, the kitchen door opens. "Oh," Mum says. "And what do *you* want?"

"Hello, Val," Mr Whetstone says. He comes in, pushing me to one side as he strides up the hall. "Brought you a present." He hands out the package but Mum doesn't move, doesn't take it. "Thought you might like some chocolates."

"I don't want your chocolates," she says. "Not staying long, are you?"

"Leave them here, then, shall I?" he says, putting the box of chocolates on the floor next to the kitchen door. "Come to see Sid. Talk over a bit o' business."

"Come in here, Harry," Dad says. "Frank, go and help your mum make Harry a cup o' tea."

The two men go into the living-room and shut the door.

"Come on, Frank," Mum says. "I don't want you having anything to do with him. Put those chocolates in the dustbin."

I open the package. "But, Mum, look! They must've cost a fortune."

"I'm not interested," she says. "If you can't do as you're told, give them here." She grabs them from me and

15

goes outside. I hear the dustbin lid being lifted up, a few noises, some loud rustling and then the lid bangs back into place.

"And if," Mum says, coming back in, "you're thinking of sneaking out later and getting 'em back, I've smashed them to pieces."

"Oh, Mum." It's amazing how she can read my mind.

She makes a mug of tea, throwing in four teaspoons of sugar. "Here, take this in to Flash Harry."

"Does he like that much sugar?"

"I hope it rots his teeth," she says.

Dad and Mr Whetstone are lounging about in the armchairs. They're laughing.

"Right," Dad says. "I'll go and get changed and we'll be off."

I hand over the tea and go back into the kitchen.

"Dad's going out," I say.

"Oh, is he?" she says, clearly worked up.

As we hear someone go upstairs, Mr Whetstone comes into the kitchen.

"Thanks for the tea," he says, making a show of pouring it down the sink. "Too bad you can't welcome your husband's boss with a bit more respect."

"Respect?" she shouts. "You get him involved with people no decent man should be involved with – "

"People?" he says, trying to look puzzled.

"He comes home here, filling the boy's head with stories of gangsters and – "

"Gangsters?"

"All that nonsense about Reggie Kray and I don't know who. It's not good for Frank to hear that sort of thing. You know how easily influenced he is."

Mr Whetstone turns to me. "Are you easily influenced, Frank? I thought you were your own man."

"Don't talk to him!" she screeches, pushing me aside as she strides up to him. "Keep away from him!"

"I'm sorry, Val," he says. "I've always thought of myself as one of the family."

"Family? *Family?* What do you know about family? The nearest you come to family is arranging abortions for those grubby tarts in those films you sell in your sleazy little shops."

"They cost me a lot of money, Val," he says. "Do you know how difficult it is to put those films together? They're artistic gems."

"Yeah, and I'm Brigitte bloody Bardot," she hollers right in his face. You've got to admire my mum, she's ain't scared of no-one, not even Mr Whetstone.

The kitchen door bursts open.

"What's going on here, then?" bawls my dad, all dressed up in shiny black shoes, suit and tie. "Val, are you upsetting Harry?"

Mr Whetstone turns to Dad. "She isn't upsetting me," he says. "We're engaging in a useful exchange of views, aren't we, Val? Are you ready, Sid?"

"As ready as I'll ever be," Dad says. "Val, apologise to Harry."

She turns her back on them and messes about with the sugar bowl and teaspoon.

"Val," he says again, "I want you to apologise to Harry."

She doesn't move, she doesn't say a word.

Now Dad's getting angry. "Val, don't embarrass me in front of Harry. Apologise."

"No, Sid," she says. "I will not apologise to that piece of filth."

He grabs her by the arm and pulls her round so she's facing him.

"Val!" he whispers.

She still doesn't move, still doesn't say a word. She stares at him, standing there, defying him, like I feel when I'm out on the street, faced with lads bigger than me, trying to make me do something I refuse to do.

"C'm' on, Sid," Mr Whetstone says. "Leave it. We'll be late."

Dad lets go of Mum's arm and half-turns to leave. "All

right, Harry." Then he twists back round and gives Mum such a slap, she falls back against the sink, her face red with marks.

"Mum!" I call out and run over to her.

"You didn't have to do that, Sid," Mr Whetstone says, as if Dad had stamped on an irritating insect.

"You keep out of this," Dad barks and he hustles him out the kitchen. The front door opens, then slams shut.

I run into the hall. "Bastard!" I shout and then rush back into the kitchen.

Mum's gathering up the tea things and putting them away. "No need for that sort of language, Frank."

Although she doesn't look at me, I see the faint curl of a smile.

After our tea, we spend the evening watching telly. Mum likes *Compact*, so I keep quiet and let her enjoy it. After that, we have a good laugh at Eric and Hattie and how Eric gets hypnotised by mistake. Then Tony Bennett comes on and Mum likes his singing so we listen to him for a bit. We wash up while *Points of View* and the news are on. Then it's McGowan vs Scarponi. I like a good bit of boxing, of course, and Mum doesn't mind, so we settle down for a good match – or at least until we hear the front door opening.

"Off to bed, Frank," Mum says.

"Aw, Mum."

"I don't want your dad to see you."

As I go upstairs, I shout out, "Goodnight, Dad."

He doesn't answer. Or maybe the grunt I hear is his answer. As I look down, I see him try to shut the door, but all he does is fall against it and slide down to the floor, his eyes half-closed, his tongue hanging out. He's lost his tie, his shirt's all over the place and his jacket's thrown halfway across the hall.

I don't want you to see your dad, more like.

Another door opens and Mum comes along. I watch her try to pick him up. She looks up and sees me. "I said, get to bed!"

"Can I help?"

"*Frank!*"

So I go off to bed.

Next morning, I'm up before Mum or Dad. As I don't want to be around, I make some sandwiches and go off over the fields to meet my mates. When I come back late afternoon, Dad's not there.

"Gone to London," Mum says, as she makes the tea.

"With Mr Whetstone?"

"We'll miss *Dixon of Dock Green*. You like that, don't you?"

* * * * *

Early one evening, a couple of weeks later, I'm in my room when I hear Mum and Dad shouting in the hall. I go out to see what the fuss is.

Dad's standing there, looking really dapper. Shiny black shoes, navy suit, white shirt, blue and white striped tie and a fancy silver tie clip shaped like a sword. His hair is greased down and combed back. When he makes the effort, like everyone says, Dad is a snappy dresser.

Mum's halfway up the hall, walking towards him. "Where you off to?"

"Up to the Smoke," he says. "It's Friday." He turns and stares at her. "Where d'ya think I'm going?"

"Well, I thought you'd stay here for once."

"Look," he shouts, "you want food on the table, don't ya? You 'spect me to pay the rent? I'm off to get some dosh. That's what the man of the house does. Provides for his family. That's what I'm doing, ain't I?"

I go down towards them. "Dad – "

"Frank," Mum says, "go to your room. This is nothing to do with you."

Dad looks at me. "Do as your mum says."

I take a few steps down to the bottom of the stairs and stand there, watching them.

"Who's stolen the car keys?" he says, fumbling in his

pockets and pulling them out. "Right, I'm off."

"Notting Hill, ain't it? Harry Whetstone and his tarts – "

"Tarts!" he hollers. "*Tarts?*"

"Don't you think I don't know," Mum hollers back. "Call yourself man of the house. You're no man. Leaving your wife and son – "

"What d'ya take me for?"

"A no-good waster, that's what I take you for," Mum screams at the top of her voice. "You're nothing but a – "

Dad takes a step forward so they're standing so close they're touching. "Now look here, Val, I'm doing the best I can."

"Oh, Sid," she says. "Why can't you get yourself a proper job, for once in your life, earn a decent – "

"I get more money doing this than going down that glass factory."

"And what else do you get?" she says. "Can't keep your trousers on, can ya?"

"Don't you ever – " he growls. He cups his hand underneath her chin and pulls her up so she's standing on her tiptoes. "For fuck's sake, Val, won't you ever understand? You're my wife."

"Dad!" I scream out. "You're hurting her!"

He glances at me. "Hurting? When I was your age… I'll show you hurting."

And with his one hand at Mum's throat, he raises her up and throws her towards me. As she flies through the air like a rag-doll, she's screaming out, her arms going everywhere. She drops down a few feet away from me.

And without looking at what he's done or where Mum has landed, he brushes back his hair, strokes his tie, straightens his jacket, takes a step out, slams the door and is gone.

I run over, near to tears. "Mum!"

For a second or so, she lays there, not moving. Then she opens her eyes and looks at me. "'S alright, Frank. I'm alright."

I burst into tears.

"Nothing broken," Mum says, "I'm all right, baby."

"I'm not a baby," I whimper, crying even more.

"No, you're not," she whispers. "You're a big and strong and fine young man."

Chapter 2. Neighbourhood

"Frank!"

I'm playing rounders with the Italians from up the road and I know it's near teatime 'cos I can smell the garlic coming from their house.

"Aw, Mum!" I call. "I'm winning."

"Come and get your tea."

We're still living with Nan and, if I don't go in now, the food'll go cold. I woof down my egg and chips. But when I get out, the others have gone. So I go back in.

Everyone's watching a nature programme on telly, about birds in Spain. Living with my nan means everywhere's always crowded. She's sitting in the best armchair. Next to her are Great-Grandma Sarah and Great-Grandpa Percy– *her* mum and dad – and Mum, not Dad – and Sheila, who's supposed to be my great-aunt except she's only two years older than me.

I sit down on the carpet next to Sheila to watch. She's not watching. She's flicking through the *TV Times*, pretending she can read. Everyone knows she can't – well, I'm not too good at it, either, but at least I can make out the words.

"What's this say?" she says, shoving the magazine in my face.

I push it away, then look where her finger's pointing.

"*The New Adventures of Charlie Chan.*"

"Is that on now?"

"That's what it says."

"Charlie Chan's on the other side."

No-one takes any notice. They're caught up in the film about Spanish birds. Like any of 'em are interested in Spanish birds. They're no more interested in Spanish birds than I am. They're more interested in ignoring Sheila.

"I want to watch Charlie Chan," she says, going red in the face.

Uh-ho. I know what's coming. I scooch away from her.

My head's still aching from a couple of weeks ago when she went at me with one of Nan's high-heel stiletto shoes and tried cracking my head open. If Nan hadn't been around, there'd be blood all over the carpet and I'd be dead.

It'd started because I was watching telly and she'd come in, seen it was Charlie Chan and had said she wanted to watch whatever was on the other side.

"What's on?" I'd said.

"A film about penguins."

I'd got up and switched over. I didn't mind penguins. But it wasn't penguins, it was women's cross-country running. So when I'd switched back to Charlie Chan, she'd gone bananas. She'd jumped up and down, pulled at her hair, snivelled, made a racket. I'd seen this before, of course, and knew all she'd wanted was to get her own way. If I'd been watching women's cross-country running, she'd've wanted Charlie Chan. She'd seen Nan's shoes up the corner, had run over, picked one up and went for me.

So when she bounces up on to her feet, screaming, "I want to watch Charlie Chan!", I'm up by the door, ready to escape.

"Sheila," Nan says. "That's enough."

That sends Sheila off even more. Nan gets up, grabs her and shakes her. Sheila's off her head again.

I leave the room and go into the back where Grandpa Wilf's sitting, reading.

He looks up and smiles.

"Grandpa," I say. "Sheila is my aunt, isn't she?"

"Yes, Frank," he says, putting a bookmark on the page, "she's your Auntie Sheila."

"Why is she only two years older than me?"

He goes back to his book. "That's the way things are."

"Why is she always screaming?"

"She thinks no-one loves her, Frank."

"I'm not always screaming."

His head bowed, he looks over the top of his glasses. "But you don't think no-one loves you, do you?"

I edge round. "What you reading?"

He closes the book and shows me the spine. "*Martin Chuzzlewit*."

"Mar-tin-chuz-zle-wit." Everyone's got funny names. John-son-mc-cuth-bert.

"By Charles Dickens."

"Charles Dickens." I lean over. "Is he any good?"

"Everything he writes is full of stories and wonderful people. Some of it's very funny and other parts are very serious." He stares at me as if he's about to say something important. "If you don't read anything else in your life, Frank, read Charles Dickens." He goes back to the book.

"I'm not very good at reading."

Grandpa Wilf lifts the book up towards me. "Reading Charles Dickens will help you improve."

We hold the book together. "Chapter Three." I look at Grandpa and smile.

He nods. "That's right. Good boy. Go on."

"Men – men – "

He doesn't lean over to see what I can't read. "Mention."

I'm not sure but I try my best. My finger follows the words. "Mention... has been already... made more than once... of a... certain... dragon – " I look at Grandpa and laugh. Dragon! It's all about dragons!

"That's the name of the inn – the tavern – "

I frown.

"'Inn', 'tavern'. Different words for 'pub'."

I know that word. "That's where Dad goes."

"Get a chair."

I go to the kitchen, pull a chair over next to him and sit down.

He turns back to the beginning. "Let's read it together, shall we?"

"But you've already read up to there."

"I've read this book three times, Frank," he says. "I can read it again. I'll read, you follow."

I nod. "How many books did he write, Grandpa?"

"More than thirty. And stories as well. I've got them all." He waves his hand towards the bookcase at the back of the room. There they are, rows and rows and rows of books. He watches me staring at them. "Every one of those is your friend, Frank. If you let books be your friends, they'll be your friends for life and never let you down. Shall we start?"

"Yes, please." I can't wait. I like being with Grandpa Wilf. He sits at the back of the house, reading his books, bothering no-one. What I like most of all is, it's so quiet. No-one bothers him. Just him and his books. "And then can we read the others?"

He laughs. I think it's the first time I've ever seen him laugh out loud. It makes me feel special. "Well, let's see how we get on with this, shall we?"

I laugh, too.

He holds up the cover. It's green and decorated with gold lettering. "Isn't it beautiful?"

I reach out and feel the leather. I don't think I've ever felt anything so soft before. It's like stroking a puppy's tummy. The gold is so pretty and delicate, I'm almost afraid to touch it.

Slowly, he flicks through the pages. "These pictures help you follow the story."

He stops at one page and there's a picture of an old man with a stick sitting in an armchair. Behind him are two young ladies dressed in Victorian clothes standing in awkward positions, smiling at the man in front of them. His hair is tufted up and he's very pleased with himself.

"That's Mr Pecksniff," Grandpa Wilf says.

Peck-sniff. Another funny name.

"You'll hear about him as we read the story."

"What's this say?" I say, pointing to the words underneath the picture.

"*Truth prevails and virtue is triumphant*," Grandpa says.

"What does that mean?"

"You have to read the book to find out."

I can't wait. I feel I'll never be as happy as at this moment.

"Right!" he says. He turns back to the beginning. "This is the title." He reads: *The Life and Adventures of Martin Chuzzlewit, His Relatives, Friends and Enemies, comprising all his wills and his ways with an historical record of what he did and what he didn't: showing, moreover, who inherited the family plate, who came in for the silver spoon, and who for the wooden ladle, the whole forming a complete key to the House of Chuzzlewit. Edited by Boz. Illustrated by Phiz. London 1843."*

"Wow!" I say, wide-eyed. "And that's just the title."

"And that's just the title," he repeats, smiling even more. It's like he can't stop smiling. He turns the page and reads.

"Chapter One. Introductory. Concerning the pedigree of the Chuzzlewit Family."

He gives a little cough, makes himself comfortable and carries on.

"As no lady or gentleman, with any claims to polite breeding, can possibly sympathize with the Chuzzlewit Family without being first assured of the extreme antiquity of the race, it is a great satisfaction to know that it undoubtedly descended in a direct line from Adam and Eve... "

We sit there for more than an hour, Grandpa Wilf reading, me spellbound by the story, following the words as best I can, loving the sound of his gentle voice.

"... for he is a fine lad, an ingenuous lad, and has but one fault that I know of; he don't mean it, but he is most cruelly unjust to Pecksniff!'"

"He was in the picture!" I blurt out.

"Yes, he was," Grandpa says. He closes the book. "There," he says, "we've got to where I was when you came in. Did you like that?"

"Wilf!" It's Nan.

"Yes, dear?"

"Why is this kitchen such a mess? Put that bloody book

26

down and get in 'ere."

"Coming, dear," he says and grins at me like we've been found out. "My mistress calls." He puts the book on a little table, pulls himself up, stretches and goes out.

As I've now got nothing else to do and it isn't bedtime yet, I go back to where everyone's watching telly.

"It's Peter Sellers," Mum says. "Sit next to me, love." She edges over to make room.

I have to climb over Sheila, 'cos she's curled up in a ball on the carpet. I try to be careful but it isn't easy and I'm nearly clear when she grabs my foot and wiggles it about as if I'm a baby's rattle.

"Mum!" I whine.

"Sheila," she says, "leave Frank alone."

But she doesn't. She giggles and grips my foot even tighter.

Great-Grandpa Percy says, "Frank, get out the bloody way. I can't see."

"Give him a chance, will ya," Mum says. "Sheila!"

"I said get out the way, didn't I," Great-Grandpa Percy says, "you London scrote, you." And he kicks me with his boot.

Of course, I go tumbling over Sheila and land on top of her. So now she's crying her head off and pushing me away.

"Behave yourself, Frank."

"But Mum, it was her!"

"It wasn't me," Sheila cries.

"Her? Who's her?" Mum says, getting up and separating us.

"It was Frank," Sheila carries on.

"She grabbed my foot," I whine, "and then Great-Grandpa Percy kicked me up the arse!"

"Less of that language," she says. "Off to bed."

While I pick myself up and go upstairs, the rest of 'em carry on watching the telly as if nothing's happened.

"Sleep well, Frank," Grandpa Wilf calls from the kitchen.

* * * * *

It's hot. Really hot. Mum's at work, Grandpa Wilf has gone out, and I've got no-one to play with. I sit on the kerb outside, watching a spider crawl about in the dust.

A car rolls up. A woman I don't know is at the wheel. Nan's next to her. Sheila and a couple of other kids are in the back.

"We're off to the swimming-baths," Nan says. "Do you want to come?"

"Ooh, yeah, can I?"

"Go and get your kit."

I run into the house, find a bag, grab a towel and my swimming-trunks, close the front door and run back to the car.

Nan says, "Have you got your sixpence?"

Opening the car-door, I say, "What sixpence?"

"Your sixpence to get in," she sighs, as if everyone knows you need sixpence. "Have you got your sixpence?"

I shake my head 'cos I haven't got my sixpence.

"Well, you can't come then," she says, pushing me away, slamming the door.

Off they go and I'm left in the middle of the street, wondering what I did to deserve that.

I go inside, put my kit away, have a pee, get a drink. I find a packet of Smith's crisps, pull out the sachet of salt, sprinkle it about and give the bag a good shake. I take the crisps into the garden and sit down.

Geoffrey, the kid who lives in the house at the end of our garden, is there with his dad. I've never liked him. Stuck up – it's always "Geoffrey", never "Geoff" – a spiteful kid. Once, when I was playing, he threw stones at me for no reason and when I shouted for him to stop, he threw more stones, hitting me in the face, laughing his head off before he ran indoors.

He sees me, smiles and waves, trying to be friendly, 'cos he's with his dad.

Well, I don't feel like being friendly.

28

I go in, upstairs, and get my catapult. Nan has left a bowl of peas in the kitchen. They're dried out. Very hard. I grab a few, go back into the garden. Geoffrey's still there with his dad and they've got their backs to me, watching some birds fly over.

I put the peas in my catapult and aim. Just then, Geoffrey bends over. I pull as hard as I can and hit him right up his short-trousered arse.

He jumps up, screaming, like he's got a flaming fire-cracker up him. In a way, he has, I s'pose. He grabs his bum cheeks and dances around. Then he runs up to his house, but misses the door and crashes into the wall.

Running after him, his dad's shouting, "Geoffrey, what's wrong?"

"I've been shot!"

"Have you been stung by a bee? Geoffrey! Come here!"

I can't stop laughing. I'm laughing so much I think they'll hear me. I run indoors, up to my bed and bury my head in the pillow, tears streaming down my face.

* * * * *

A couple of weeks later, it's bright and sunny and I'm in the back garden on the lawn, kicking the football I got for my eighth birthday not so long ago.

Great-Grandpa Percy comes out. "Hey, boy! D' ya wanna feed the hens?"

"Can I?"

"Here y'are," he says, walking down the path, handing over the feedbag.

When we get to the coop, he undoes the door. As I throw in the food, a dozen hens run up to me.

"Not like that, you idiot," Great-Grandpa Percy says. "Give it here."

I step out, give him the bag and he gets inside.

"You don't toss the stuff any old where," he barks above all the noise. "Throw it gently in batches so everyone gets a good go at it."

Now that he's shown me, I step forward. But he carries on, talking to the hens as if I'm not there. When the bag's empty, he holds it out for me to take. He steps towards the cockerel perched at the back, watching everything that's been going on.

"C'm' on, Cocky," he says, bending over to pick him up. The bird squawks but soon calms down. Great-Grandpa Percy carries him out the coop. "He can have a good rootle around on his own."

We watch Cocky strut about, pecking at the grass, picking up the odd morsel. He's a fine old bird, what with his comb and bright feathers, and it's nice to see him enjoy freedom, instead of being squashed up with those squawking hens. I know how he feels.

"Cocky," I call, holding my hand out. "Here, Cocky, Cocky, Cocky!"

He looks up and strides towards me, his head bobbing backwards and forwards. Then he makes a jab at me and pecks my fingers.

"Ow!" I scream, jumping back.

He goes for my foot, then the other one. I kick back. "Geroff!"

Great-Grandpa Percy laughs. "Go on, boy, get him!" I don't know if he's talking to me or the bird.

Cocky dives at me and gets my shins and, 'cos I'm wearing shorts, he nicks the skin and blood starts to seep out. I'm flailing around which upsets Cocky even more. He flaps his wings, lifts off the ground and then he's having a go at my willy and my what-nots.

"Get him off me!" I screech, trying to brush him away.

But Great-Grandpa Percy's laughing his head off and doesn't move a muscle to help.

Cocky carries on, first my legs, my hands and then anything else he can get at. I give a great big kick and he's off me long enough for me to escape up the path.

Great-Grandpa Percy can't stop laughing. "That's my boy," he says, getting hold of Cocky and stroking him.

"You got the bloody runt."

I bump into Grandpa Wilf, who's standing in the doorway. Crying my eyes out, I throw my arms around him. "Oh! Grandpa! Cocky tried to kill me!"

He folds his big hands about me. "What're you up to, Dad?" he calls. "Frightening the boy like that."

"He's a coward," Great-Grandpa Percy calls back. "He's nothing but a lily-livered lump o' London shit."

"Either you put the bird back in the coop," Grandpa Wilf shouts, "or we have him for dinner."

Me and Grandpa Wilf watch as Cocky goes back into the coop.

"Say, Frank," Grandpa Wilf says, pulling me on to the lawn, "Let's have a kick-about."

Soon me and Grandpa Wilf are passing the ball to one another and it's sunny and warm again and we're having a good time. We laugh and chuckle when Grandpa Wilf misses the ball, 'though we both know he's doing it deliberately to make me feel better.

Great-Grandpa Percy stands in front of the coop, hands sunk in his pockets, scowling 'cos we're ignoring him.

"Wilf!" Nan comes down into the garden. "There's someone at the door."

"Well," shouts Great-Grandpa Percy, "answer it, you lazy crone!"

"Shut your face, your miserable old git," she shouts back. "Wilf! The door! "

His foot on the ball, Grandpa Wilf stands still and sighs. His shoulders heave up and fall down, to make sure someone a mile away can see how he feels. "Sorry, Frank."

Footie over for the afternoon, he plods off the lawn and goes in.

Leaving the ball wherever it is, I sit on the grass and examine Cocky's handiwork. I don't hurt any more, but little dried rivers of blood streak down my arms and legs.

Great-Grandpa Percy and Nan stand at opposite ends of the garden, glaring at each other, saying nothing, waiting for Grandpa Wilf to return.

He comes out. "They want to talk to you," he says. Then he heads straight for me. "You all right, Frank?"

Two men come into the garden.

"'Allo, Flo," one of 'em says. He's big, with a mop of thick curly black hair and wearing a navy suit, blue shirt and dark blue tie.

The other's about the same height, blond hair, younger and well turned out. Sharp light blue suit, white shirt, green tie. Unlike the big one, this one keeps himself fit.

Nan says, "'Allo, Ron." She leers at the blond. "Who's your pretty friend?"

"Him?" Ron says, as if surprised to find him there. "That's Ted Kingsley."

"Mrs Peters," he says, getting out a notebook and pen.

"What do you want, Ron?"

"Do you know John Frye?"

I don't know who these men are but it's obvious everyone else does. Great-Grandpa Percy comes up from the coop. Grandpa Wilf stands up. Nan's not moving. Me, I stay on the grass.

Mum comes out. "What's going on?" she says. "Oh, it's you."

"'Allo, Val. So, Flo," Ron says, turning to Nan, "John Frye. You either know him or you don't."

"'Course she knows him," Great-Grandpa Percy says. "Johnny comes round here a lot."

"Keep your trap shut," Nan snaps.

"Mr Frye says you stole his dole money," Ron says.

Great-Grandpa Percy says, "How much?"

The other man opens his notebook. "Twelve pounds, ten shillings and fourpence."

"John's not very good with money," Nan says. "I help him out."

"You sure you're not helping yourself?"

"Quite sure," she says.

For a minute, no-one says a word. No-one moves. They remind me of when we went to Madame Tussauds.

Grandpa Wilf, Mum, Nan, Ron, Ted Kingsley, Great-Grandpa Percy. All in a row. And everyone's so serious and dumb-faced. Even I feel serious, although I've no idea what's going on.

"Flora Peters," Ron says, "I'm arresting you on suspicion of fraud and theft. You do not have to say anything unless you wish to do so – "

But he's cut off. From the bottom of the garden comes a loud cock-a-doodle-doo. Cocky strides out of the coop, runs up the lawn and hurtles himself at Ron's bits.

"Oh, Percy!" Nan yelps, collapsing in laughter, "what have you done!"

Ron's jumping around, swearing his head off and Ted Kingsley's kicking at Cocky, getting nowhere fast.

Great-Grandpa Percy's only gone and left the coop door open, hasn't he?

* * * * *

"What's going to happen?" I ask Mum when all the fuss has died down and they've taken Nan away.

"Who knows?" she says, handing me a glass of orange squash.

"Will she go to prison?"

"I don't know," she says. "I wouldn't've thought so."

"Well, I hope she does," I say.

"Frank! That's not a very nice thing to say."

"I don't care," I tell her. "I don't like her. She's horrible to Grandpa Wilf."

Mum puts the kettle on. "She's had a hard life."

"Why does she boss Grandpa about so much? She sits around all day while he does all the work." I gulp down my drink.

"She hasn't had it easy," she says, getting a cup and saucer. "Your nan used to work in the West End in... well, a few of the clubs up there. She was a hostess."

"Serving drinks and things?"

"Mostly things. Anyway, never mind," she says as the

33

kettle boils and she brews a pot, "I've got some important news."

I put my glass on the draining-board. "Dad's coming home!"

"That, too," she says, sitting down at the table. "We've got a house for ourselves. So it'll be Dad, you and me, living together like a proper family." She's smiling her head off like she's won the pools.

"Can I have a gun?"

She frowns. "What do you want a gun for?"

"So I can kill Cocky."

She laughs. "Oh, Frank."

"I'll still be able to see Grandpa Wilf, won't I?"

"It's only a couple of streets away. Oak Tree Avenue. You'll have your own room and there's a big garden as well."

I can't believe it. I can put up pictures, sleep in my own room and have some peace and quiet.

"It's going to be lovely," she says. "But you're going to have to help me 'cos we've got to pack up all our things – "

"Can I have another drink, please?"

She nods.

I mix myself some orange squash. "Sheila's not coming with us, is she? 'Cos if she is – "

"She's staying here."

"When we moving?"

"End of next week."

Dad's coming home, we're moving into our own house, Sheila's staying put, no more Nan, no more Great-Grandpa Percy, I'm getting a gun and Cocky will die a horrible death. It's gonna be great!

* * * * *

Grandpa Wilf helps us move. Everyone else keeps out the way. Dad comes home and we get some new furniture. Like Mum says, I get my own room. And she's right about the garden. It's massive. Mum gets her own kitchen and

34

finally, as she says, her own bathroom. I don't think I've ever seen her so happy.

It doesn't take us long to settle in. And it's not long, either, before I'm off out. I know we're only four streets away from Nan's but it's a different territory. New neighbours, new people, new pavements.

A week or so after we've moved in, I'm scouting about, walking around the houses, sizing up the streets. We live in Oak Tree Avenue, then there's Cedar Rise and Plumtree Road.

I'm strolling along Plumtree Road when a boy, twice my size, steps out and blocks my way. It isn't difficult for a boy to be twice my size 'cos I'm a little lad but he blocks my way, all the same.

"Where you going?" he says.

"Nowhere."

He grabs hold of my arm. "Come with me." He pulls me into a front garden where a gang of boys is lounging about on the lawn.

"What's your name?" he says.

"Frank Peters."

"Well, Frank Peters," he says. "I'm Steve and these are my brothers. That's Arnie, that's Stu, that's Harold, that's Bob, that's Cliff and that one there is Ken."

As their names are called out, each of them nods or gives a little wave. Arnie's a big bloke with black uncombed hair. Stu's a smaller version. Harold and Bob look like twins, only Bob hasn't washed in a week. Cliff's playing with himself. Ken, the smallest one, has the gingerest hair I've ever seen.

Steve's obviously the leader. While he's got the same black hair as Arnie and Stu, he towers over the lot of them. He's got thick arms and his chest bulges out of a shirt a size too small for him.

"We're the Bartram brothers. What d'ya think?"

"What d'ya mean, what do I think?"

"Can you beat us in a fight?"

"All of you?"

35

"No," he says, "that wouldn't be fair, would it? Choose who you'll fight."

He pushes me into the middle of the lawn so I'm surrounded. I turn to go but Steve, once again, blocks me. I'm going to have to fight my way out.

"Who do you want to fight?" he says again.

If I go for the smallest, they'll call me a coward. If I go for Steve, I'll be beaten to a mash. "Him," I say, pointing at no-one in particular.

Steve says, "Cliff, leave your dick alone for once and get up here."

As Cliff gets up, everyone cheers him on. Someone says, "'bout time, too." They move around the edge of the lawn.

He strides into the centre and bends over, his arms forming a semi-circle in front of him, ready to catch me when I fall. Steve steps to one side.

Although I've been in a few scraps before, this is the first one that's set up like a boxing-match. We're in a ring, we've got an audience, Steve's the ref.

Everyone keeps quiet as we circle, two hungry bears sizing each other up.

Cliff lets out a shout as he dives for my legs, getting me to the ground. As he climbs on top of me, I pummel his chest with my fists. But he grabs them, pushes me down and thrusts his knees on to my arms.

I can't move. I'm trapped.

He leans back, stretches his arms back and grips the back of my knees. He's got long arms! Grunting, he pulls my legs up so my feet stretch up in the air. Holding on to my legs, he lifts his knees off my arms.

Before I can get at him, he stands up, my legs either side of him. He gets up straight and raises me up so I'm upside-down, my head now the only part of me touching the ground.

His brothers are cheering him on. "Now swing him," Steve shouts, "like I showed ya!"

Cliff hoists me off the ground and looks around. "Shall

I?"

Someone shouts, "Give him the merry-go-round!"

Everyone bursts into song. "Here we go round the mulberry bush, the mulberry bush, the mulberry bush – "

He swings me round and round. I'm a fairground ride, my arms flying everywhere. Everyone's singing and shouting. I close my eyes. I can do nothing. I feel sick. But he carries on. Round and round and round as they cheer him on. It's never going to end.

"Over here, Cliff!"

"To me! To me!"

"Give him to me!"

He throws me through the air and I land on all of them. Their hands dive in. They scream, they shout, they screech. One pulls my tee-shirt up and pinches my tits 'til I can't feel them. Another's scratching my legs up and down. A hand grabs my bits and holds hard. Someone tries to pull my hair out. Another sticks his fingers up my nostrils so I have to open my mouth to breathe, then the same fingers go down my throat.

I'm trying not to cry. I'm really trying.

"All right, boys," Steve calls out. "Let the kid go."

Without a sound, they stop at once.

Steve pulls me up. "Off you go, Frank Peters. See you soon."

Only when I'm round the corner and they can't see me do I fall to the ground. I breathe fast. I try not to cry. I don't want them to see me snivel my way home. I don't want Mum to see me like this. Besides, I have to get home to make the tea for when she comes in from work.

The next week, it's the same. Steve pulls me into the garden. They make me choose who I'm going to fight. I pick Stu, thinking he's so big I can crawl between his legs and pull him down, get on top of him and smash his face in. But he picks me up and, his arms stretched upwards, carries me around in the air like the FA cup, Stu 5 Frank 0. Then, like before, I'm thrown at the others, who scratch and maul me like hungry lions.

A couple of weeks after that, it's Bob, who still hasn't washed. He's a scrappy fighter, a dog who's not eaten for days. In no time, he does me in.

"Frank," Steve says, "you're not trying very hard, are you?"

"Sorry, Steve."

It's not 'til I'm on my way home, cleaning myself up, that I wonder why I apologised. Then I wonder again why I keep going back for more. I mean, why do I keep going past their house? Maybe I like being beaten up.

One weekend, a month later, Dad's home, it's late Saturday afternoon, and he says he's off out for a couple of hours.

"Frank can come along," he tells Mum, handing her a fiver. "The shops are still open. Go buy some smellies and have some time to yourself. Have a bath or something."

She smiles at him, she hugs him, she kisses him. Don't know why. It's only a bath, for goodness sake.

"Where we going, Dad?"

"You'll see," he says, unwrapping himself from Mum's clinging arms.

We go to the speedway track. Some bikes are already there and a few more are coming in.

"Frank," Dad says, "I've got to see someone. Here's – " And he dives into his trouser pockets.

"Why can't I come with you?"

"Grown-ups only," he says. "Get yourself a hot dog. Have a good time." He hands over some coins.

"I thought we were going to watch the racing."

"You watch the racing. Meet you here in an hour."

Fifteen and sevenpence ha'penny. Loose change from his pocket. Buying me off, like he did Mum with the smellies. He thinks I don't know.

I wander around, buy a hot dog and a drink. On my own, the racing's not very interesting. It's not long before I'm bored and desperate for a pee. But I can't find the toilets. I find my way round the back of the stadium and, in some long grass, let it out. The relief!

As I turn from the shadows and weeds, I see some big boys coming towards me, two from one end, three from the other.

"Too stuck up to use the proper bog, are ya?"

They lay into me. I'm on my own and these are bigger and better at it than Steve Bartram and his brothers. These know what they're doing and, unlike the Bartram brothers, it isn't a game, this time it's for real. They thump me in the stomach, kick me between the legs, punch me in the eye, stick their fingers in my ears.

"Get his dosh!"

Another feels my jeans pockets. "There's something there." But he can't get his hands in properly.

"Hold on a minute," the first says. "Lift him up, boys."

Two get hold of my arms and pull them back while another pulls my jeans down.

"Try that."

Hands go into the pockets and grab whatever's there.

"'bout twelve bob, I reckon. That's a burger each. C'm' on."

They let go. I fall back into the grass.

"Thanks, mate." They run off.

Snivelling, I get myself together and, I don't care if the hour's not up yet, I go to where Dad said we'd meet.

He's already there.

"What happened to you?"

As I don't know what to say, I stand there while he looks me over.

"You've got a black eye, you have," he says. "Someone set on you?"

I can't speak.

"Not again," he sighs. "First, the boys in Plumtree Road. Now this."

How does he know about the boys in Plumtree Road? I haven't told a soul.

He gets out a cigarette and lights up. "Right," he says, letting out the smoke, "this has gone on long enough."

Next day, he says, "Get your coat."

39

He takes me to a large wooden hut the other side of town.

"I ain't joinin' no youth club," I holler. "I hate table tennis."

"You'll do as you're told," he says, pushing me inside.

The main hall is full of boys in judo kit. All I hear is the sound of men, also in judo kits, shouting instructions and the thud of bodies landing on large mats.

"Jed!" my dad calls across the room.

"Sid!" A lean, muscled man with Brylcreemed hair, his judo coat undone, runs over.

"This is Frank," Dad says.

Jed smiles as he leans down and holds out his hand. I can smell the sweat from his hairy chest. We shake.

"Hello, Frank. Come to join us, have you?"

I shrug. I've no idea what's going on.

"I've got some kit for you." He darts away and comes back with a pile of clothing. "You can change over there." He points to a corner.

"Change?"

"'S 'bout time you learnt how to defend yourself," Dad says. "Get over there, take your clothes off and put your kit on."

"*Gi*," Jed says.

"What?"

"The name for your judo kit is *gi*."

"Frank," Dad says, "get over there and put your *gi* on."

Jed's holding the *gi*, smiling. "You'll be fine, Frank. You'll love it."

After I've changed and Dad's cleared off, Jed pairs me up with a freckle-faced kid called Tim. It's his first session, too. We're the same size and height so well matched. We spend the hour learning *ukemi*, breakfalls, 'cos Jed says *ukemi* are what stops you from hurting when you fall. Without them, he says, we'll be black and blue very quickly but if we do it properly, getting thrown won't hurt.

After an hour, Jed gives Tim and me towels and we go

back to our clothes, strip off, wipe ourselves down and get dressed. We can't stop talking about what we've done, we're so excited.

Jed comes over with cups of orange juice. "Make sure you drink this before you go. Dehydration is the enemy of the sportsman."

Open-mouthed, Tim and I stare at each other. Sportsmen! We're sportsmen! Wow! We drink up, stopping between mouthfuls to enjoy grinning at each other.

Next thing, Dad's standing over me, smelling of beer. "D'ya want to come again?"

I nod. "Can I?"

"That's why I brought you," he says.

Tim nods, as if my dad's his dad. He looks across the room. "My mum's here. Gotta go. See you next week."

"See ya, Tim."

"Well?" says Jed, who's joined us.

"How did he do?" Dad says.

"He's a natural, Sid," he says.

Dad beams at me as if I've won an Olympic gold medal. "Course he is. He's my son, ain't he?" He pulls out his wallet. "Let's settle up."

While I'm folding the *gi*, they have a chat and Dad hands over some notes.

"The *gi* and the white belt are yours, Frank," Jed says. "Your dad's paid you up for ten lessons."

"Will you show me how to throw someone over my shoulder?"

Jed laughs. Dad laughs.

"First, you perfect *ukemi*," Jed says, "and then I might – *might* – teach you *ippon-seoi-nage*."

I get him to say *ippon-seoi-nage* again and again until I can say it without thinking.

"Thanks, Jed," I say as we leave. "See you next week."

After that, there's no stopping me. Every Sunday afternoon for the next ten weeks, Dad drives me to judo classes, goes off somewhere, comes back stinking of beer and takes me home. In the meantime, I steer clear of the Bartram brothers, even if it means staying indoors or in the garden.

I finish the ten weeks and Dad signs me up for another ten weeks. And then another ten. That's more than six months without bumping into the Bartram brothers. Life is easier this way, I think, and it's easy not to see them. But I've decided to get my revenge.

One Sunday afternoon, after training, Jed says, "How would you like to enter a tournament?"

"Me?"

"You've come a long way," he says. "Like I said, you're a natural. It's for novices. I'm entering Tim as well. If you win, they'll upgrade you. That's the prize. Yellow belt."

Of course, I have to ask Mum and Dad but they agree at once.

A month later, the big day arrives and Jed, Tim, me, Mum, Dad and the rest of the club go up to Tottenham to a championship event. It goes really well. Tim and me get through and, there and then, we're both upgraded to yellow belt!

A couple of days after that, I walk by the Bartrams' house, pretending I don't see them in the garden. They pull me in and form their usual circle.

This time, I pick Arnie. When I last saw him, he was bigger than me. Now, he's like a brick shithouse. Must've been muscling himself up.

We circle each other for a few minutes, getting our measure. I don't let on what I've learnt. I let him think it's going to be easy for him.

As the boys cheer him on, he makes a lunge, picks me up, hoists me over his shoulder, ready to throw me over his head on to the ground.

But I don't let him. I curl my arms round his neck and hang on for dear life. Then I get him in the *hadaka jime*, or naked strangle. Then it's easy to manoeuvre myself into the rear naked choke. Going for the blood choke variation,

I curl my left arm around his neck with my elbow at his throat. My right arm grasps my left and I squeeze.

And I squeeze. I mean, hard.

I know I've got him when the back of his neck goes deep red and he's struggling to breathe.

He's starting to pass out.

I can render him unconscious if I want.

Everyone else has gone quiet.

If I want, I can kill him. For a while, I'm wondering if I will.

"Frank."

I'm interested to find out.

"Frank."

I leave off dreaming, let go, slide down Arnie's back.

As he falls, Steve and Stu catch him and help him down on the grass.

Someone says, "I'll get him a drink."

I stand there, watching what's going on, getting my breath, not really bothered whether Arnie's all right or not.

Now he's sipping water, everybody's standing back to give him air and I'm figuring what to do next. Arnie's on the grass. The boys are hovering over him. I decide to go. Don't need to stay. I've proved myself. I turn to go.

Steve says, "Hold it there, Frank."

One of the others pulls me back. I'm back in the Bartram circle.

"You coulda killed him."

I nod. I can't deny something that's true.

"Would you have killed him?"

I shrug. I don't know, do I?

He steps towards me.

I don't move. He knows what I'm capable of. I'm not afraid.

His right arm comes out and grabs my left shoulder. He holds it iron-tight. "You're goin' nowhere."

I slowly turn my head, stare at his grip and then, equally slowly, turn back and gaze up into his face.

"Well done, boy," he says, releasing me.

Everyone else cheers, claps, pats me on the back. Arnie's on his feet, smiling, nodding, applauding.

For the first time in my life, I'm the kiddie, I'm the boy. I've got the power.

And I love it.

* * * * *

I practice throwing bricks, lobbing them about the garden, because my arms get stronger that way and it's good for judo. Also, I have to be fit enough to fight the Bartrams. But I need something to aim at. Otherwise, I'm Eliot Ness on *The Untouchables* shooting a gun without a target. How do you know if you're any good if you don't know where the shots land? So, when no-one's about, I get a pile of bricks, carry them upstairs, stand on my bed, lean out the window and aim at things in the garden.

But as I'm aiming one brick at a pebble on the lawn, I slip and twist my ankle. The brick zooms out, smashes through Mr Kowalski's greenhouse next door, lands on a tomato plant and crushes it to pieces.

This is great. I've found my targets! I'm so excited, my head goes light and I nearly wet my pants. When I come back from the bathroom, I'm upset I've got no bricks left.

But I decide not to get any more. Not yet. I figure it's better to see first what Mr Kowalski does about the broken glass and smashed tomatoes. After all, if he finds out it's me, Dad'll beat me up like he does Mum. Don't want that. I can't do judo on Dad.

Nothing happens. Not a peep from Mr Kowalski. I never see him inspect the damage but, mysteriously, it's cleared up and new glass put in.

So, a few days later, I get the bricks, go upstairs and aim at the greenhouse. I hit my targets every time. Soon, I've smashed every pane. Once again, the mess is always cleared up and new glass is put in. I don't understand it.

But, next day, Mr Kowalski comes round when Dad's home and says our fantail doves make too much noise.

Worse, he says, when they're let out, they shit on his vegetables.

"They're doing nothing illegal," Dad tells him. "Bird shit is good fertiliser."

"*Feathers* are not fertiliser."

"You're wrong," Dad says. "They're the best fertiliser you can get."

"My carrots are ruined!" Mr Kowalski shouts. "Nothing grows. As if I don't already have enough trouble with my greenhouse."

"What's wrong with your greenhouse?"

"The windows, they break for no reason," he says, near to tears. "I do not understand it."

"Nothing to do with me," Dad says. "Tell you what, mate. Why don't you get your wife to suck on your carrot and see if it grows? That'll take your mind off your windows."

Mr Kowalski goes bright purple. "I will call the police, you see if I don't."

Dad says, "Fuck off, you fat Polish git," and slams the door in his face.

A couple of weeks later, everyone goes to the pub. My cousin, Robbie, comes round to look after me and, 'cos our Sheila's staying with us, that nutter as well. We're watching *The Benny Hill Show*.

I get up. "Going outside to check the birds."

From the kitchen light, I can see Mr Kowalski's beautiful garden. Rows of runner beans, rows of carrots, rows of onions. Every vegetable known to man, all in their little rows. He must be proud of what he's achieved.

I switch the light off so it's pitch black outside. I creep down the path, jump the fence and get into his garden.

Methodically – 'cos I am always methodical – I rip every runner bean off the frames and pull up the frames. I place everything on the path.

Then the carrots. Every one of 'em goes on the path with the beans.

Then the onions.

The parsnips.

The potatoes.

Beetroot. I don't like beetroot. Up they come and on the path with the rest.

Up comes a great big marrow.

When I finish, there's a huge pile of vegetables on the path. I've arranged them very neatly. After all, there's no need to make a mess. All ready for Bonfire Night.

I jump back over the fence, run into the house and sit down with Robbie and Sheila. Benny Hill's finished. It's *Perry Mason.*

"All right?" Robbie says.

"Yeah," I say. "I think so."

"Have a choc," Sheila says, handing over the box.

"Birds all right, are they?" Robbie says.

My mouth full of nut praline, I nod two or three times. I've forgotten all about them.

Next day, Sunday, when I get up and go into the garden, the police are inspecting the pile on Mr Kowalski's path. He's in tears. Mrs Kowalski's in the doorway, arms folded over her pinny, chin jutting out, like Norman Evans leaning over the garden wall.

"I told him," she's calling out, "it's his own fault."

One of the coppers looks up from the rubble. "How's that, Mrs Kowalski?"

"Came in the other night, didn't he," she says, "muttering how he can't get his marrow to grow and would I give him a hand."

The copper draws his hand over his face. "And," he says, trying not to laugh, "what did you say to that, Mrs Kowalski?"

"I told him," she says. "I told him straight. I said we're not having that sort of talk in this house. He did this himself, just to spite me. And that's the truth of it."

* * * * *

Mr Sears lives on the other side of our garden. He's as

46

cantankerous as Mr Kowalski. Not that he grows vegetables. No. Keeps pigeons and ferrets. Raises chickens to sell the eggs.

And he's got a cockerel.

It goes off at four o'clock in the morning. On and on and on. Every day. You never heard anything like it.

This particular day, it starts up in the morning and doesn't stop.

Dad bought me an air rifle for Christmas, lovely it is, a .177. So I lean out the window, as I did with the bricks, aim and shoot the noisy thing in the head. Corker of a shot.

Next day, Mr Sears raises merry hell. Well, I would if someone'd shot my cockerel.

He calls the police and accuses Dad. Then he accuses me. Then Dad accuses me. I accuse Mr Kowalski. Mr Kowalski accuses Mrs Kowalski. Mrs Kowalski accuses Mr Sears. Everybody accuses everybody they've ever met since the day they were born. You can hear the row ten miles away. The Old Bill give up and go away.

Gotcha, Cocky.

Up yours, Great-Grandpa Percy.

Chapter 3. School

"Frank, you sure you know what you're doing?"

They're standing around in the playground like they've never done this before. I mean, look at 'em: Tommy Owens – he's my lieutenant 'cos he's my mate – Mickey Golightly, Charlie Milliken and Stiffy Oswald. My gang. Do I have to show them everything?

"Course I do," I say. "I used to do this at junior school, didn't I? It's a cinch."

Irene Lloyd saunters by.

"Y' all right, then?" Stiffy shouts out, humping himself at her.

She takes no notice. Walks on, letting us see her fake coy smile.

"She's up the duff," he says.

"Not her as well?" Mickey says. "Who did it?"

"Who didn't?" Tommy puts in. "One o' them pikeys."

"Not again," I say.

"Not the same one, I don't s'pose," Stiffy says.

"You know what," Charlie says, pulling himself up tall. Charlie's taller than the tallest fourteen-year-old in the school and he's only eleven, like the rest of us. "You know what," he says again.

"What, Charlie?" I say. "We ain't got all day."

"I worked it out. If they take all the pikeys, showmen, fairgrounders, pregnant girls out of this school – "

"And those who've been to borstal – "

" – then us five'd be the only ones left!"

"This ain't a school." I say. "It's a lunatic asylum."

They nod. They'd nod if I told them Father Christmas lived in a marzipan factory.

"Right, let's do it."

Casually, separately, we move towards the tuck shop, keeping our eyes open for teachers, prefects and Mr Robbins, the caretaker. As I hide behind them, they form a huddle in front of the door. As I open it, Charlie reaches up and catches the bell. I crawl in under his arm. I scurry across the floor, go under the wooden flap and get to the till. It isn't locked. Even better, the drawer isn't properly closed. There's more than twenty quid. I shove it in my pocket, grab a load of sweets and crawl out.

Charlie closes the door real quiet. Me and the gang stroll away as if nothing's happened and at lunchtime we go round the back of the Portakabins and share everything out.

* * * * *

We're in geography class with Miss Chapman. There's more than thirty of us and she's talking about isles of the Pacific Ocean. I mean, when am I ever going to need to know about isles of the Pacific Ocean? Here I am, trapped in the Thomas Ellwood School with more chance of sunbathing on the Isle of Sheppey than dancing the hula-hula in the isles of the Pacific.

Everyone's ignoring her. Like they always do. They're either chattering or drawing or something. Someone throws a paper aeroplane across the room. Someone else throws it back. Tommy and me are talking about what we're going to do after school.

"Peters!" she shouts so loud everyone on the isles in the Pacific Ocean must have stopped what they were doing. "Come to the front!"

Everyone hushes and stops what they're doing. I'm always good for a bit of drama.

"Oh, what now?" I sigh, getting out from behind my desk and ambling up the aisle.

"What was the last thing I said?" she says.

"'Peters, come to the front'," I recite. I've heard it all before.

"Don't get cheeky with me," she says. "When I'm teaching you a very important subject, you pay attention. Do you understand?"

"Yes, Miss Chapman."

"And how many more times do I have to tell you, it's *Mrs* Chapman."

"Yes, Miss Chapman."

She goes bright red. She's ready to combust. "Mandy," she says, turning to one of the goody-goody girls sitting in the front row, "go and ask Mr Openshaw if he can spare me a moment of his valuable time."

Mandy gets out of her chair.

"And ask him to bring his slipper."

Not again. I've lost count of how many times I've had the slipper.

"Yes, *Mrs* Chapman." Smirking, Mandy marches out of the classroom.

While she's gone, no-one speaks or moves. It's like we're waiting for a bomb to explode without knowing when it'll go off.

A few minutes later, Mr Openshaw comes in. Mandy trots in after him. He's carrying his size-twelve slipper. It's long, thin and brown. Like him. He's long and thin and with brown hair combed over to hide his bald head. He smells of fish paste. And teaches chemistry. And talks like a lost sea lion. So we call him 'Stonky'.

"You wanted me, Mrs Chapman?" he honks, waving his weapon about. "Not Peters again."

"Go to your desk, Mandy. Yes, Mr Openshaw," she says, her voice rising to match his. "This boy – *once again* – is full of himself. He thinks he's more important than the education we're trying to instil into him."

"Full of himself, eh? Well, we'll soon get rid of that."

As Grandpa Wilf and me are in the middle of reading about Dotheboys' Hall in *Nicholas Nickleby* by Charles Dickens, I can't help but smile.

"Think it's funny, do you, Peters?" Stonky barks.

"No, sir."

"So what're you smiling about?"

"Nothing, sir."

"Right," he says, "you know what to do."

Mrs Chapman moves away.

50

Stonky takes a few steps so he's up against the door. I turn my back on him, close my eyes and bend over. I hear his shoes pitter-patter as he runs up to me, thwacks me right across the arse and pushes me a few feet along the floor.

'Cos I'm taking this in front of my mates, I make sure they don't see me wince in pain, even though it hurts like hell.

"How's that, Peters?" he growls.

"Thank you, sir."

"Do you want another?"

"No, sir."

"Well, as you insist, let's do it again."

"Thank you, sir."

His footsteps paddle across the room. He takes another run and smashes at me again.

Boy, does that hurt. I can feel tears trying to force themselves out my eyes. I shut them even tighter as I feel my face go bright beetroot.

"To your desk, Peters," Mrs Chapman says.

Everyone is silent as I walk back. Once again, seeing as I know they're watching, I sit down as casually as I can, my bum still stinging.

"Thank you, Mr Openshaw," says Mrs Chapman.

"Not at all, Mrs Chapman," Mr Openshaw says. "I am always at your service."

"You all right?" Tommy whispers, rubbing my shoulders.

I shrug as if it doesn't matter. But I'm so angry I can't speak. Tommy and me were talking. That's all we were doing. Why didn't he get the slipper? Everyone else was messing about. Why didn't they get the slipper? Why me? It's not fair.

Mrs Chapman gets back to her isles of the Pacific Ocean and, for the rest of the lesson, everyone pays silent attention. I write things down when she says, "Class, write this down," and pretend to pay attention when she says, "Pay attention, class."

But all the time I'm planning my revenge.

Exactly a week later, when I'm home getting ready for school, I pick up yesterday's *Daily Mirror* and shove it in my bag. Morning at school goes slowly. Summer's here, the sun's shining, the windows are open and everyone wants to get outside. Even the teachers are irritable.

At last, the bell goes and we're free for an hour.

I eat my lunch with the gang, then tell them to get lost, I've got something to do. They want to know what it is but, when they see I'm in no mood to argue, they clear off.

I slip out the school grounds and walk around the streets, keeping my eyes on the pavement. It doesn't take long to find what I'm looking for. There is it, by a broken-down fence in front of a garden filled with a couple of worn-out tyres, a busted pram and a clapped-out oven.

I get my *Daily Mirror* and crouch down. Then I spread it out over the heap of dog shit and wrap the lot up into a neat bundle.

When I get back to school, I go into the corridor that leads to Old Ma Chapman's classroom. In the wall next to the door is the air vent leading to the heating and cooling system. Making sure no-one's around, I open the vent and ram the bundle in. I ram it in really tight. Then I shut the vent and leave.

First lesson after lunch is geography, as I knew it would be.

"I know it's hot," she says, "so I've asked Mr Robbins to turn up the air conditioning. Now, today, class, we're going to study some more isles. This time, those around Africa."

She rolls down the blackboard to show a coloured map of Africa that must've taken hours to draw. It's so beautiful that, for a moment, I feel sorry for her.

We open our exercise books and start copying.

After a while, one of the girls at the front shouts out, "What's that funny smell?"

"Be quiet, Alexandra," Mrs Chapman says, "and get on with your work."

But before long, others are piping up.

"Ugh, Miss!"

"Miss, Jack's farted something awful."

"Miss, Jack's shat himself."

And even she can't pretend there isn't the worst smell in the whole wide world filling the room.

"Alexandra," she says, "go and find Mr Robbins."

Mr Robbins comes at once. "I'm on the case, Mrs Chapman."

"Miss, I think I'm going to be sick."

Mrs Chapman waves her arms about as if she's semaphoring to a Lancaster Bomber. "Class, we'll go out on to the school field. Calmly but quickly, please."

There's no calm but lots of quick. In fact, it's a stampede. Some are feeling ill, of course, but more are hamming it up, carried away with the drama. Others keep calm. I'm one of the calm ones.

Quacky – that's Mr Duxford, the headmaster – finally puts in an appearance. While he and Mr Robbins search the school, Mrs Chapman shouts at everyone to sit down and keep calm. But everyone's too excited, or too sick, or pretending to be sick, to pay attention.

And me?

I sit a few feet apart from all the silly kids. Watching. Smiling.

Mrs Chapman keeps looking at me out the corner of her eye. I can see she thinks she knows what it's all about. But without the evidence, she can't do a damned thing.

* * * * *

"Ready?" I say to Tommy, my mate, when he opens his door.

"Got everything?"

"Yeah." I open my bag. Glass cutter, screwdrivers, hammer, two trowels, gloves, a money bag and a few other little things.

"Got your gloves?"

"Yeah," he says. "Let's go, then."

It's eight o'clock on a Tuesday evening. Mum's out at the bingo, no idea where Dad is, Tommy's parents don't care where he is.

We get to the Labour Club along Shillingbury Close. We know it's closed on Tuesdays because we checked it out last week. We go up the side alley, get a beer crate and put it under one of the windows. I stand on it and cut out the glass. We clamber in.

As streetlights glow into the place, we crawl along the floor to the bar and the till. It's empty.

"Shoulda known," Tommy says.

"Yeah."

We go out the same way we got in.

"Where now?"

"We stick to the plan," I tell him.

Handy Hardware is down the road from the Labour Club. A lot of people go there so we know there's going to be some cash to take. After all, that's where I lifted the glass cutter. It was easy. The shop was crowded, the assistants were busy, nobody saw me.

We get round the back. Same routine. Cut the window, climb in, get to the till. £5 2s 7d.

"At least that's something," Tommy says.

"Not much, though," I say, putting the cash in the blue felt moneybag.

When we're out of the place and in the empty street, we light up our smokes.

"Now the Polish shop," I say.

"Let's go," Tommy says.

Once again, we go round the back.

"You'd think," Tommy says, as I'm cutting the glass, "these people would be a bit more careful."

When we get in, we have a good look round. The place stinks of cheeses, chickens, hams and there are loads of jars and bottles of stuff. But mostly sausages. So many different huge sausages. I've never seen so many sausages. A rack of a dozen or so knives stands by a sink. They're like the sausages. Huge.

"Look at these," I say.

"Can't carry 'em," Tommy says. "Let's do the till and get outa here."

It's easy to break into. There's a wodge of dough and that goes into the moneybag.

When we get outside, we count it. £32 4s 1ld.

"Who leaves that sort of money in a till overnight?" I say.

"This bloke does," Tommy says. "Stupid idiot."

Altogether, we've bagged £37 7s 6d.

We go back to Shillingbury Close. Using the trowels, we dig up the turf near the Labour Club, we make a hole, bury the moneybag and replace the turf. Then, and only then, now it's all over, Tommy gets nervous and has to pee. I'm all right. We have another smoke, then leg it home.

Next day at school, morning goes on forever. At last, the dinner bell goes. Quick as we can, Tommy and me go to Shillingbury Close and dig up the money.

As there's about three-quarters of an hour before we have to be back in school, we go into town to treat ourselves. We're hungry, Tommy's always hungry, so we go into the Wimpy Bar and order double cheeseburgers. That's with tomato, lettuce, ketchup and onion, of course. Followed by toffee sundaes.

We're sitting back, relaxing with strawberry milkshakes and smokes when Tommy says, "Look at the time!"

We stand up, gulp down the rest of the shakes, stub out the fags.

"We're gonna be late," he says when we get outside.

I count the money. "Nah, let's have a taxi." We pile into the first one that comes along and tell the driver to take us to Thomas Ellwood School.

"Phew!" says Tommy as we're riding along. "That was close."

"Worth it, though," I say. "I'm stuffed."

"How much we got left, Frank?"

"'Bout twenty quid."

Staring out the window, he says, "That was a good night's work."

"And there's loads of other places we can do," I say. "How many shops are there in this town? I tell ya what, Tommy, if we bag that sort of haul every week, we're laughing."

The taxi driver drops us at the gates and I pay him. We get into school as the afternoon bell is ringing. We make it to gym. In the changing-room noise and clutter, no-one notices us slip in.

After school, I'm home, settling down to enjoy *Top Cat*, when there's a knock at the door. Mum's making tea. "See who that is, love," she calls.

"Hello, Frank." Ron Chantrell and his mate, Ted Kingsley. The police. "Can we come in?" Before I can say a word, they're pushing me aside and are on their way to the kitchen. "Your mum through here, is she?"

I call out. "Mum! It's the – "

"You," Kingsley says, grabbing hold of me, "come with us."

Mum's making a pot of tea.

"Looks like we got here just right, Ted, "Chantrell says. "Fancy a cup o' tea?"

"Mine's two sugars," Kingsley says.

"What's Flo been up to now?" she sighs, putting the lid on the pot.

"It's not Flo we've come about, Val," he says. "It's your boy here."

As Mum's getting some more cups and saucers, I say, "It wasn't me!" and I laugh, like it's a joke.

Not in the least smiling, Chantrell looks down at me. "What wasn't you, Frank?"

I feel myself go red. "Dunno," I mumble.

Mum's pouring out the tea. "Well, let's all sit down, shall we? Whatever it is you're saying Frank's done, I'm sure we can sort it out."

The three of them sit round the kitchen table. I stand at the end, where they can see me. While Kingsley's watching me, he gets out his notebook and pen.

"Tell me, Frank," Chantrell says, "is it true you got a taxi from town to school this afternoon?"

I shake my head. "No."

"Really?" he says. "That's odd." He turns back to face Mum. "You see, Val, two lads, one of them answering Frank's description, and one called Frank, the other called Tommy, took a taxi from town to the Thomas Ellwood School this afternoon at about... " He looks at Ted.

Kingsley flips a few pages of his notebook. "One thirty."

"Frank," Mum says, "where did you get the money to pay for a taxi?"

"This morning," Chantrell goes on, "we received two reports of break-ins. Handy Hardware. Paul's Polish Emporium. Windows cut out, tills broken into. Nearly forty pounds taken."

Everyone's quiet as they look at me.

Mum's trembling. "You didn't, did you?"

"Mum!"

"Frank Wilfred Peters, I'm arresting you on two counts of shopbreaking and stealing, contrary to the Larceny Act of 1916, Section 2." He cautions me.

"You missed out the Labour Club!" I blurt out.

"Oh, Frank!" Mum says, bursting into tears.

Pushing back the kitchen chair, Chantrell stands up. Kingsley closes his notebook, gets to his feet.

"Get your coat, Frank," Chantrell says. "You're coming with us. Val, you should come too."

While Mum's getting our coats, I say, "How did you know it was us?"

"Well, son," he says, looking round to make sure Mum can't hear, "next time, don't talk about it in the back of a taxi. And if you do, don't use your names, eh? You are such a stupid oaf, you know that?"

Three months later, me and Tommy are put on

probation for three years and have to pay £1 2s 6d restitution each. Dad makes me pay it myself. But that's no problem, 'cos I've still got the twenty quid left over from the break-ins. I hadn't dared spend it and nobody thought to search my room. I fork out for Tommy as well.

"You know what, Frank," Charlie Milliken says a week later, when he shows me the local paper reporting my court appearance. "You know what," he says again.

"Spit it out, Charlie. Christmas is only three months away and I got things to do."

"This means," he says, waving the paper in the air, "you're now officially a criminal."

"Yeah," I say. "I s'pose I am."

"You're the first criminal I ever met."

"Well, whaddya know."

* * * * *

If there's one thing I hate about school more than anything, it's gym. They call it gym, but really it's running across muddy fields in the rain. Me and Tommy, we're always last 'cos we stop for a rest or a smoke. We can't understand how the eager beaver blockheads at the front never have to stop for a pee, either. Sometimes, we get so fed up of the whole thing, we walk most of the way. But however late we are getting back, Jonesy, the PT teacher, is always waiting for us.

"Why haven't you gone home, sir?" I say one afternoon when Tommy and me come in from the rain.

"Have to make sure everyone's back safe and sound, Peters," he says. "Come on now, get those things off and into the showers."

"Haven't got a towel, sir," Tommy says. He's never got a towel. He's never got any kit, come to that. He's my best mate, I know, but he's a poor little thing. He doesn't even come to school in a uniform. It's always grubby tee-shirt, unwashed V-neck sweater, mucky jeans and plimsolls with holes in 'em, whatever the weather, summer or winter.

He peels off his gear and hands each item to Jonesy, who's waiting patiently to take them off him. Jonesy gives him a towel. "Okay, lads, get cleaned up."

I'm in and out in ten minutes. A few minutes later, while I'm drying and getting dressed, Tommy comes out, no cleaner than when he went in.

"Here's a bar of soap, Owens," Jonesy says, "back in that shower, lad. You'll have another twenty minutes until you're clean."

While Jonesy and me are waiting, I say, "Look, sir, we don't like doing this cross-country. So how d'ya feel about having a nice fresh chicken for your Sunday dinner?"

"Yeah, that'd be lovely."

So next day, Tommy and me go out, nick the chicken and kill it. We get Jonesy to drive us to where we've hidden it and he's a happy bunny.

After that, we're excused gym, providing we keep quiet and don't wander too far from the changing-rooms for the hour. He tells us to shower near the end of the period so it looks like we've been out. From then on, of course, it looks as if we always beat the best runners in the class. Which puzzles them no end.

Three or four weeks later, a day after we've delivered another chicken, Tommy and me are playing cards in the changing rooms. Everyone else is out on their run. It's about five minutes to go to shower time when Baxter, one of the prefects, wanders in.

"What're you up to?" he shouts across the room.

"Minding our own business," I say.

He strides over and examines our card game. "Why aren't you out with the others?"

"Get lost."

"We'll see what Mr Hyde has to say about this," he says.

Playing my cards and without looking up, I say, "Don't bother. He knows all about it."

"Don't you tell me what to do," he says, thumping me in the back. "What's your names?"

Tommy edges away. "Uh-ho."

Baxter stares at him. "What's up with you? Scared?"

Tommy shakes his head. "I wouldn't do that, if I were you."

"You mean this?" he blurts. And he thumps me in the back again.

Tommy stands up. "I'll go and get help, Frank." He runs out the changing-rooms.

"So it's Frank, is it?"

Slowly and carefully, I gather up the cards, stack them in a neat pile on the bench and stand up.

He thumps me a third time. "Like that, do you?"

That's it. I've had enough. I spin round, throw him a right-hander and catch him in the eye. It's a corker of a punch, it really is. Screaming out, he jerks backwards, leaves the ground, goes a few feet and lands on his arse. He's clutching his eye as if it's fallen out.

Tommy bursts back in, followed by Mr Channing, the pottery teacher, and, and I don't know why, Mickey Golightly, one of my gang. The three of them stand there for a few seconds, taking in the scene and then Mr Channing rushes at me, grabs me around the throat, slings me up against the lockers and punches me in the stomach.

"You're a delinquent!" he shouts. "Do you know that, Peters? You're nothing but a bloody half-cracked hooligan."

Tommy and Mickey run at him and drag him off me.

"Get off me, you ruffians!" Channing shouts, trying to get at me.

"Sir!" Tommy shouts. "Sir!"

"Get off him!" Mickey hollers.

Channing calms down. They let him go. Now that it's all over and he doesn't have to do anything, Baxter gets up. I brush myself down.

Next day, Mickey, Tommy and me are in Mr Duxford's office.

"Well," the headmaster says, looking at the three of us across his desk. "This is a fine mess. Peters, you assault a school prefect – "

"Sir, he thumped me three times."

"I don't want to hear it, Peters. You, Owens, and you, Golightly, you manhandle a teacher – "

"He was thumping Peters, sir," Tommy says.

"We were trying to stop him," Mickey says.

"There seems to have been," he says, "a whole lot of thumping going on." For a few minutes, he reads the file in front of him. "And you, Owens, and you, Peters, should have been out on your weekly run, anyway... Mr Hyde tells me you're permanently excused that particular activity." He looks up at us. "He's vague as to the reason." He closes the file. "So I'm not blaming you for that... but this other stuff. Peters, we can't go on like this."

"No, sir."

He takes a few minutes looking at the three of us, standing in front of him, hands behind our backs.

"Well, Peters?"

"Sir."

"What do you think you deserve?"

"Sir, I'll take whatever Owens gets, sir."

"And you, Owens?"

"Sir."

"What do you think you deserve?"

"I'll take what Peters gets."

"Golightly."

"Sir."

"What do you think you deserve?"

"Me, sir?"

"Yes, you, sir. What do you think you deserve?"

By now, Mickey's shaking. "Nothing, sir."

Quacky doesn't say a word, runs his hand through his hair, shakes his head.

Mickey says, "I was only trying to help." Then he starts blubbing. He rubs his fists over his eyes, leans forward and soon he's crying his eyes out. It's quite an exhibition and I'm not best pleased. One of my gang crying his eyes out over getting the cane.

61

"Peters," Quacky says, "it's obvious you were provoked. But you should have backed off and reported Baxter, not gone for him. You'll get two of the cane."

"Yes, sir. Thank you, sir."

"Owens, you'll get the same."

"Thank you, sir."

"Plus one more. You did what you could, I know, but you should have come for help, not manhandled Mr Channing. That's three altogether. Do you understand?"

"Yes, sir, thank you, sir."

Tommy looks at me out of the corner of his eye.

We smile.

Mickey stops his snivelling.

"Blow your nose, Golightly," Quacky says.

"Haven't got a hanky, sir," he says.

Quacky sits back, folds his arms, waits as Mickey wipes his nose and cleans his face on his sleeves.

"Golightly."

"Sir."

"What a sorry sight you are, Golightly."

"Yes, sir."

Quacky shakes his head. "Not good, Golightly. You get two for manhandling Mr Channing."

"Yes, sir, thank you, sir."

"And you get another two for not sticking with your pals here. You're in Peters' gang. Peters expects you to behave like a member of his gang. Don't you, Peters?"

"Yes, sir."

"Uphold the code, eh, Peters?"

"Yes, sir."

"And when you're called in front of your headmaster, you stick together, like members of a gang should." He stands up and barks, "What you don't do is let down your mates! For disloyalty to them, you get another two."

"Sir." He starts blubbing again.

"And you get another two because you're a coward, Golightly," he says. "You take your punishment like a man. You do not cry. And if you do cry, you do it when

62

you're on your own. You've embarrassed everyone. You've let Peters down. You've humiliated yourself. So, you get six altogether."

"Sir, thank you, sir."

Quacky goes to his cupboard, gets out his cane and gives it a few swishes.

"Peters, you first. Show Golightly how it's done."

"Yes, sir, thank you, sir."

Afterwards, Quacky lets Tommy and Mickey go but keeps me behind.

"Give this to your parents." From under the file on his desk, he pulls out a sealed envelope. "We need to sort you out once and for all." He hands it over. "And it's no use hiding it. If your parents don't come, I'll go looking for them. Understood?"

The following week, Mum and me are in Quacky's office.

According to him, I'm always fighting. I'll fight anyone who so much as looks at me. I organise my gang so well Al Capone could take lessons. I terrorise the playground. I attack prefects and my gang attacks teachers. I commit crimes. I'm put on probation. I maliciously infect the air conditioning. "You thought I'd forgotten about that, didn't you?"

But worst of all, he says, are my school marks. They're some of the worst marks he's seen in his thirty-two years in teaching. If I want to get on, I must get my head down. I show no signs of doing that.

Mum takes all this in. "Okay," she says, "what do you want me to do, Mr Quacky?"

He falls back in his chair. He doesn't know what to say. It's all I can do not to laugh out loud. Finally, he gets his breath, opens a file, pulls out a sheet of paper and hands it over.

It's a letter expelling me from the school.

"Oh, Frank," Mum says. She looks up. "I'm so sorry, Mr – er – "

"Mrs Peters," he says, "I've had a word with the head

63

teacher at Lee Valley Comprehensive. He's willing to take your son, 'though God knows why. As it's only two weeks to the end of summer term, your son will leave this school today and start at Lee Valley in September. But be advised, Mrs Peters, he'll be fourteen then, so he hasn't much time left to straighten himself out. You and Mr Peters have six weeks to decide what you want his future to look like." He stands up and shows us out.

As we leave, I think if Jonesy hadn't said he liked chicken, I wouldn't a got expelled.

* * * * *

We move to a village a couple of miles from Lee Valley Comprehensive. So getting there is an easy walk and I can keep in touch with my mates at Thomas Ellwood.

As far as I'm concerned, Lee Valley Comprehensive is a joke. It used to be a grammar and behaves as if it still is. The kids are stuck up. They come to school from the posh end of town, dressed in brand new sheepskins. They flash their money around and talk about parties, clothes, music and dates with the latest lover-boy or bit o' skirt. They live in big houses. Their dads drive Jaguars and Bentleys. Their mums go to the hairdressers twice a week. The girls are really good-looking. With all that money floating about, they should be.

I make a couple of friends and, when I go round to theirs, I walk across their lovely carpets in their lovely houses. I've never seen carpets like that. Must've cost a fortune. Their mums and dads sit on plush sofas, smiling, sipping sherry, calling each other darling, watching their colour TVs.

This is how to live. I really like it. I've gotta have some. Of course, the only way I can get anywhere near it is by thieving. 'Cos I reckon, for me to mix with the rich girls in the clubs or in the pubs or wherever, I have to have a few bob. 'Cos they don't want a skintbob round 'em, do they?

I don't do very well at that school.

After a while, the headmaster, he takes me into his office and says, "You're running this school from the outside. If you don't like someone, or a prefect tells you to do something, you have them beaten up. You will not run my school from the outside."

When I leave his office, I don't feel like going back into lessons, so I go for a walk in the park, sit down on a bench, light up a fag and have a think. I'm fourteen, in my fourth year, and ready to do something else. It's March. Spring is here. I decide to take six months off. That'll take me up to September when I'll be fifteen, school-leaving age. So I figure it doesn't make much difference if I go to school or not. I'll spend my days fishing in the Lea.

I tell Mum and Dad what I'm going to do.

"Just keep yourself out of trouble," Dad says. "And if you can't do that, don't get caught."

Mum says, "Make sure you get enough to eat."

So that's what I do. Nobody bothers me, nobody comes looking for me. I think they're glad to be shot of me.

September, on my first day back, a prefect who doesn't know me tries to tell me what to do. So I thump him in the face and his nose spouts blood like I've never seen before. Someone else lays into me and soon the three of us are scrapping on the ground.

The headmaster comes out. He picks me up by the collar and frogmarches me to his car, slings me in and takes me home.

Mum and Dad come to the door.

The headmaster says, "I do not want this child in my school any more. Take him. He's your responsibility."

Mum says, "What are we supposed to do with him?"

"Do what you like. I don't want him."

Chapter 4. Town

Mum arranges for me to work Saturdays at the glass factory. Only Saturdays, mind, 'cos I'm not old enough for a full-time job. But I earn a few bob and I really enjoy it. They say when I'm older, if I'm interested they'll teach me to be a glass blower. I'm up for that. I like art.

The thing is, though, during the week when Mum and Dad are at work I've time on my hands so, to supplement my earnings, I do a little thieving. I don't rob people's houses, 'cos that's not right. But when everyone's gone home, I get into offices, factories, warehouses, that sort of thing. It's shocking how many people leave dosh lying around on their desks and how easy it is to break into cupboards and cabinets where they keep the petty cash. Money for old rope.

A couple of weeks later, on the way from doing a job I stop by to see Grandpa Wilf. What with one thing and another, I haven't been round for a while. One of the reasons is he and Nan have bought a big house, done a deal with the glass factory to take in some of their workers and have been setting everything up. Mum tells me they'll have seven lodgers with rooms for two more.

I go round the back into the kitchen. "Grandpa Wilf!"

"He ain't here," Nan shouts from somewhere over the noise of a vacuum cleaner.

"He ain't here," says a fella standing by the kitchen sink, drinking a mug of coffee and smoking a fag.

"Where is he?" I shout again.

"Joined the Bowls Club, ain't he?" Nan shouts. "Christ knows why."

"Oh… " I look at the fella in the kitchen. "You're Bobby Crick."

"You're Frank Peters," he says, drawing on his fag, stubbing it out. "You're the bloke who beat up that teacher – "

"I didn't beat up no teacher."

66

" – and they threw you out of school." He smirks and nods at the same time. "Good on yer."

I've heard about Bobby Crick, everyone's heard about Bobby Crick, but this is the first time I've met him.

When he was thirteen, they put him in a Remand Home. He thought the milkman was having it away with his mum, so he hit him in the balls with a hammer. Turns out the milkman *was* having it away but the judge said that was no excuse. Everyone else said it was, but their opinion didn't count.

When he came out, some lad won five quid off him in a snooker game, so Bobby snatched his cue off him and broke it over the lad's head. He shoved half of it down the lad's throat and whipped the barman about the face with the other half. It took four coppers to hold Bobby down while they cuffed him. He was sixteen.

And here he is three years later in my nan's kitchen, dressed in a dark wine-red leather three-quarter coat, white shirt, narrow black tie, black trousers, black socks and black loafers. He looks fit and stylish. He's a Mod.

"What you doing here?" I say.

"I live here."

"With my nan?"

"I'm renting a room. Just got out, didn't I?"

"Oh yeah?"

"Yeah."

We stare at each other for a while, then, suddenly, his face breaks into a broad grin and he shows off sparkling white teeth like he's modelling for a Gibbs SR toothpaste advert. You can see why all the birds go after him.

A young woman in her early twenties carrying a mug comes in.

"Sally," Bobby says, "this is Frank." He nods in my direction. "Mrs Peters' grandson."

"Pleased to meet you," she says.

She's a good-looking bird. Flip-flops, Levis, sparkly pink top nicely stacked, long black hair. I watch her fill the kettle and switch it on. "Well," I say, "if Grandpa Wilf ain't here, I'll go."

"Yeah," Bobby says, "why don't ya?"

"I will then."

Sally says, "Nice to meet you, Frank."

* * * * *

After four months or so, seeing Mum and others shut in all day every day, I go off the idea of glass blowing. I don't intend to be locked up for most of my life.

"Mum, Dad," I say, "I'm going to join the Merchant Navy. I wanna see the world."

Mum says nothing, gets up, makes some fresh tea.

Slowly, Dad slowly lights a fag. "And how are you going to do that, son?"

"I looked it up in the Library," I say. "I go down to Prescot Street and register. I'm going tomorrow."

"You'll wanna bit o' cash," he says, reaching into his pocket.

"'S all right," I say. "I can manage."

I catch Mum and Dad looking at each other. But they keep quiet.

Next day, I get on the train up to Prescot Street where they offer me a job with P&O as a steward on the Canberra.

"That's a bloody good job," I say.

"Too right, lad," the officer says. "But first you have to go on a sixteen-week course at sea-training school in Gravesend."

"Sounds good to me."

"We don't have any vacancies at present, but if you'd like a job with the British Shipping Federation as a courier until one arises – "

"Yeah, okay."

"That's 'Yeah, okay, sir'."

"Yeah, okay, sir."

"Good lad."

A couple of weeks later, every day I'm going up to The

Minories, next to the Tower of London, where the British Shipping Federation has its offices. It's my job to deliver the letters, memos and messages they write to shipping companies. I have to walk everywhere, of course, and when you're doing that, you find out how big the City of London actually is.

Soon, I know the place like the back of my hand – every office, every address, every building, every café and everybody in all of 'em. It's a great little job and I love it.

But then one Saturday afternoon, I'm round Brian's, my mate's, and he's showing me his dad's new sunbed and says would I like to have a go. So I strip off and get on. He switches it on and goes off for a fag. Well, I don't know how long I'm supposed to stay on there, do I, and before you know it, I'm the colour of a burnt chipolata. Brian comes back, sees what's happened, calls his dad and they get me to the hospital, where I get a sick note for four weeks.

The Shipping Federation has to keep paying me, of course, but while I'm at home, I do a bit of thieving here and there – to keep my hand in, you understand – and then realise, while I love the job itself, I don't like the journeys to and from the City. I figure I've swapped being shut up in a factory for being cramped in a train two hours a day with all the other packed sardines.

To top it all, two weeks into my sick note I get a letter from Gravesend, saying they've got a place for me at sea-training school to start in four days' time. Only I can't go, can I, 'cos I'm on the sick.

So I can't go sea-training and I can't go to work.

"Never mind, Frank," Dad says. "Blowing glass, serving drinks in glasses. You're obviously not meant to be working with glass. I'll have a word with Sean Underwood."

Sean's another of Dad's mates – Dad knows everyone – and Sean and a bloke called Bandy own a massive scrapyard in the Lea Valley. Dad fixes me up to go and see them.

"You'll be working with my son, won't ya now," Sean says. "He'll show you the ropes. Are you good with dogs?"

"Dogs?"

"Woof woof, bow-wow."

"I suppose so."

"If you're not, you're no use to me."

We go out into the scrapyard. A lad my age is nearby, sorting through a heap of metal cuts. A giant Doberman sits, watching. His tongue, the size of a leg of lamb, hangs out of his mouth. His paws are big enough to clobber a fella over the head and leave him in a coma.

"This is Smiffy," Sean says.

I hold out my hand. "Pleased to meet you, Smiffy."

"Smiffy's the dog, you twerp," Sean says. "Rory, this is Frank, the lad I told you about. He starts Monday. He's Sid Peters' boy." He turns to me. "Seven sharp. Any morning, if you're not here, we start without you and you're out of it. We can't be doing with hanging around. Understand?"

I nod.

"It's tough work," he says, "but if you stick at it, you'll be doing fine. Right. Dinner time." He takes a few steps away and shouts at the top of his voice at a chap operating the shredder, "Bandy! Are you ready now?"

"You bet," a wood-alcohol voice calls back.

Sean says, "Stay for the day. Look around. Rory'll see to you."

With Sean and Bandy gone, Rory eyes me up and down. "So you're Frank Peters."

"'S right."

"You're the idiot who got thrown outa school for thumping that teacher."

"I didn't thump no teacher," I say.

"That's not what I heard."

"Well, you heard wrong."

I eye *him* up and down.

He's taller than me, in jeans, Doc Martens and a black

70

tee-shirt with white lettering. "United Skins". His head's shaved completely bald.

"You a skinhead?"

"You gonna make something of it?"

I shrug. "What do skinheads do?"

"We meet up, get pissed, go to matches and kick the bollocks off anyone we don't like the look of."

I spend the rest of the day with Rory. It's a big place, all right. Cars piled on top of each other all over the place. The equipment, cranes, shredders, grapples, magnets, cutters. Portakabin office. Portakabin kitchen and canteen. Portakabin toilet.

He says, "We keep a few dogs around the yard – "

"Yeah."

" – 'cos we can't be everywhere all the time. They guard the place. Tell us when punters are about."

Putting his fingers to his mouth, he lets out three sharp whistles. For a couple of seconds nothing happens, then clanging and rattling noises come from up the tops of piles of scrap and metal nests. Then more than a dozen Alsatian dogs are running at us.

Rory's watching me, sizing me up, waiting for me to back off, to be shit-scared.

As these dogs the size of wolves thump their way through the scrapyard, I'm careful to let Rory and them see me stand my ground. "How many are there? Thirteen, fourteen?"

"Seventeen," he says, "if you don't count Smiffy."

Like wild animals tamed to perform in a circus, they reach us at exactly the same time and stand in front of Rory, tongues hanging out, panting, ears perked, tails wagging.

"Sit!"

There they sit, never once taking their eyes off Rory. One or two gently woof or growl. They're magnificent.

"All right?" Rory says.

"Any reason I shouldn't be?"

"Anyway," Rory says, "you won't see my dad or

71

Bandy for the rest of the day. Once they get to The Angler's Rest for their dinner, that's it. So it's you and me and the dogs in the afternoons. You all right with that?"

I've got a job, it's outside, I'm not shut in, and once Sean and Bandy have gone, Rory and me can do what we like. We knock off at four, which means I can get the 4.15 bus home, have some tea and I've got the evening to go out thieving. And I get paid. I mean, what's not to like?

Soon it's as if I've been there all my life. I love it. Rory and me become good mates and he teaches me quite a lot – how to cut up lorries and one thing and another.

I get on really well with all the dogs. Each one has its own individual personality and I treat them all as separate characters. Before long, I take to two in particular, Magnum and Candy, and they take to me. They follow me wherever I go and if they're not there, I call 'em and they come running. My personal bodyguards.

One day a couple of months later, I ask Rory, "How do I get to be a skinhead?"

"You get your head shaved," he says, "you get the gear, you get yourself along to a meet."

"That don't sound difficult."

"Interested?"

"Might be."

"Tomorrow's Saturday," he says. "Come round to mine, I'll shave your head, we'll go up the Smoke and get you kitted out. How about that?"

Next day, he sits me down in his kitchen, covers my shoulders with a bath towel and, like an expert barber, shaves off my hair. He does a really good job. He's gentle and soft and caring, like you'd expect a woman to be. 'Cos my head's a bit raw when he's finished, he massages my bald pate with some cream to take away the sting. When I look in the mirror, I see a short guy with an ostrich egg for a head and ears sticking out like two handles on a soup dish.

"You'll be fine once you get the gear," he says, running his fingers over his handiwork. "C'm' on."

We get the train up to The Last Resort in Goulston Street, Aldgate. We're in there at least a couple of hours. First, I try everything on, then I buy the full outfit.

The black Fred Perry shirt sets me back £12 19s 11d. The red and white check Ben Sherman shirt is another £12 19s 11d. Red braces are £2 10s. Black Sta Prest trousers, £9 19s 11d. Doc Marten's black steel toe 14-hole Ultra High-liner boots, £29 18s 0d. A tee-shirt with "The Power and the Glory" on it, £3 19s 11d. A tee-shirt with "Strength through Oi!", another £3 19s 11d.

"That's the real business," Rory says as I catwalk up and down the shop, dead proud.

"You look good," Micky, the owner, says. "Now, the suit, shirt and tie. And the Crombie, of course."

I choose a dark Prince of Wales suit going at £39 18s 0d, a white shirt for £12 19s 11d and a black tie for £2 19s 11d. The black Crombie overcoat with red silk lining and red hanky is £28.00, a pair of black loafers £28.00 and two pairs of socks, 7s 0d.

"Thanks a lot," Micky says, as he wraps everything up. "That comes to £195 5s 5d, please."

"And cheap at the price," Rory pipes up.

I must say, as I hand over the cash, I agree.

We get the train home, feeling very pleased with ourselves. Over the noise of the rumbling train, Rory shouts, "Now all we gotta do is get you to a meet."

I nod. I can't wait to get home to try everything on again.

A couple of weekends later, I'm in my gear in Hertford with about thirty or forty other skinheads. The next weekend it's Nazeing, or Harlow, Cheshunt, Waltham Cross, Letchworth or Stevenage. Sometimes we go as far as Luton, Bedford or even Northampton. Wherever, it's always the same. We find the local disco, crash our way in, cause mayhem, bash everyone to a pink-bloodied pulp and skedaddle.

When we get back, we have a few beers, crash out wherever we are and go home on the Sunday morning. We spend the rest of the week cleaning, polishing, washing and ironing our gear ready for next time.

One Saturday night, for a change, we stay local. The Come On Inn, Broxbourne. Jimmy Steele, a good friend of mine, has a disco at the back. All the skinheads go there. Jimmy has all the right music, too. My favourite is Derrick Morgan, *A Night at the Hop*. There's more than enough fights for everyone.

Afterwards, we're walking home along the high street – me, Rory and maybe thirty others, when suddenly we're being escorted by a couple of police squad cars. We're orderly. We don't cause no trouble. We don't fight the filth. That's out of order. But it's a fine sight. Thirty skinheads in their Ben Shermans, Crombies and Doc Martens walking up the High Street, followed by squad cars.

"This is the business," I say.

"It's always good to have some fuzzy protection," Rory says, handing me another spliff.

As we're passing the police station, two men jump out from behind the trees, like they're marauding kangaroos. The squad cars stop. A dozen uniforms come out the station.

The kangaroos leap forward and one of 'em says, "Okay, everyone, empty your pockets." It's my old mates, Ron Chantrell and Ted Kingsley. I was only thinking of them the other day, wondering where they'd got to.

Before you can say "Mack the Knife", everyone's thrown their weapons away in the trees. I get rid of a small fireman's axe and a chain with balls of lead on the end that I always use for bashing people's heads in. I snatch Rory's spliff off him and drop it and mine down a drain.

It's quite an awesome sight, seeing all the skinheads and pigs socialising like they're old mates. Everyone's polite. Everyone wants to get on their way. Fuzz included, I suppose. No-one relishes the thought of a run-in.

Ron comes up to me. "Oh, Frank, you're not playing this game now, are you?"

"Hallo, Ron," I say, "long time no see."

"I thought you, of all people, would know better than get mixed up with this lot."

"Well, you know how it is, Ron," I say. "You go where you can find it, don't ya?"

"Still working for that double-dealing Sean Underwood? 'Allo, Rory, y' all right?"

"Yes, thanks, Mr Chantrell," Rory says. "And yourself?"

"How d'you know I'm working for Sean?" I say, shocked.

"Oh, come on," he says. "We know everything. You should know that. Let's search your pockets." While he's crouching, having a rummage about my person, he says, "You know, Frank, we'll get you one day. Don't know where, don't know when."

Rory bursts into song. "But I know we'll meet again – "

Ron looks up at me. "What's he on?"

I shrug. Nothing to do with me.

Ron stands. "But we *will* get you, Frank. That's as certain as you think the sun shines out your cocky little arse." He steps aside. "On your way."

* * * * *

A couple of months later, Nan and Grandpa Wilf hold a party to introduce their lodgers to the neighbourhood. She clears out the main room, puts in a record-player and a couple of tables for food and drink. Everyone brings a bottle so there's more than enough. I bring some dope to help liven things up a bit.

Soon everyone's sloshing it back and stuffing their faces with cheese and those little white onions on Ritz crackers, sausages wrapped in bacon and pineapple chunks on cocktail sticks stuck in grapefruits. Grandpa Wilf puts some music on and all us young 'uns dance the night away. It's a good do. I'll say this about my nan, she knows how to give a party.

Eventually, Bobby turns up, still in his red leather coat, white shirt and black trousers.

"Is that the only thing you've got to wear?" I ask him as I pour him a glass of red.

"More or less," he says, "'til I organise some dosh. You got any you don't need?"

I put the bottle down, pull out my wallet and peel off a couple of tenners. "There y' go. Buy yourself a clean shirt."

As he takes it, he puts his arm round my shoulder. "Thanks, mate. I'll pay you back."

"No need," I say. "Look on it as a token of our friendship." I hand him the glass.

"Yeah," he says, leaning on me, slightly sloshed. "'Cos we're mates, ain't we?"

"Course we are, Bobby," I say. "Now, if you'll excuse me, there's a lady over there I have to talk to."

I free myself and go to where's Sally's listening to some fat bloke.

"Oh, hi, Frank," she says. "This is, er… Sorry, I don't know your name."

The fat bloke mutters something into his pineapple chunk on a stick.

"Shall we dance?" I say, grabbing her hand, as *This Guy's in Love with You* by Herb Alpert comes on.

"Oh," she says, "I love this. It's so romantic."

Then it's *Honky Tonk Women* by the Rolling Stones, *Goodnight Midnight* by Clodagh Rogers and *On the Road Again* by Canned Heat. By the time *My Cherie Amour* by Stevie Wonder is blasting out, I fancy Sally something rotten and she obviously likes me.

Later, when the party's winding down, I'm tired and need a lie-down. I roll a spliff, grab a bottle of wine and wander upstairs. On the second landing, a door's open and I go in. No-one's there. The double bed is empty.

I shove off my shoes, put the bottle on the bedside cabinet and, spliff in mouth, throw myself on to the eiderdown. As I pick up the bottle, I see a photo of a middle-aged couple. "To our lovely Sally, Love Mum + Dad xxx."

Well, well. What a surprise. I take a swig of wine. If she's not here, at least I can be close to where she *will* be. I put the bottle down, get off the bed, take off my clothes and slide in. My hard cock feels good against the sheets, really good. When I've smoked the spliff, I fall into a doze.

It must be, I dunno, half an hour later when she walks in. "What you doing?"

"I'm in your bed," I say, opening my eyes, "that's what I'm doing. What do you think I'm doing?"

"Do you mind getting out?"

"Well, I do really," I say, "'cos there's nowhere else to go. All the other rooms are taken and I'm not sleeping on the sofa, I can assure you."

"Get out my bed."

"Why make a fuss?" I say. "It's late… Tell you what, you sleep down the bottom and we'll sleep topsy-turvy, all right?"

"Mmm," she saying, half-smiling. "All right. But no funny business."

"Let's crack on with the zees, eh," I say, edging up and turning over. I close my eyes. I feel a pillow go from behind me, some rustling about and, after a few minutes, the light goes out, the sheets are pulled away, a pair of legs sidles up against my back and the sheets are dragged back over.

After a while, one of her feet rubs up against my backside, which is nice, and I open my legs so she can get a proper feel. Her other foot comes over and plays with my inside thighs and balls. As I turn on to my back, she pulls her feet away but I grab an ankle and slowly rub her foot over my cock. Using my other hand, I play with my balls and before you know it, they're tight. By now, I'm big and rock hard.

After a few minutes, she pulls away and, in the darkness, I see the sheets lift up like a wigwam. Her body rises and falls. Her hands grab my cock and I feel her warm breath on my balls. She's licking them all over, taking them in her mouth, her fingers are up between my legs, her lips are around my cock, my cock is in her mouth and it's like my cock is the first cock she's ever had.

Which it can't be. She's got three kids, for God's sake. I've had girls before – of course I have – but Sally's different. She's a woman, not a girl. A real, live, beautiful, seductive woman. Although I'm only fifteen, I know exactly what to do. I do it well. All night. 'Til the sun shines through the window. That's the thing about speed. When it's in your system, your cock stays monstrously big and hard and your energy pumps away all night.

* * * * *

Despite what Ron Chantrell says about Sean, I'm still at the scrapyard six months later when, for a change, I pop over the road to Cal's Café for late breakfast. Sean and Bandy have gone off for the day to meet someone interested in signing a deal. Rory's struggling with paperwork. Everything's quiet. The dogs are loping about, so he says I'll be all right for an hour.

As I make my way across the yard to the gates, I realise Magnum and Candy are following me.

"Ya fancy a fry-up?"

They wag their tails, creep up close and let me pat their heads.

"C'm' on, then," I say and wave them on.

They jump all over me as if I've given them a couple of bones the size of a dinosaur's ribcage.

We cross the road and go into Cal's. It's packed with lorry drivers having breakfast. As there's a table left in the corner at the back, I go through and take my seat.

The place goes quiet as the dogs, taller than the table-tops, follow, sit down either side of me and stare at these drivers with bellies as big as your arse, daring them to approach. They're wolves guarding the Keeper of the

Gates of Hell.

Cal comes over. "Yes, Frank. What can I do you for?"

"Two eggs, bacon, black pudding, tomato, mushrooms, fried bread, a couple of slices of bread... And a cup o' tea."

He nods at the dogs. "What about Sooty and Sweep?"

"They're fine, Cal, thanks."

The great thing about Amber, Cal's cook, is she doesn't hang about. Within ten minutes, the plate's in front of me and I'm digging in.

One or two of the drivers get up and leave. Then a few more.

As I'm dipping bread into the yolks, a fat bloke with no hair comes over to me and sits down at my table.

"Look, son," he says, "do you mind getting these dogs out?"

"They're not my dogs," I say, concentrating on my food. "I don't own 'em, nothing to do with me."

"Don't mess with me," he says.

"Look, mate, they do what they like." I grip my knife and fork upright in my fists on the table. "I can't tell 'em what to do. They're scrapyard dogs. You sort 'em out."

He sits for a minute, saying nothing. Then he gets up and leaves. Soon everyone's gone and there's only me, Magnum, Candy, Cal and Amber left. I finish my meal, pay up and the three of us head back to the scrapyard, where all hell has broken loose.

Smiffy, the Doberman, is going berserk, terrorising the other fifteen Alsatians. They're running about, barking their heads off, trying to defend themselves. Smiffy doesn't see me, thank God, as I dive into the Portakabin where Rory's hunched up against the window, watching what's going on.

I look out. One punter's crouched on the top of a lorry cabin, another's climbing up the crane and another's clambering over crushed cars trying to get away. Smiffy's trying to get at them all, rushing from the lorry to the crane, then the cars, then back again. He's all over the place with no idea of what he's doing.

"Have you called the Old Bill?"

"The guns are on their way," Rory says, stroking his bald head.

"They're gonna shoot Smiffy?"

"'Course they're gonna shoot Smiffy!" he yells in tears. "What d'ya think they're gonna do? Take him in for questioning?"

There and then, I decide I don't wanna be a skinhead any more. I face off a café full of angry lorry drivers and this so-called hard nut's blubbing his eyes out over a mad dog.

* * * * *

"Frank!" a voice shouts out from across the road.

I turn round. It's Bobby Crick. He runs over.

"How ya doin', Bobby?"

"Fine," he says. "Great... I'm okay... Not so good, if you want the truth, my old mate."

"What d'ya want?"

"Oh, nothing," he says. "Pleased to see you, that's all."

"And you, Bobby," I say. "I'm late. Gotta go."

As I walk away, he grabs my arm. "Hey, Frank. You don't know of any accommodation, do ya? Only I'm in a fix. Your nan's throwing me out at the end of the week – "

"What did you do?"

"Nothing much," he says. "I borrowed some dough off her and didn't pay it back."

I look up and down the street, then at my watch. I really am late. "So what's the problem? Pay it back when you can."

"Yeah, well," he says, staring at his shoes, "only problem is, I didn't tell your nan I'd borrowed it."

"Bobby, you are dead."

"That's what she said," he says. "She's kicked me out."

I look at my watch again. I look at Bobby. I can see he's desperate. "There's my old room. I'll ask my mum

80

how she's fixed."

"You're a mate, Frank," he says, grabbing my hand and shaking it 'til it hurts.

"But no borrowing off my mum," I tell him. "Or you will be more than dead. My dad'll personally arrange your funeral. You understand?"

"Sure, sure," he says. "When can I move in?"

"Bobby, I said I'll have to ask my mum. It ain't up to me," I call, walking away. "Meet me in the Angler's Rest tomorrow night. Half nine."

"Why not tonight?" he shouts.

"'Cos I've gotta talk to Sal and then I'm out tonight, that's why."

I've arranged to have a meal with Dad while Mum's out at bingo with some women from work. As I've told Dad I want to discuss something, I take him for a meal at the Wig and Gown in Bayswater.

After Marco's taken our order and we're drinking a couple of beers, I light up. "Nan's thrown Bobby Crick out," I say, leaning over to give Dad a light.

"Was he a naughty boy?"

"Borrowed dosh without permission," I say.

"I tell ya," Dad says, "if he did that in my house, I'd be arranging his funeral."

"That's what I said." I wait.

Dad shakes his head. "You haven't offered him your old room, have you?"

"I said I'd ask."

"And what if you want to come back?"

"It's a big enough room," I say. "We'd share."

He draws on his fag and shakes his head again. "'S okay with me," he says. "But it's up to your mum. Depends what Bobby wants, what she's prepared to do for him and how much he'll pay her." He looks at me. "That's it?"

"What's it?"

"You've brought me 'ere to ask me that?"

"No, course not," I sneer but laughing at the same time.

81

"Bobby's the business all right, but I'm not buying you dinner to ask you that."

"I should hope not," Dad says.

Marco appears with the first course. I'm having fresh large brown mushrooms with parsley and garlic covered with grated cheese grilled nice and crispy and Dad's having baked fresh asparagus served with Parmesan cheese. We choose the house white to accompany.

As we watch Marco pour the wine, Dad says, "Sal all right, and the kids?"

"I finished with her today."

"Oh?" he says, tasting the wine and nodding to Marco to pour. "Why's that, then?"

I take a deep breath and start my rehearsed speech "As I see it, Dad, there's them and there's us."

"And who's them?"

"Sal's all right," I say, "but she's got no ambition, she's happy as she is. She doesn't want to better herself, get ahead, you know? She likes to go to work, look after her kids, wait for me to go round for dinner and a bit of how's your father – "

"Like your mum."

"Besides," I add, "last week, her kids called me Daddy."

Dad looks at me, asparagus poised. "Oh, as bad as that, eh?"

I nod a couple of times.

"You've still got your flat over the fishing-tackle shop?"

"I'm happy there."

Shaking his head, he scratches the back of his neck.

"Dad, Bobby and me go to parties in these posh houses with drives longer than your back garden. Everyone pulls up in cars that Daddy's bought them. There's colour tellies in every room. You find speed, LSD and condoms in separate bowls in every room. Girls with loose dresses and big tits wander about like they've left a fashion-shoot to grace us with their presence – "

82

"Probably shoved a pair of football socks down their bras."

"They don't wear bras. That's the point. Lads with muscles bulging out their silk shirts and trousers two sizes too small so everyone can see what they're offering – "

Dad shoves some asparagus in his mouth, chews and swallows. "Probably shoved a pair of football socks down their pants."

"They don't wear pants. They like to display everything. But, Dad, the thing is, I like what I see. And I want some of it. Now," I say, my mouth full of garlic mushroom, "I figure the only way to get in on it is either you gotta be a bit clever and work in the Stock Exchange in London, or wherever, have a cream job – "

"You tried that, Frank."

"Well, it didn't work out, did it?" I say. "If it hadn't've been for that bloody sunbed, I'd've been all right."

"If you say so."

"Well, all right," I say, putting down my knife and fork, taking a glug of wine. "Maybe that was an excuse. But the thing is... "

We stop talking while Marco takes away our plates and brings the next course. I've gone for the Welsh lamb meatloaf with a selection of seasonal vegetables while Dad fancies the beef Bourguignon with buttered carrots. We request a couple of bottles of Mateus Rosé.

"Dad, if I want what them up the road have, I have to do something I'm good at."

We carry on eating for a few minutes while he takes this in.

"And you know what that is, do you?" Dad says, demolishing his buttered carrots at the same time. "First, you're going to be the greatest glass-blower the world has ever seen. Then you're going to sail the world in the Merchant Navy. Then you're swanning up and down the City Road. Next, you're planning to buy out Sean and his scrapyard. What you doing now? Loading lorries? You're not improving, son. In fact, you're on the decline. How old are you?"

I nod. "I know."

"First, you're with Sal," he continues, pointing his fork at me. "Then you're a skinhead. Then you're not a skinhead. Now you tell me you're no longer with Sal." He takes another mouthful of beef. "I dunno, Frank, it's about time you sorted yourself out."

"That's exactly what I'm saying." I stop eating. "Look, Dad, there's no two ways about it. I like thieving. In fact, I love thieving and I get some nice little earners out of it. I put a bit of work together, it comes off, I get a nice few quid and there's no better feeling... " I put down my knife and fork. "Dad, I wanna be a villain."

"Hmm, well," he says, "it's about time you found yourself a proper career." He pops the last carrot in his mouth, has a chew and swallows. He looks at me and smiles.

As I finish off my selection of seasonal vegetables, I smile back.

We finish the course in silence. Marco takes the plates away.

"But how the hell," I say, once Dad is going at the Peach Melba roulade and I'm into the custard tart with nutmeg pastry and cream, "do you break into a safe?"

"As I see it, Frank," he says, "you need three things to set you up. You're right about safes. I know a bloke who'll teach you. You'll have to pay him, o' course – "

"Course."

"Proper training don't come cheap."

"And the other two things?"

"You'll need some wheels."

"Wheels?"

"What you gonna do?" he says. "Go by bus? Taxi? We all know what happened the last time you did that."

As I enjoy a mouthful of nutmeg pastry, I chuckle at the memory.

"As it happens," he carries on, "your mum and I *were* wondering what to give you for your sixteenth birthday.

How d'ya like a set o' wheels?"

"But I can't drive!"

"I'll teach you," he says. "And I won't charge."

"What about a licence and insurance and stuff?"

"Oh," he says, finishing his roulade, putting down his fork and spoon, "I wouldn't worry too much about that. As long as you don't get caught. And you're not gonna do that, are you? I mean, not with you on probation from that shop-breaking you did a few months ago."

I don't know what to say. I'm overcome. Never has a fella had better parents, never has a fella had a better start. Dad's watching me. My head's down, pretending I'm concentrating on my custard tart. I can't speak.

"So that's decided," he says.

"Thanks, Dad." I put down my spoon and fork. "And the third?"

"Third?"

"You said I needed three things to set me up."

"You need a partner. Someone you trust with your life. And I mean *your life*. You can't do every job on your own. You'll need a partner for the bigger jobs."

* * * * *

I've been in this factory, on my own, for two hours now, trying to get this bloody safe open. I've got the tools, I've had the training. But it's hard, it's *really* hard. But then it opens. I'm in, for Chrissake. I'm in. I've done it. All on my own. The wages I came for are there all right. But there's also wads of cash tied up with rubber bands. A cash box filled to the brim. A jiffy bag stuffed with fivers and tenners. I look at everything. I can't believe my eyes. My first safe. Bloody hell. I've done it.

Chapter 5. County

"Bobby," I say, "I wanna tell ya something."

It's a week after my first safe job and I'm driving along in the Ford Zodiac Mark 1 Mum and Dad bought me for my birthday a month ago. Bobby's beside me and we're going to Fine Fare. I'm too young to buy booze but I've got the dosh and Bobby's legal, so we're set up.

I pull into the car park, see a space and edge along. There's a woman driving a blue Jag coming towards us, so I slow down to let her pass. But, instead, she turns to go in.

I wind my window down and wave at her. "Hey! You're not goin' in there, that's mine."

She stops, winds her window down. "No, you're not. I am."

I'm not having that. I jump out and stride towards her.

She's sitting there in her dangly pearl earrings, her leopard skin hat and her leopard skin coat.

She pops her head out the window. "You can take that bashed-up jalopy o' yours, my son, and shove it up your arse."

I stop for a second, shocked to hear her speak like that. "I tell ya what," I say as calmly as I can, "you're not takin' that space. I was here first."

"On your bike, Shorty," she says.

"'Ere's what I'm gonna do," I say. "You go in that space and I'll ram your motor."

I walk back to mine, get in and wait for her to back off.

But she doesn't. As I watch her manoeuvre her way into the space, I say, "Bobby, I ain't having that."

"Go for it, mate," he says.

So I drive straight smack bang into the side of the Jag. I reverse and go smack bang again. While Bobby's laughing his bollocks off, I reverse and go at her one more time. The snotty cow's screaming her head off.

"Screw you, lady," I shout out the window.

I reverse until I'm clear. I turn and off we go. "We can

get the beer at that new Tesco down the road."

"Sure thing, Frank," Bobby says, lighting up a couple of fags for us both. "I hope you ain't damaged your motor."

"Built like a tank, mate," I say, taking the smoke.

"What was it you were going to tell me?"

I tell Bobby about Dad setting me up to learn safe-breaking and my first job.

"I'm impressed," he says. "I didn't know you had it in you."

"You did."

"Yeah, I did."

We get to Tesco's. As we're loading the booze into the boot, I say, "Thing is, Bobby, like my dad says, I need a partner. I can't do it all on my own."

"Don't suppose you can."

"Dad says it's like mountaineers and the Old Bill."

"I ain't climbing Everest for you or nobody," he says, "and I most definitely ain't joining the rozzers."

"Someone I can trust with my life."

"You can trust me, Frank."

* * * * *

We rob every safe we come across. Every office block, every factory, every warehouse right across the Thames and Lee Valleys, Enfield, Waltham Cross, Edmonton, Bayswater, Tottenham, Wembley, Hackney, Dalston, Hertford, Ware, Cheshunt. You name a safe stashed with money and we cane it. We get ambitious and go after one or two big safes. We try one on a railway station. But as it's cemented into the ground, we come away with nothing. But it doesn't matter 'cos we're learning all the time, earning good money.

On a normal day, if we've been thieving the night before, we have a lie-in and, if it's summer, lie out in the garden. Then we go to the Capstan, a pub in Hoddesdon, for breakfast and a drink. Then we roll to a betting-office and spend some money on the gee-gees.

Late afternoon we go home, have a shave and a bath and go up to Bayswater to The Artist's Easel for some dinner. We like it there 'cos they have these naked birds who stand around while artists paint on them. Sometimes, for a change, we go to Romford Dogs where we pull the birds. Every time, it's a different bird.

Soon the money's coming in from so many directions, we realise we don't need to go out on a job every night. Instead, we keep to a weekly routine. Friday, we plan the job down to the last detail. Saturday, we take a last look at the place. Sunday afternoon, we do it over. The rest of the week we enjoy ourselves.

With Bobby now becoming a reliable mate, we don't put a foot wrong. By the time I'm well past sixteen, we've got a Zodiac, a Consort and a Transit twin-wheel. And we're renting a yard with a lock-up.

All the time, the law's running around in ever-decreasing circles, trying to nick us. They know it's us. They know what we're up to. But there's nothing they can do. They can't get the evidence and we're too slippery for 'em.

* * * * *

"Okay," I whisper. "Here we are."

"Hey! Yeah!" Bobby yells.

"Shut up! Do you want everyone to hear?"

"Sorry, Frank," he says, still shouting.

"*Bobby!*" I hiss.

"Sorry," he hisses back as loud as before.

Shaking my head, I switch on my torch. It's not very good security. No Yale. Padlock only. I stand back, let Bobby do his thing and after a minute or so, we're in.

I flash my torch around to get a feel for the layout. On the side is a high bench with a couple of stools underneath. On the wall above, there's a row of about a dozen hooks. On the hooks are keys and underneath each one is a label.

There's a reg number written on each label. These are the lorries we walked around in the loading-bay.

I run my torch under the bench and between the stools. I find the safe.

Bobby's taking a look further along past the office. "Look at this."

He's eyeballed a large locked cage with a sign over it that says "Secure Area". In it, boxes upon boxes of cameras, video recorders and similar cargo. I do a quick count. There must be about two hundred. Retail – who knows? Anyway, we'll get two grand for 'em. That's a grand each.

"Oh, Frank, this is too easy," he laughs, ambling towards two pallet trucks and three sack barrows neatly parked a few feet away. His torch tucked under his arm, he gets his jemmy and with a snap he's broken into the cage.

"Let's do the safe first," I say. As I move the stools out the way and get down on my knees, Bobby comes over.

"Can we shift it?" he says, "or will you do it there?"

I feel its size and weight. "We'll take it," I say, edging myself out and standing up. I point the torch at the keys.

Bobby says, "And which wheels?"

We go out on to the loading-bay. Two or three lorries along is a BMC VA Noddy removal van. Dark green, needs a good clean, right size for the load. We note the reg plate, go back into the office and find the keys. Bobby grabs a sack barrow while I get back under the bench and start edging the safe out. Once Bobby's helping me, it's not too heavy. We get it on the sack barrow, go out to the van, push up the roller shutter and shove it on.

We don't need to talk about what we do next. We already know. Bobby goes into the cage and loads a sack barrow. While he's taking it out, I'm loading up a second. By the time I get to the Noddy, he's cleared his barrow. I leave mine there for him to unload and wheel the first back inside to load up. We carry on doing this until the cage is empty and the Noddy is full.

Then we put the sack barrows in the back. Might as

well. They'll be useful the other end.

While Bobby's pulling down the shutter and securing it, I go back to the office, close the cage door, put the stools back in place, shut the door and put the broken padlock back on the locking bar.

All done, I go back to the Noddy where Bobby's waiting for me.

He says, "Me for the Noddy?"

"I drove the Zodiac last time," I say, "so it's my turn with the van. You're in the car."

It's about forty miles from Sawbridgeworth to Canvey Island where Bobby's mum has a café with an empty garage. We don't hurry. It's one-thirty in the morning. No point drawing attention to ourselves. It takes about an hour and a quarter.

While we're off-loading the gear and loading up the dozen cans of petrol we prepared earlier, his mum cooks us eggs, bacon, mushrooms, fried bread and a cup of tea. We're back on the road shortly after three. We know where we're going, a little country lane near Dungeness.

While Bobby's soaking the cabin and back interiors with the petrol, I'm dousing the bonnet, sides and tyres. I tidy up and put the empty cans in the back while Bobby reverses our Transit a good few yards clear in the getaway direction. He leaves the engine running while he brings the newspapers and matches over. We throw our gloves, balaclavas and coats in the back.

It's two minutes' work to light the paper and throw the torches into the cabin, inside the back and on the tyres. And two seconds for the vehicle to be blazing away. We don't hang around. We drive off in the orange and blue glow of the fire. We don't stop to watch. We've destroyed the evidence. That's all that matters.

Ten days later, we take the Transit to Canvey Island. I'd arranged a buyer before doing the job, so it's easy to shift the stuff. It's three trips up to the Smoke but worth it.

We get £2,100 for the gear. Takes me half an hour to get into the safe. That's another £550-odd smackeroonies.

That's £1,325 each.

Bobby and me, we always go 50-50 with every job. Sometimes it's me that does the most, sometimes it's Bobby. We agreed at the beginning that, rather than sit down each time and work out who's the brains and who's the packhorse, it balances itself out. That way, there's no fighting or falling out.

What I like about this job is no-one got hurt and no-one got tied up. We looked over the place, we went in, nicked the load, nicked the lorry and scarpered. That was it. The End.

* * * * *

Bobby and me are in Hatfield and I'm pulling out of a side turning to go right. I don't know what we're doing here. 'Cos Bobby says he wants to take a look at a betting-shop, he's giving the directions. But he's got no more idea of where we are than I have.

"Back up," he says. "Go the other way."

I back up but do it really sharp and hear a bang.

"What you done?"

"No idea, mate."

I pull forward, look in the mirror. Bobby looks round to see what all the fuss is about. "You've run somebody over."

"I haven't run anybody over," I say. "I hit him with the boot, that's all. Is he dead?"

A bloke in a suit and bowler hat is sitting in the middle of the road. He's clutching his umbrella, which is bent into a V, with one hand and rubbing his groin with the other.

"No," Bobby says. "But he can't find his balls."

I roll down the window and lean out. "Don't get behind my car, you stupid idiot." I go left and drive on, still looking for Bobby's betting-shop. We find it up the road.

"Wait here," he says, getting out.

I have a smoke while he goes in. Ten minutes later, he comes back.

"What was that all about?"

"I'll tell you when we get home."

When we're in my flat, Bobby says, "Look, Frank, I've worked this bet out."

"Oh, yeah?"

He goes into some spiel about cross-doubles and accumulators and he gets so excited he knocks his coffee over. He doesn't care – I do, it's my carpet – he carries on, pulling out bits of paper from his pockets, trying to get me to understand. Well, I don't. But he's convinced.

"When we place one bet," he says, "it's really six bets."

"How can one bet be six bets?" I say. "That makes no sense."

"Course it does. Look, I'll explain it again." And off he goes, making my head swim. I tell you, he loses me after the first two minutes.

"Bobby, do *you* understand it?"

"Course I understand it. What've I just been telling ya?"

"Will it bring in the readies?"

"Can't lose, mate, can't lose. It's not only the cross-doubles, you see, it's when we do the accumulators as well. That's the trick. You see – "

"I give in," I say, holding my hands up. "Bobby, it's a very, very clever bet."

"It's a 108 bets in one," he says.

"What? First, it's one bet, then it's six bets, now you're telling me it's 108!" I shrug. Still, Bobby knows his stuff when it comes to betting, so if he says it'll work… What the hell do I know?

"This is what we do," he sighs, finally – *finally* – realising I'm never going to understand. "I have to write the bet out exactly. If I miss out a word or get a word wrong, the bet is void. I do that, you place it and collect the winnings. We do it with dogs. Agreed?"

"If you say so, Bobby," I sigh.

He gets to work. First, he goes to W H Smith's and buys a ledger-book and a cash-tin. He heads each page with the bet we're going to place, where we're going to place it and the date. We put a couple of ton in the cash-tin. He takes great pride in his record-keeping.

"Minimum bet is £4.90," he says a few days later, handing me a piece of paper and some cash from the tin. "Off you go."

I take a look. He's written the date, 14 March 1972, the name of the betting-shop and the bet. All I want to know is where I'm going and as Bobby's sending me to a local shop it doesn't take long. They don't look at the bet, they just put it on.

"There's no way on God's earth we can lose," Bobby says when I get back, half an hour later.

We doss around for the rest of the day, waiting for five o'clock, which is when I collect. I take the ticket up to the window and the fella hands over a ten-pound note.

"No," I say, "that don't come to no tenner, my old son. Look at the bet."

He looks again. "My Christ! That's a ton!"

"Yeah," I say. "Hand it over."

"That's the pay-out limit for this sort of bet."

"Yep."

"I'm not sure," he says.

He scratches his head, ums and aahs, asks the woman in the next window. She shakes her head. He calls the manager. They have a conflab. In the end, of course, he has to hand over the hundred 'cos the shop accepted the bet. He's got no choice. This takes nearly an hour.

When I get home, Bobby's asleep on the settee.

"What you doin'?" I say as I shake him.

"Eh? What?" he says, coming to.

Grinning, I pull out the hundred smackers.

It takes us a couple of weeks to draw up a list of all the betting-shops in Hertfordshire and north London. With about forty in the county and more than two hundred in north London, we reckon a total of about 250 at a hundred quid a time will give us £23,775 profit. We jumble up the list so we're not moving in a pattern from one office to the one next door.

In the next few months, on and off, we hit 93 shops and, according to Bobby's ledger, make £8,844.30. We open a separate bank account to keep track. This is on top of the dosh we're raking in from the robberies, lorry jump-ups and everything else we're doing. For a while, I also team up with another mate who only does drums. But I soon find that breaking into private houses ain't my thing so I let it go. Just as well. Three weeks after I tell him I don't want to do it no more, he gets himself nicked and ends up with four years.

"You know, Bobby," I say one morning when we're sunbathing in the garden – beats sunbeds any day – "why don't we do a betting-office that ain't got a limit on it?"

"'Cos there aren't any," he says.

"I know where there's one."

Bobby opens one eye. "You sure?"

"Course I'm sure."

"Where?"

"I'll take you."

"All right," he says, getting up. "C'm' on, then."

We go in, get dressed properly and I drive him there. I stay in the car while he goes in. About ten minutes later, he's back. He slumps into the passenger seat, lights up and closes his eyes. "You're right. We can't lose. Drive on."

Bobby spends the next couple of days working on the bet.

"What's taking you so long?" I say.

"Frank," he says with the air of a surgeon working on a life-saving operation, "we only get one go at this. It's gotta be right."

I leave him to it. There's nothing I can do. As I've already said, I don't understand what he does. But I don't have to as long as he does. Anyway, I'm in the middle of organising a little job of my own so I got people to see and he's better off on his own. When you're working on something, there's nothing worse than being watched by amateurs. And with what Bobby's doing, I'm definitely the amateur.

Three days later, he's knocking at my flat. "Right," he says, barging in, not noticing I'm in my underpants or the bird in black bra and panties sitting on the settee is eating toast and Rose's lime marmalade. "I've checked and re-checked. We're ready. Here you are."

He hands me an envelope. Inside is a sheet of paper with his carefully written out bet.

"Well, what you waiting for?" he says.

"Well – " I say, waving towards her.

"Today's the day," he says.

"Sorry, sweetheart," I tell her. "Business."

Without a word, she puts the half-eaten toast on the arm-rest, gets up and goes into the bedroom. A few minutes later, she's out, fully dressed. "See you, honey." She kisses me and goes.

"Who was that?"

"I've no idea," I say.

"Well," he says, "are you gonna put some trousers on or aren't ya?"

I place the bet and a lot of the dogs come in. Bobby says it doesn't matter if they come in or not because, the way he's worked it out, we win anyway. But a lot of the bets come good.

"Now then," he says next day, "I've worked out how much we collect."

"How much?"

"I've written it down." He hands me a piece of paper.

"Are you sure?"

"Course I'm bloody sure," he says. "You sayin' I don't know what I'm doin'?"

"No, course I'm not, Bobby." I know how Bobby can get if he thinks someone's having a go at him. "It's just… well, let's see what the bookie says, eh?"

First, we go to a photocopier shop and get a copy of the betting-slip. Then we drive to where we placed the bet. Bobby stays outside in the car while I walk up to the window.

"Can you pay this?" I say, handing over the betting-slip.

"Yeah," he says. He's wearing specs like those Michael Caine wears in *Alfie* and his hair is Brylcreemed back. Hair sprouts out from his red and black check shirt. A roll-your-own sticks to his lower lip. He takes the slip, opens his drawer and hands over twenty quid.

"Hold on, mate, "I say. "I think you better look again."

He picks it up again and holds it while he reads it. His jaw opens and the roll-your-own falls on to the bench. He takes off his specs to see if they're working, puts them back on and stares at me. "Bloody 'ell," he says. "I can't pay this."

"You've got to. You accepted the bet."

"I'll have to call the guv'nor," he says, standing up. "This comes to a fortune, son. That's more than a hundred grand."

"£122,467.91."

"I can't pay this out."

"You've got to," I say again. "You accepted the bet."

He disappears for about twenty minutes. I'm still there when he comes back with another fella.

"Look, son," says the other fella. "I'm the manager. You gotta understand we don't have this sort of cash lying around. I'll have to talk to my boss. Give me your name, address and number and we'll be in touch."

I give 'em my mum's details where Bobby's still staying, 'cos I don't want 'em knowing about my flat. Later, we get a call to say the betting-shop guv'nor's coming round the next day at about two.

He pulls up in a Rolls-Royce Silver Shadow. It's a bit over the top. What's he trying to tell us? Once he's handed over the dosh, I'll be able to buy five of 'em and still have some cash left over.

I let him in. He's a tall bloke with black hair and a thin moustache and he's wearing a navy suit. He'd look smart if it weren't for the cigar ash straddling down his front.

"All right, lads?" he says when we're sitting down in

the front room. His voice is like a St Bernard with a sore throat.

"Do you wanna a cup o' tea?" I say, getting up.

"No, thanks, son," he says. "Let's get down to business."

I sit back down next to Bobby and light a fag.

"Right," he says, nestling in the armchair. "I'm Bill Strangelove, the governor of the betting-office. Before we go any further, let's get something straight. Do you think we're all divs or something? You two have been at this bet all over the county and north London."

"Have we?" Bobby says.

"We're all in touch with one another," he says, "and we know you've been at it everywhere. And now you've hit my betting-office.

"Oh yeah?" I say.

"Yeah," he says.

Without flinching, I tell him, "If you don't pay this bet out – "

"It was an illegal bet!" he snorts. "I'm paying you nothing."

"What do you mean 'illegal'?" Bobby says. "How was it illegal?"

"Just take my word for it, son," Mr Strangelove says. "*It was illegal.*"

"So if you knew it was illegal," I say, "and you accepted the bet, you broke the law, didn't you? I'll tell you what, we'll 'phone up *Sporting Life* and we'll report you. Get your betting-office in *Sporting Life* and everything."

He didn't speak for a while. We've got him over a barrel and he knows it. "Okay, boys, I'll pay you the 120-odd grand – "

"£122,467.91," Bobby pipes up.

"I'll go back to the office," he says, "and write out the cheque. My associates will deliver it tonight. Is that okay?"

Bobby and me look at each other and nod.

"That's fine, Mr Strangelove," I say. "Thank you very much."

"You haven't met my associates, have you?" he says. "They're a good bunch o' lads. There's Wes, who's a bare-knuckle fighter. Oh, the stories he could tell you. And there's Duggie. Just got out of Strangeways has Duggie. Fourteen for doing his old woman in. Then there's Sammo. Now he's a very interesting character. You'll like him – "

"We're going out tonight," I say. "Tell 'em to push it through the letter-box."

"Or," he says, "I give you £500 here and now, we say no more about it and you never, ever, go into any of my betting-offices again."

Bobby and I look at each other. We don't know what to say.

"Your choice, lads," Mr Strangelove says. "I give you £500 now or my associates deliver the cheque when you're next at home."

So I say to Bobby, "Let's turn it in, eh? We're playing around with some naughty people here."

And he says, "What do you think?"

"I think we should take the monkey and call it a day."

"Yeah," he says, "I think you're right."

Mr Strangelove stands, pulls out a wad of notes, counts out a monkey and hands it over. "A pleasure to do business, gentlemen. We won't shake hands, if you don't mind. I don't like to imagine where you've had yours."

* * * * *

"Eh, lad!"

He's a big fella with a belly the size of a beer barrel, jaws to match and hasn't shaved in days. As he swaggers over towards me, he's swinging an iron bar, making sure I see it. He's like Desperate Dan without the cow pies but with the GBH.

"'Ow do."

I ignore him. After all, I'm not doing anything. I'm only standing there by his artic, sizing up the tarp, what's the best way to get it undone and trying to work out whether the load under it is worth the effort.

"What be thee doin'?"

If I understood him, I'd answer. But what with his wheezing, his wobbling jowls and thick northern accent, I can't make out a word he's saying. I understand his iron bar, though. At the same time, I'm sweating under this ski-mask and gloves, I've had a long night, it's getting light and I want some shut-eye. I'm not in the mood for bother.

"Look, me old son," I say, "don't you shoot me with that iron bar. This is a jump-up. We're nicking the load. That's all we want."

Desperate Dan moves from one foot to the other. It's obvious he doesn't know what to do for the best.

I try to help him out. "Don't be clever, mate. You'll get hurt, I'm tellin' ya. Get back in your cab. Forget what's happened. Give it half an hour and then 'phone the filth, if that's what you want to do."

As he swings his iron bar from hand to hand, his face is going from pale pink to bright purple.

I can see he's working up to trying something on. "And you can put that down for a start." I turn to face the grassy slope behind us. "Yo!"

Three geezers the size of combine harvesters and wearing black ski-masks come over the top like zombies arising out of a misty sunrise. They've got jemmies in what pass for hands, 'though they're more like breezeblocks covered in outsize black leather gloves.

I say, "Look, mate, you start and they'll break your back."

He takes a long look at them, relaxes his grip on his iron bar and, without a word, goes back to his cab, climbs in and shuts the door.

I go to the back end of the lorry and wave to Bobby, who's been patiently waiting for me in the van to give the signal. He gets out and runs over.

99

"Get your mask and gloves on, you idiot!" I shout.

He goes back, puts his gear on and comes to help with the tarp. It's heavy and takes us quite a few minutes to get it clear.

"Okay," I say. "Let's see what we got."

"Good idea," says Bobby, only his voice is muffled 'cos he hasn't got his mask on straight.

Daz soap powder. Fairy washing-up liquid. Flash floor cleaner. Domestos bleach. Boxes and boxes of 'em stacked and tied on pallets.

"What a load of old shit," Bobby says.

I turn back to the three zombies still standing on top of the slope and wave. "That's it, fellas."

They disappear as smoothly as they appeared. Bobby and me put the tarp back in place. As he goes to the van and starts the engine, I walk to the cabin, bang on the door and wait while the driver finishes blowing his nose. He slowly winds down the window and pops his head out. His eyes are red like he's been crying.

"Okay, son," I call up through my mask. "Get out of here. And no looking back."

I bang on the door again, stroll over to the van, climb in and we drive off.

We meet up with our three lookouts at the Lucky Hat Transport Café where we have a good breakfast. Then, of course, I have to pay each of 'em the ton I promised. After all, it's not their fault Bobby and me don't get a result.

"You know," I say after they've cleared off, "how about a night out tonight? After this almighty cock-up, I feel like a Chinese."

"Yeah," he says. "A mate o' mine's opened a Chinese out Enfield way."

"Who's that, then?"

"Gustav Choong Lon, if you must know."

"And what's his gaff called?"

"Mein Chinesisches Restaurant."

"You're havin' me on."

"No, I ain't," he says. "I'm a very cosmopolitan

fellow… I'll give him a bell and book a table."

"Are you bringin' whatsername?"

"Trixie."

"Yeah, okay, Trixie. You bring her and I'll see if Kenny Maugham wants to come along."

"You wanna bring Kenny along?" he says.

"Why not?" I say. "He's always good for a laugh."

I go back to my flat and Bobby goes to my mum's. After five or six hours' kip and a bath, I call Kenny and he says he wouldn't mind a night out. An hour or so later, Bobby calls to say he's booked the table and Trixie's coming and, from what I make out, Bobby's coming there and then.

At seven, I pick Kenny up in the Zodiac, then drive to Mum's. Bobby jumps in the Consort, we go to Trixie's and before you know it we're all zooming down the A10 on the way to Gustav Choong Lon's Mein Chinesisches Restaurant.

We cruise along, Bobby driving in front, when we come to a roundabout. A Morris Minor is ahead of him, dawdling along. I slow down.

Kenny says, "Look at that!"

"What?"

"A snail overtook the old biddies."

But Bobby doesn't slow down. He's trying to overtake before the roundabout. If there's one thing Bobby hates, it's crawling along. He parps on his hooter but the old biddies don't take a blind bit of notice. On they trundle. They think they're out for a Sunday afternoon drive. They don't give a monkey's about our spring rolls, chow mein and Peking duck. Bobby's up their backside, hooting away, trying to get past.

"Uh-ho," I say.

"What?" Kenny says.

I slow down even more. I can see what's going to happen and I'm not gonna get involved.

True to form, Bobby slows down and then suddenly spurts forward, shoving the Consort's bumper right up the

Morris Minor's back end. No thought for the Consort, no thought of how the damage is going to affect our future operations, no thought of how much it'll cost us to get the repairs done. The old biddies are in Bobby's way. That's enough for him. If they won't move, he'll move them anyway.

When it comes to a battle between a 2.5 litre estate Ford Granada Consort Mk1 and a 1000cc two-door Morris Minor, the contest is over before it's begun. After Bobby's second shove up its arse, the Morris shoots across the road. It's only the driver who stops it from crashing into the central lane and ending up as a pile of crushed tin.

Now Bobby's got the bit between his teeth. Instead of overtaking, as Kenny and I expect, he slows down to give the old biddies enough time to get back on the straight. He coasts along, not letting them out of his sight, ready to shunt again.

Kenny mutters, "Dickhead."

I say, "Bloody lunatic, more like."

We go a few miles, me following some distance behind, when Bobby slows down and signals me to overtake. Which I do. But then I'm stuck between the Morris Minor in front and Bobby and Trixie in the Consort behind.

Without warning, the Morris Minor signals left and pulls into a lay-by.

I follow in.

"What you doin?" Kenny screams.

"Well," I say, putting the hand-brake on and getting out, "someone's got to apologise to the old folk for Bobby's performance. He's not going to, is he? Might as well be us."

As I stand up, Bobby pulls in as well. I make towards the Morris Minor. The driver's door opens. It's like those tiny clown cars in the circus. Out climbs the biggest Hell's Angel you've ever seen in your life. Then another. And then another. Blow me, another. They're like Jolly Green Giants dressed in denim, covered in tattoos with little crucifixes dangling from their earlobes. And they're carrying axes you use for chopping down trees in Epping Forest.

"Swipe me!" I say to Kenny. "We've bit off more than we can chew, mush."

Then, in the distance comes the faint rumbling of buffalo trundling across the open plains. Only it's not buffalo. It's thirty or so Hell's Angels on bikes coming down the A10 and heading straight for me, Kenny, Bobby and Trixie. They start pulling up.

"For Chrissake," I say, "we're bang out of order here."

Kenny and me run back to the Zodiac, get in and lock the doors. But the four axemen, having clocked Bobby, walk straight past us. When they get to the Consort, they slam the axes through the bonnet.

Wham! Wham! Wham! Wham!

Bobby's having none of it. He drives straight at 'em. They dodge out the way and he's off down the carriageway with the axes lodged in the Consort. A couple of Angels start up their bikes but others hold them back.

While they're doing that, I grab Kenny's arm. "Across the road!"

We fall out of the car, sprint across the road into a geezer's garden where we crouch down behind his hedge. I spot some empty milk bottles on his doorstep, creep over and get two of 'em. I give one to Kenny.

"They ain't seen us," I say. "If they come over here, we'll have it with 'em."

"Frank," he says, "we're gonna get murdered."

I bob my head up. They're standing there in the lay-by, chatting as if they've met up for a cup a tea and an iced bun. When one of 'em looks in my direction, I bob back down. By now, of course, our bollocks are sweating buckets.

"They've seen us," I whisper. "Get ready."

We don't move.

We don't move for fifteen minutes, listening, waiting for the onslaught.

After a while, Kenny whispers, "What's keeping 'em? Where the hell are they?"

I slowly raise myself up and peep over the hedge.

The Zodiac stands in the lay-by. A few cars are whizzing past. Apart from that, nothing. They've only gone and bloody scarpered. I stand up. Kenny stands up. We look up and down the A10 to make sure they're not coming back the other way to get us.

"Quick," I say, stepping into the road. "Let's get out of here."

We run over, get in the car and zoom off, me driving as fast as I can, Kenny keeping his eyes peeled. As soon as we can, we turn round and head back home.

Next morning, Bobby turns up as calm as the Dead Sea.

"Where were you?" he says. "Gustav's got a good gaff."

"We could've been killed!"

"But you weren't, were you?"

Chapter 6. Shop, Garden

He's dressed in a dark three-piece pinstriped suit, white shirt and a navy tie with little pink roses and he's holding tightly on to a rack of watches resting on the counter. I can feel him watching my eyes. It's an old trick. You watch where the customer is looking and whatever he settles on, you know that's the thing to push. To confuse him, I dart my eyes all over the place.

"Have you got one o' them digital things?" I say, staring at the clocks in the cabinet behind him.

"They're just in, sir," he says, "and not cheap." He's looking me up and down, trying to work out whether I've got the dosh for his sort of prices.

"Let's take a butcher's, then."

Without a word, he takes the watches away. I use the opportunity to have a quick shufty around the shop. A minute later, back he comes with a very small rack with three identical watches.

"Is this all you got?"

"As I say, sir, they're just in." He picks one up. "This is the Hamilton Pulsar P1. It uses a light emitting diode behind a synthetic ruby crystal." He hands it over.

"How's it work?"

He takes it from me. "To read the time, you push this button and the display lights up." He pushes it, the light flashes up the time and disappears just as quick. He takes a deep breath. "As sir can see, the case is eighteen-carat gold."

"Oh, yeah," I say. "Thought I recognised it."

He hands it back. I make a show of examining it. I try it on. I stretch my arm out so I can see it from a distance. It's the business, all right. Top-notch timepiece. Real quality.

All the time, he's watching me as if, any second, I'm going to take it out the shop without paying.

"How much?" I say as carelessly as I can manage.

"That, sir," he says, trying to match my carelessness,

"is £804.54."

"Mmm." I look at the others on the rack. "What's wrong with it?"

"Wrong with it?" he says, gulping. "I assure you there's nothing wrong with it."

"Then why is it so cheap?" I say, taking it off and laying it flat on the counter. "I mean, if it's supposed to be the latest thing and all that, no other like it on the market, I'd expect it to push me back at least a grand, wouldn't I?"

"I don't know, sir," he says.

"Show me how to tell the time again."

He picks it up and presses the button. It flashes on and off before I've had a chance to lean over and see what it says.

"That was quick."

He takes another deep breath. He can see he's losing the sale. "That's the only problem, sir. There's a complex 25-chip circuit in the works. It's so power-hungry, that's the most it can manage."

"Not a lot o' use, then, is it?" I say. "What good's a watch that don't tell me the date?"

"A watch tells the time, sir," he says, straining now, "not the date."

"So why have a date thing there? If it's got a date thing there, it's supposed to work, ain't it? If I'm gonna pay eight ton for it, I expect the date thing to work, don't I?" I take a step back from the counter. "Nothing doin', mate," I say, leaving the shop.

I walk a few streets back to the Zodiac. Bobby's behind the wheel and, like always, snoozing his head off. As I jump in, he comes to.

"Well?" he says, reaching for a smoke.

I light one up as well. "Yeah. That'll do nicely. Good layout. Good lot o' gold and jewellery. Their watches are a con, though. Nearly a grand and they don't work… wouldn't mind one, all the same."

"Well, you'll be able to help yourself, won't ya?"

"Nah," I say, shaking my head. "If I snatched one o'

106

them and wore it about the place, we'd be nicked in no time, wouldn't we? Use your noddle, my son, use your noddle."

We sit there for a few minutes, finishing our smokes.

"Right," I say. "What's the time?"

Bobby laughs. "If you'd bought one o' them watches, you'd know, wouldn't ya?"

"Ha-bloody-ha. What's the time?"

"Half five."

"We keep to the plan. We go for a burger and chips, then take a walk around town."

He grunts.

"Come on, Bobby," I say, bopping him on the top of his head, "That's not the attitude I look for in my partner in crime. Never been to Welwyn Garden City before. Let's see what it can offer two young lads with nothin' much to do and an evenin' to spare."

"I need a piss."

"That's okay," I say. "I'm sure this wonderful town can accommodate you."

Except it can't. We wander the streets looking for a public toilet and don't find one. And if there is one, it's well hidden. And if there ain't one, what's a fella to do? He does what Bobby does. He finds an alley and pisses up against the wall, that's what he does.

By the time he's done that and we've found a burger place and had a good feed, it's rolling up to seven or thereabouts and starting to get dark.

We stroll back to the jeweller's, which is now closed, o' course. We make sure no-one's about before ambling round the back. There's a fire escape leading up on to a flat roof. We don't need to go up. We can see there's a fire door and, next to it, a sloping roof.

"Door's no use," Bobby says. "More trouble than it's worth."

"Yeah," I say. "We'll take the tiles off."

Back to the car and home by eight. I draw a plan of the shop, then we make a list of the gear we'll need, size up

107

what we've already got and what we need to buy. Then we go off to The Angler's Rest, talk a bit about the job on Saturday night but for the most part, have a game of darts – Bobby wins 'cos he's taller than me – and chat to a few geezers we know.

An hour after the barman's called time, Bobby and me decide to go home. It's a cool, late summer evening and, as we're walking out to the Zodiac, we see this fella walking by. He's dressed like a gunslinger. Black hat, black shirt, black leather waistcoat, black jeans, black leather boots halfway up his shins. He's even got a pair of silver spurs on his boots. To top it all, he's got a holster round his waist with a gun. He's on the plump side and got a droopy moustache. If he was bald, he'd look like Telly Savalas in that film about Pancho Villa I saw last week.

"That's Kenny Maugham," Bobby says.

"How do you know?" I say. "You can't see his face under that hat."

"Frank," he says, "how many people do you know who go around looking like the Rumpo Kid outa *Carry On Cowboy*?"

"Except he don't look like Sid James," I laugh.

Bobby shouts, "Hey, Kenny!"

Kenny stops and looks all around him, sees nothing, carries on walking.

"Kenny! Over here. Car park."

Then the penny drops. I suddenly know who this playground cowboy is. It is Kenny Maugham. Bobby's been doing nothing but talk about Kenny Maugham for the last two weeks. Kenny and Bobby have window-cleaning rounds, different territories, o' course, but Bobby's got it into his head that Kenny's accusing him of stealing his customers. And with Bobby, that rankles.

Kenny slouches over like he's on his way to the OK Corral. "Who goes there?"

"It's me – your friend and colleague, Bobby Crick."

Kenny leans forward. I think he needs a pair of specs 'cos it ain't dark, not by any means.

"Hiya, Bobby," he says. "Tell me, if I put two birds in a bush, how much are they worth?"

"What?"

"If a bird in the hand is worth two in the bush," he says, "then how much are they worth in the bush?"

"What you goin' on about?"

"And while we're on the subject – "

"Which we ain't."

"Who is this Bill Stickers and what's he done?"

Bobby steps towards him. "I don't know nothing about Bill Stickers but what I do know is you bin goin' around sayin' I'm a thief and thug."

"But, Bobby," I say, "you are a thief and a thug."

He turns to me, fag dangling from his mouth. "Frank, you know I'm a thief and a thug. Kenny here knows I'm a thief and a thug. I know I'm a thief and a thug. For all I know, the whole world knows I'm a thief and a thug… but that's no reason to go around tellin' everyone, is it?"

"Crick the Kid," Kenny says, standing back, his hand hoverin' over his gun, "you bin a-stealin' ma customers. And ah don't like it. No, sir. Ah'm gonna have to mow ya down."

"Oh, Kenny," Bobby guffaws. "For Chrissake. Everyone knows it's a water pistol."

This is nothing to do with me. I'm not getting involved. I make my way to the motor.

Next thing, Bobby's screaming his head off.

I turn and see him with his hands over his face as Kenny's squirting him all over with his toy gun.

Bobby's head's dripping, his shirt's drenched and he looks like he's wet himself. He wipes his hands over his face, shakes his head a few times, watches Kenny for a few seconds and then goes for him.

I mean, he goes for him. Pulls his hat off, headbutts him on the nose. Grabs his hair, tugs out a clump. Knees him where it hurts most, shoves him to the ground. Kicks him in the balls again. Then again. And again. Bends down, pulls him up by the armpits and slugs him in the mouth, fingers his eyes, thumps him in the mouth once more – and then again.

Kenny falls backwards and lands on the tarmac, flat out, blood pouring from his nose, mouth and God knows where else.

Very slowly, Bobby picks up the water pistol and dowses Kenny in the face with what's left of the water.

And all through this, Kenny hasn't made a sound, not said a word. It's as if he's a lump of dough on a baker's bench.

Bobby turns away, walks towards me and the motor. "Shall we go? We got a lot to do tomorrow. Early night, eh?"

He unlocks the car, we get in and he drives off. He says nothing. I keep quiet.

Next day, Friday, while Bobby's going over the van to make sure it won't let us down, I do the shopping.

Saturday, Bobby says he needs some time with his girl – he always needs a good shag before a job – and, as that's not a bad idea, I ring up a girl I know and we get together for the afternoon. She's a good girl, she is. She don't ask questions. Neither do I. If it's all right by her, it's all right by me. Her pot and pan is her problem, not mine.

Bobby and me meet up about nine for a Chinese takeaway. Well fed, we change into our work gear and set off for Welwyn Garden City. We get there about midnight.

Bobby reverses the van up the alley so the back end is a few feet from the fire escape. We're not quite hidden from the street but near enough. I go up with my torch while Bobby opens the van and sorts out the gear. We've packed it in the order we'll need it but it's always a good idea to double check before we start. We don't want any hitches or delays.

Once I'm up there, I switch off the torch. There's enough light from the sky and neighbouring streetlights. I pull my gloves out my pocket and put them on.

Bobby comes up with the kit – a bag holding a couple more torches, a jemmy, ropes and pulleys – just in case –

some picks to get into the glass cabinets in the shop, some spare gloves and a couple of big strong bags. We've decided what we're after. Anything that ain't that, we don't touch. Not many tools, I know, but then, I've seen inside the shop, I know the layout. None o' this should be hard.

I'm already taking off the tiles and laying them on the fire escape landing. Bobby takes them one by one and stacks them out the way. We don't need to take off too many – enough for us to get through. Maybe a dozen or so.

Then it's straight into the building. As I'm smaller, I go first. I jump down and I'm in some sort of storeroom, an attic, something like that. I switch my torch on. There's a metal rack with two or three shelves filled with files and small boxes. A big box of cables and plugs has been shoved up the corner. Another big box, this time full of manky Christmas decorations and an artificial tree with a tatty angel perched on top, in another corner. The usual stuff.

I look up at Bobby's face watching me. "Everything's okay. C'm' on."

I edge away to give him room to land. His feet come first, then his legs. He drops down and he's standing next to me.

I shine my torch towards the door. He opens it. A wooden staircase leads down to another door. He reaches round the door frame and flicks on the light. I switch the torch off.

He goes down, I follow, shutting the attic door behind me. When he's there, he opens the door and, lo and bloody behold, we're in the office. And very nice and tidy it is, too. Everything neatly packed and filed away.

Bobby points to a safe scotched up a corner.

"Yeah," I say, "on the way back if we've time."

Now we're only a few steps away from the stuff we've come for. Bobby goes over to the office door. This place is all doors.

"Hold it," I say. I close the door we've come through,

so the light doesn't shine into the shop.

He opens it and we stand in the doorway. A short staircase leads straight into the shop.

"Yeah!" Bobby says.

I refresh my memory from a couple o' days before – where everything is, where the stuff we've come for is, how to get to it, how to get to it easily and safely – while Bobby stands behind me, waiting for my instructions. This is how we decided to do it. Bobby's in charge of getting us there and away, I'm in charge of being there.

About two feet away from the third stair from the bottom is the first of the glass-topped counters. They go round the shop in a horseshoe shape. Once you're standing on one of 'em, you can get round the shop without needing to step on to the floor. The only problem now is to make sure the glass tops can take our weight. O' course, I'd sussed 'em out when I went in to look at the watches, so I know they're about an inch thick. Should be strong enough. But this next step is crucial to everything.

"Okay, Bobby," I say, "give me your arm and don't move."

He holds out his arm and I grab hold of it. I lower my left foot on to the counter. Put my other foot down. Steady myself while I get my balance. Seems okay. Take a step forward. Still okay.

"Like I said before," I tell him, "only one of us at a time on any one counter."

"Sure thing, Frank."

I look down at the floor and see what it's about. "And for God's sake," I say, "do not, whatever you do, put your foot on the floor."

Grabbing his arm again, I get off the counter and back on to the stairs.

"There's the gold," I say, pointing to some cabinets three counters away, "next to the clocks. That's where you go."

When we were munching the chow mein, we agreed Bobby gets the gear and I check it out 'cos I know what

112

gear we can shift. I open the tool bag, get the picks and hand 'em over. We change places on the stairs, he grabs my arm and gets down on to the counter.

Funnily enough, although Bobby's taller than me, I weigh more. I've got the muscle, I've got the weight and Bobby doesn't go in for keeping in shape. Me, I'm pecs and six-pack. All Bobby does is sit, sleep, smoke, shag.

But, to my surprise, he tiptoes his way over to the gold. He's a gnat ballet-dancer on a tightrope.

He's lost weight, though. His jeans sag like an empty bag of chips. And when I think, the snappy sharp dude he was when we first met has turned into a thin, loping, wheezing geezer. Don't know why I didn't see it before. Me, well, I mean, look at me, I'm – but enough of that, gotta concentrate on the job in hand.

"Easy does it," I say.

He's at the clocks, gold rings, watches and bracelets, picking the locks on the cabinets.

I take a few steps closer, bags open, ready.

"These clocks are amazing," he says, pulling one out and handing it over to me. "Look at that."

"The gold, Bobby," I say, putting the thing down.

He takes out another clock, some eighteenth-century bobby dazzler, and hands that over.

I don't even look at it. "Forget it, will ya," I hiss, placing it next to the other one.

"You sure?"

"We're not doin' the Greenwich Observatory," I tell him. "It's gold we can move, not dickory docks. Stop messin' about, Bobby. Get the gold."

"Right," he says, taking a sideways step. "The gold it is."

"About time, too."

So what does he do? Instead of going to the top of the cabinet to get the valuable gold first – any fool knows the high-end stuff is always kept at the top of a display – what does he do? The numbskull decides to go for the cheap range first. On the bottom shelf. And to get to the bottom shelf, he jumps off the counter.

On to the floor.

On to the bloody floor.

Well, that's that, ain't it?

That is well and truly that.

The alarms go off, don't they?

I look at him. "What the hell are you doing? There's pressure pads under there, you prat. What did I say?"

"Sorry, Frank."

"Too late for that," I shout. No point in trying to keep quiet. The whole of Welwyn bloody Garden City has heard us. The Old Bill'll be here before you can say, "Hold hands, this is an upstick."

We don't hang around. Bobby runs around the counters and up the stairs. I jump over and follow him. It's only a couple of minutes to get through the office, run up the steps to the storeroom, out through the hole, down the fire escape and into the van. Bobby's got the keys so he drives and we're away.

When we're on the main road, we slow down so as not to attract attention.

It's only then Bobby says, "Frank, we left our tools there."

"Yeah," I say, finally lighting up a couple of smokes and handing one to him, "I know."

"But – "

"But nothing. Too late to worry about that."

"Sorry about that, Frank."

"Drive on, my fat-headed fool, drive on."

When we get to my mum's, we have a drink and a smoke. "Get your kit off," I say. "Don't want no forensics connecting us up to the scene, do we?"

"What?" he says. "This old clobber?"

"That old clobber," I say, "can land you inside. Give it here and I'll dump it."

While he goes upstairs to change, I find a sack in the garden shed. When I get back indoors, his scruffy old jacket, jeans, tee-shirt, Y-fronts, socks, plimsolls and gloves are in a pile on the floor.

As I bundle 'em up, I say, "Get some kip and first thing tomorrow, tell my mum you need to take a bath. Wash every part of you clean. We stay out of contact for at least a couple of weeks. No 'phone calls, nothing. When it cools down, I'll call Mum and she'll tell you where and when we meet. Do you understand?"

"Okay, Frank," he says.

I stand up straight. "And keep out o' trouble, will ya? Do nothing. Don't even pick your nose. When you go for a crap, check the bathroom first. The Old Bill are everywhere. Make no mistake, son, we are in the deep dippy doo-doo." I let out the biggest sigh ever recorded in the history of sighing. "For Chrissake, Bobby, what was the last thing I said?"

"Don't put your foot on the floor."

"So what do you do?"

"Put my foot on the floor."

Some minutes later, I'm back at my flat. I strip off and put my gear in the sack with Bobby's. By now, it's four in the morning and, God knows, I can do with some sleep, but first I have to get rid of the sack. Then I figure walking around at that time of day with a sackload of stuff ain't wise, so I have a bath and scrub instead and get some kip. I dump the stuff later.

Next day, I'm having a bit of breakfast and the 'phone rings. It's my mum jabbering away in a showcase of spectacular panic.

"Whoa!" I say. "Slow down, Mum. What's going on?"

She can't talk proper, she's so upset.

"Okay, don't leave the house. I'm coming over."

The fried eggs stay where they are, the tea stews, I get my jacket and drive over. Mum's at the door before I've opened the garden gate. She's near to tears.

"They've taken Bobby!" she cries.

"Calm down, Mum," I say, putting my arms around her. "Let's go indoors, have a cup o' tea and you tell me what's gone off."

The police come, she says, to our home in Oak Tree Avenue, where Bobby's still lodging, of course, asking for him and me. My mum's there and Bobby's there. We have a corner unit, like a settee, and there's a gap between the corner and the wall, and Bobby leaps over it and hides.

Two CID walk in and say, "Have you seen Crick? Where's Frank?" And, of course, she says she don't know where we are, knowing Bobby's behind the settee.

And they say, "Right, we believe they done a jeweller's. Can we look upstairs?"

Without waiting for permission, they go upstairs and a few minutes later come down with a Crombie, which they take away. Now, Mum knows Bobby's not wearing a Crombie on the night of the robbery but, obviously, she can't say nothing. But she knows all right, 'cos she swears blind that, however bent the Old Bill are, she knows that Bobby never wore it. Anyway, she says, they take this Crombie away.

This is about seven this morning, she says. Three hours later, just before she calls me, they come back, 'cos they've found some forensic on it. It's clear to Mum, and it's clear to me, they take it to the scene of the robbery, rub a bit of whatever in it and now they say as Bobby's coat was at the scene, so was he.

"Didn't take 'em long, did it?" Mum says.

And, o' course, Bobby can't turn round and say he wasn't wearing that, he was wearing the clobber I disposed of.

So they take Bobby away.

No sooner has Mum finished telling me this than there's another knock on the door.

"Come on, Frank," – it's my old mate, Ron Chantrell – "your turn."

They shove me in a car and before I know it, I'm in an interrogation room with Ron and his sidekick, Ted Kingsley, staring at me, smiling all over their fat faces like they've just arrested Jack the Ripper.

Ron bends down, picks up a polythene bag of tools and

plops it on the table.

I take a good look. Everything's there all right. Our bags, torches, picks, screwdrivers, the rest of it. The lot. Kingsley hauls up paperwork proving I'd bought them.

"Well, as far as I'm concerned," Ron says, "you bought all these tools. They're yours."

"Yeah, okay," I say, "they're mine."

"Frank," he says, "what's going on?"

"I'll tell you what's going on."

Chantrell looks at me and says, "Go on, then. How are you going to explain this lot?"

"I'll tell you exactly what happened, Ron," I say. "You know that yard we got up the road?"

"Yeah… "

"Well, we parked the Transit there the other night."

"Oh yeah?"

"And all them tools," I say, "was in the back of the Transit."

"Oh yeah?"

"Now all them tools," I say, looking him straight in the eye, "we use in our work in the yard for the cardboard rounds. The tools you have in the yard. But now you're confronting me with all this bollocks, that you found 'em at the jeweller's and on the roof. Well, it all makes sense."

He looks at me and says, "Whaddya mean, it all makes sense?"

"When we got to the yard, someone had broken into the Transit, hadn't they?"

"Had they?"

"Yeah. I noticed my tools had gone. Now you're telling me you found 'em on top of the roof of the jeweller's." I lean back and fold my arms. "Whoever broke into my Transit has used my tools to do the jeweller's."

He looks at me like I've grown another nose on my startlingly handsome face. "Are you serious?"

"Yeah. Definitely."

He looks at Ted Kingsley, back at me, back at Kingsley. He can't believe what he's hearing.

Kingsley leans forward. "So how come you didn't report the break-in?"

"Yeah," Chantrell says, also leaning forward. "How come you didn't report it?"

"Well, Ron," I say, "Ted. It's like this. We've known each other a few years, ain't we?" Ron nods. "If I'd reported a break-in, would you a believed me? Let's face it, if I say it's pissing down with rain, you go outside and check, doncha?"

He goes red and, despite himself, nods.

"So let's see what happens here," I say. "I report a break-in. A few days later, a jeweller's is robbed and you find my tools on the scene. What you gonna say?" I unfold my arms and lean over so our faces are three inches apart. "You, my friend, are gonna say I reported the break-in to the van to give an alibi for my tools in the unlikely event I cock up the robbery and you lumber me for it. What's the point o' that?" I pull back. "Nah... too clever for me. Keep it simple, that's how I do things, you oughta know that."

"And what about Crick?" he says. "He's your mate. You go everywhere together. How come we found some forensics on his Crombie?"

"Yeah," Kingsley says, not wanting to be left out. "What about him?"

"Haven't got a clue, mate," I say, looking at one of 'em, then the other. "That's between you, him and his solicitor. Nothin' to do with me. The only thing I can think of is you've fitted him up."

I know if I stick to that and it goes to court, I've got 'em. I know that. They know that. So I get out of it. I leave the station a couple of hours later and that's that.

For me, anyway.

They keep Bobby, charge him with the GBH on Kenny Maugham, he pleads not guilty and gets three years. Turns out he's broken Kenny's jaw. He has to have wires inserted and ends up with a permanent grin.

So for the first time in I don't know how long, I'm on my own. It's not bad. I don't have Bobby hanging about, me not knowing what stupid thing he's gonna do next. Mum misses the rent, o' course, but both she and Dad say it's nice to have the house back to themselves instead of sharing it with that psycho.

I don't move back in. I've got my flat, I can do jobs on my own. Much better that way in the end 'cos now I've only got myself to worry about. I can bring the birds back without thinking I'm always gonna be interrupted by Bobby drunk and at half-cock. I like a bit of order, some structure. Bobby's been messing all that about.

A couple of weeks after he's sent down, who should I come across but Mickey Golightly. I haven't seen him since he blubbed his eyes out in Quacky's office and got six of the best for letting everyone down.

He hasn't turned out like I thought. He's lost a lot of weight, got rid o' that fat from round his belly, working as an apprentice plumber, doing very well for himself – and become a hippie. Who'd a thought it? Mickey Golightly a hippie!

Apart from smoking the weed, he's as straight as a stalk of wheat on a summer's day. And smoking grass isn't bent. Not really. Before you know it, we're going around the country to all the music festivals – Cambridge Folk Festival, Cornwall, Windsor. And the best of the whole lot, the Weeley Festival at Clacton. What's not to like? The Faces, the Groundhogs, Edgar Broughton, Arthur Brown, Mungo Jerry, Barclay James Harvest, Lindisfarne.

Mickey provides the weed, LSD and booze and I provide transport and petrol. Turns out he's one for the ladies, too. I think I'm pretty good at getting 'em but him... Well, you have no option but to stand back and watch the master at work. All he has to do is look, smile and his kit's off and he's stuffing the chosen bird like a crazed chef in the kitchen of a hospital for the criminally insane.

In the meantime, Ron Chantrell has decided I shouldn't've got away with the jewellery robbery and becomes a bit obsessed.

For instance, one night, I'm on my way to Harlow to do some thieving and the Old Bill stops me. It's obvious they know who I am. "You're not coming into Harlow," they say. "Go back to where you came from." So I have to turn round and go home. So no more Harlow.

And then there's that time I was going out with a girl in Broxbourne.

At the top of Broxbourne is the posh houses and I'm going out with this au pair girl, French she is, nice-looking bint. One night, more very early morning, I'm coming out of this drum, this house, 'cos I've been with her and I'm coming out down the drive out into the main road, I hear, "Oi, you! In the motor."

It's Chantrell and Kingsley.

"Right, Frank, what you doing?" Chantrell barks. "Are you casing that gaff or what?"

"Don't talk stupid, Ron," I say. "I bin with a bird, ain't I?"

"Nah, nah, nah, we're not having that," he says. "You're casing that gaff. You're gonna turn it over."

"No, no, no, Ron. I don't do drums, you know that."

"Believe that and you believe anything," Kingsley says. 'Cos Kingsley's gotta have his say, ain't he, even though he don't amount to nothing without Chantrell by his side.

They're forever pulling me in on the least little thing. That's how it goes. When you're as well known as me, you have to take the flack that goes with the fame.

Nine months later, Bobby's freed on appeal 'cos it turns out there were no witnesses to the GBH. I mean, I was miles away shacked up with the au pair, wasn't I, so it was Kenny's word against his and, as Bobby's brief says, it isn't clear in the evening darkness who it was who done Kenny.

The day after Bobby gets out, we go for a little celebration at The Angler's Rest. A good plate of steak, chips and a side plate of veg with a nice bottle of Mateus Rosé perks Bobby up so much that prison grub is soon just a funny story he tells when he's pissed.

While we're sitting there, our plates clean and the bottle empty, enjoying a couple of smokes, Mickey comes in. I wave him over. Of course, Bobby and Mickey don't know each other but soon the three of us have opened another bottle and we're having a laugh like the two of 'em have known each other all their lives. In a way, o' course, they have. I've known both of 'em since I was no taller than an amputated ant so we've got dozens of stories to share.

Next thing I know, Mickey's invited a mate of his to join us, a Jamaican geezer called Leroy Maypole. Seems they're both apprentice plumbers with the same outfit.

"'S matter o' fact," Leroy says when we've had a few glasses, "I'm on my way to a birthday party over at Hoddesdon. Why don't you come along? Bring a bottle." He reaches for a napkin, pulls out a pen and writes down the address. Then he stands up, gets his fags and lighter. "Gentlemen, urination approaches. Already I anticipate the later pleasure of your company."

"What a charmer," I say, watching him head for the toilets.

"Yeah," Mickey says.

"He wouldn't know a copper if one hit him on the head with a rubber duck up a dark alley."

"Nah," Mickey says. "As straight as they come, mate."

"Anyone know where this is?" Bobby says, picking up the napkin and reading the address.

"Have some Lucy," Mickey says, pulling some pills out of his shirt pocket, handing them around.

So by the time we're at the address, we're as high as crazy circus clowns on twelve-foot stilts. But that's okay. Puts us in the party mood.

We park the Zodiac in the street, quite a walk from the party, 'cos everyone else has parked in the street as well. We've all got a bottle of Blue Nun, the cheapest plonk we can get from the offy.

At the front is a big, bright green lawn bordered by orange, purple and yellow flowers. No idea what they are

121

but they're really pretty. We walk up the drive towards the bungalow. A massive place. You can drop my mum's ground floor in it and lose it. Whoever's living here has bankrolls o' dosh, I tell ya.

We walk round the side into the back garden. Again, another enormous lawn, this time with about fifty or sixty people there. The garden's decorated with coloured lights, red Chinese lanterns and blue and yellow flags. It looks really lovely. There's loads of chairs and on each side of the lawn is a table and each table is weighed down – I mean, the middles are sagging, you can see where they bow – with food.

Think of some food you'd like at a party and it's there. Sandwiches, sausage rolls, crisps, them little puff pastry things filled with shrimps and soft cheese, pineapples and pieces of cheese on sticks, bowls of grapes, oranges and bananas. Behind everything, bowls of punch, bottles of wine, cartons of orange juice, jugs of water. On one table, wine glasses, tumblers, cutlery and paper plates.

Some loudspeakers, spread all around the place, are giving out one of my favourite songs, "The Girl from Ipanema".

I thought my nan knew how to throw a party but she's a beginner compared to this. It's amazing. I've never seen anything like it. We put our bottles with the rest of 'em.

"Where's Leroy?" I say, looking around, seeing beyond the lawn where someone's building a conservatory.

Mickey looks around. "Dunno."

"Who cares?" Bobby says, stuffing coconut macaroons in his mouth like he's at an eating competition. "Didn't get this inside." Then, on another table, he spots the biggest Black Forest Gateau you've ever seen and he marches over to help himself.

I'm not very hungry 'cos I've just pushed a big meal at The Angler's Rest – like Mickey – like Bobby, come to that – so we pour ourselves a couple of glasses of wine, light up and stand there, enjoying the music. Harry Nilsson. "Without You." Great song, great singer.

"'Scuse me, mate," someone says from behind.

I turn round and see this enormous fella standing there. He's a younger version of Jackie Pallo, except he's completely bald. Can't be more than six years older than me but, my Christ, he's big. He's dressed in a pair of beige trousers, moccasins and a blue and white striped shirt, open down to his waist with a gold chain dangling over his hairy chest.

"Evening," I say.

"Evening," he says, very polite. "Who are you?"

"More to the point, my son," I say, "who are you?"

"I'm Malcolm Pettifer," he says, "and this is my wife's birthday party. I don't remember Joyce inviting you."

"Who's Joyce?"

"My wife."

"Well, happy birthday, Joyce," I say, raising my glass.

"Thank you," he says. "That's very thoughtful. So. Who are you?"

"I'm Frank, this is my mate Mickey and that," I say, waving in Bobby's direction, "that's Bobby. Leroy Maypole invited us. Great party, Malc, great party. You done yourself proud, son, you done yourself really proud."

'Cos now, o' course, the mixture of the wine and speed is playing around in my head.

"Who'd you say invited you?" he says, leaning forward.

"Leroy Maypole," I say. "Good friend o' yours, I believe."

"I've never heard of him!" he screams at the top of his voice. "Why do you think I'd know someone with a name like that? Leroy Maypole! You've made it up. Nobody has a name like that! Come off it, mate, you're gatecrashing." He puts his drink on the table. "Get out." Then he stands straight and faces me. "And take your drugged up pals with you."

I look at Mickey, then back at this imitation wrestler. "No," I say. "It's a very nice party. We ain't going nowhere, son."

Next thing I know, his fist is coming at me and he socks me in the face. Straight on the mouth. No messing. Wham! A pile o' bricks slams into my guts. I go backwards and fall against a table full of coconut macaroons, a dish of Angel Delight scattered with hundreds and thousands, a gigantic trifle and a chocolate blancmange that should've been eaten hours ago. The table collapses and I'm covered in mashed bananas and strawberry jelly.

Bobby comes running up, his mouth full of salmon and cucumber roll. "What's going on?"

I'm splayed out on the ground and Mickey's crouched over me, not knowing what to do except be concerned. I'm licking the chocolate blancmange off my chin, wiping some coconut out my eyes, tugging at the Angel Delight that's stuffed itself up my nose.

"He chinned me," I gurgle through the gunge. "That geezer chinned me."

"Oh yeah?" Bobby goes close up to him so their faces are touching. "Oh yeah?" he says and steps back a couple of paces. Now one thing about Bobby is he's got a lovely right hand when he has a mind to use it properly. He slowly clenches his fist and lets him have it. Right on the chin. Boy, can he do the business.

The fat fella falls back, bangs his head against another table that doesn't collapse. The sandwiches jump up and down like firecrackers, go all over him and he's out for the count.

"Stop this!" Mickey cries out as he helps me up. He pulls out his handkerchief and starts wiping my face.

I shrug him off and grab the hanky. I don't want no bloke wiping my face for me. I can do it myself.

By now, everyone's trying to come out of the bungalow to see what's going on. Bobby's quicker, though. He runs inside before they can get out and goes at 'em, fists and feet everywhere like an enraged octopus.

I run over, cream still dripping out my hair and off my nostrils, and I see through the kitchen window girls otched up against the units, their arms flailing everywhere, screaming their bee-hived heads off.

Bobby's going at the blokes, hittin' 'em, shovin' 'em, bashin' em. They're crouching over in agony but he don't care. He carries on. He's lost it, I tell ya, he's well and truly lost it.

"Frank!"

I turn round.

"Help!"

Two guys have got hold of Mickey. One's got a lumberjack beard, two brass rings in his ears. He's got his shirt off and he's covered in tattoos – swords, flaming torches and the Angel of Death on his back. The other's wearing a plaid shirt with no sleeves and his jeans are splattered in – well, whatever it is, it's very bright red – jam… jelly… wine… blood – who knows?

A most unrefined set of suburban party guests they've turned out to be, I must say.

They've knocked Mickey to the ground and the one without the shirt is pummelling him about the head while the other's kicking his balls in. And, from what I remember from the school showers, Mickey's got big balls so this fella's getting his money's worth.

Bobby's managing quite well on his own. It's Mickey who needs my help. On the other hand, if Bobby gets hurt, I'm gonna be next. Something's got to give. Or I've got to make it give. I look around and over there, where the conservatory's being built, among the tools, there's a four-pound club hammer.

So I go over, pick it up and stroll over to the yahoo who's bending over and thumping Mickey in the head. I raise the club hammer and smash him straight in the back. He gives out a yelp like a strangled puppy and falls over on to Mickey's chest.

The other one stops kicking Mickey in the balls and stares, mouth open, at what I've done. I don't hang about. I step over the two bodies, swing the club hammer and smash him right across the head. It opens up and blood goes everywhere. Over my face, down my shirt, on the grass. A few of his teeth spurt out. I don't know where they land. His hands go up to his face. He screams one almighty scream, falls down to his knees, keels over and that's him done.

Everyone rushes out of the kitchen – Bobby too – blubbing, crying, screaming, shouting, yelling, yelping, yowling and Christ knows what else.

I'm as calm as an axe-murderer on sedatives, the club hammer by my side.

Some girl comes running over, stands in front of me and says, "Put it down, put that down!"

Mickey's pulled himself from under the shirtless tattooed moron and is lying there, getting his breath. The bodies of his two attackers are splayed out at my feet. Another bloke slumps against the kitchen doorway, his arms stretched out, his hair soaked in blood. Through the kitchen window, I can see someone else drooping in the sink, throwing up. A tap's running water over his head.

The girl's holding out her hand for the club hammer. She's nodding and trying to smile at me. She's the bravest girl I've ever met and, just for a second, I'm in love with her and want to lay down there and then and give her a bloody good shag.

So, for her, just for her, I drop the club hammer, help Mickey up, wave over to Bobby. Without a word, we walk down the drive and over to the car.

"So," Bobby says as I'm driving us away, "where can we find this Leroy Maypole?"

"He sometimes hangs around Hoddesdon Clock Tower with his mates," Mickey says, sitting in the back, checking his wounds.

"Frank," Bobby says, "Clock Tower. Now."

When we get there, the place is deserted. According to the clock, it's about one-fifteen. We pile out and take a stroll around. That's all Mickey can manage, to be honest, what with his wounds playing him up.

"Leroy Maypole," Bobby shouts, "where are you!"

"Dunno, mate," Mickey says, sitting down on a bench, struggling for breath. "Maybe he was here and now he's scarpered."

"You all right, mate?" I ask, sitting down next to him.

"Scarpered," Bobby says, striding about the place. "When I get my hands on him, I'll scarper him all right."

"Yeah, Frank," Mickey says. "I'll be all right."

But he don't look all right to me.

And then the square is filled with God knows how many squad cars. Chantrell and Kingsley get out the first one and, along with about a dozen rozzers, run over to us. Chantrell's shouting, "Nick 'em!" and Kingsley's screaming, "Nick 'em, nick 'em, nick 'em!"

Chantrell points at me, "Him. Nick 'im."

A copper rushes over to me, grabs my arm, pulls me to my feet.

Chantrell points to Bobby. "Him. Get 'im. Nick 'im."

But Bobby don't give in so easy. It takes four of 'em to hold him while a fifth cuffs him.

Chantrell looks at the copper who's holding me. "Why haven't you cuffed him? Cuff him, for God's sake!"

The copper cuffs me.

Now Chantrell's standing over Mickey. "And you, my son, you're nicked."

They don't cuff Mickey. They don't need to. He's so weak he couldn't start a riot at a teddy bears' picnic.

Chantrell comes up to me, puts his face right in mine. "You've done it this time, Frank. You've really done it."

Bobby's standing in the middle of the square, surrounded by the five plods. But that don't stop him. "You all right, Frank?" he says. "They doing you over?"

At that, Chantrell looks at him and knows, even if Bobby's cuffed and restrained, he can do some damage. "Split 'em up," he barks. "Put 'em in different cars, don't put 'em together."

I shout over to Bobby, "We're in a bit o' trouble, mate."

"Looks okay to me," he says. "'S all a misunderstanding."

"I lay at that geezer with an 'ammer, didn't I, a four-

127

pound club 'ammer."

"You didn't?" he calls over.

"Yeah," I says. "I did a bit."

"Oh my sweet lord," he says. "Fuck."

Luckily, we ain't been cautioned yet so they can't use what we just said. But they waste no more time hangin' about.

The first thing they do at the nick is charge me with attempted murder, which I think is a bit strong, to be honest, and they bang me up in the cells. I'm in there for five days and they have to release me after that. But, instead, they hold a special court, don't even take me to the proper court, they take me to a special court that sits in the police station. The magistrates come to the nick and remand me for another five days.

While I'm in the cells, the Old Bill give me plenty o' stick. They go through every unsolved crime on their books for the last two years to see what they can shove on me. They don't tell me anything about Bobby or Mickey. The only thing they tell me is, one o' the blokes I hit with the hammer has lost a kidney. Yeah, I think – and what about Mickey, eh?

By the time I get out, they've dropped the attempted murder to wounding with intent which, as my brief tells me, is the same as attempted murder. No different, he says. They also lump me up with the jeweller's.

By now, I know Bobby and me are going down. We're stuffed. Bobby'll be off to prison and, my brief says, I'm due for a couple of years in Borstal. He also tells me to plead guilty – too many witnesses, too much evidence. The date for the trial is set.

My mum and dad kick Bobby out of his room, I give up my flat and move in with them. I spend the time dossing about, carrying on, going fishing, keeping away from Bobby and Mickey. Waiting. Mum and Dad don't talk to me about it. There's nothing to say. We get on with things.

Most of all, I keep away from The Angler's Rest, 'cos I know that's where Bobby'll be most. I've had it with him.

Only now do I see it's been Bobby all along that's dragged me down. Whenever I've tried to do anything with him, it's always ended up wrong. He's a loser. Now I see he always was.

Mickey tries to keep in touch but I tell him to stay away. I don't want any more to do with him, either. I can't take him always crying down the 'phone. Ever since I've known him, he's tried to cry his way out of things. It was the same in Quacky's office that day. It's the same now.

And before you can say "Devil's Island", it's the day of the trial and I'm in the dock at St Albans Crown Court with Bobby and Mickey beside me. It doesn't take long.

Bobby gets four years for the ABHs at the garden party and breaking into the jeweller's. Bobby doesn't say a word, doesn't look at me. Nothing. So stuff him, that's what I say. They take him down. Good riddance.

The judge turns to Mickey – Mickey, who'd done nothing, absolutely nothing at all. All he'd done was get beaten up by two yobs who should've known better. "Golightly," the judge says, "it's unfortunate for you that you got mixed up with the others. But you chose to and you have to pay for the consequences. I sentence you to one year's imprisonment. And may it teach you a lesson."

"What!" Mickey screams. "You can't do that!"

"I can," the judge says. "I have. Take him down."

But Mickey can't take it. He looks up to the gallery.

A woman's voice calls, "Mickey, my son, I love you."

At that, Mickey collapses into a crumple, bleating and sobbing his heart out. Then he passes out. I mean, the poor bugger loses consciousness. Three guards have to pick him up and drag him out of the place.

"Francis Wilfred Peters," the judge says.

I stand up.

"You indulged in violence in a most vicious way. There is no justification for your conduct at the party nor for the break-in."

He gives me a year for the jeweller's. Three for the wounding with intent. Another two for ABH. Another two for ABH on the other bloke. Six months 'cos I'm in breach of my probation. And then he throws in another three months for altering the tax disc on the Zodiac. Everything to run concurrently. That's three years in Borstal.

Well, that ain't so bad, I think, considering what I got nicked for. I can do three years in Borstal all right.

I grab a look up at my mum and smile. She waves back. I turn towards the guards, ready to go down.

But the judge hasn't finished. "Peters," he says, "you are aged eighteen years and one month."

What's he going on about? What's my age got to do with anything?

"Under normal circumstances," he says, "you would be sent to Borstal to serve your sentence. But you are nothing but a vicious vandal. Let me make it clear, Peters, society will not tolerate this type of behaviour. Because of your crimes and because you have reached the age of eighteen, you will serve your sentence in prison. Take him down."

Chapter 7. Aylesbury

In the slush room, there's a big butler sink but about four times the size. It's completely blocked with piss and turds floating around the top. About thirty turds. You really need that at half past six in the morning. The gut-wrenching stench, the belching stink, the faecal fragrance of buckets of piss and shit swimming in a pond of vomit-heaving crap.

But, like everyone else, I throw my slops in without a thought and now I've been in HMYOI Aylesbury for six months – it's May, 1973 – I don't even notice it. The first morning I slopped out, I threw up. No-one took no notice. Now I don't notice new cons doing the same.

I get out as soon as I can and walk through the noise – screws screaming at cons to get a move on, other cons running to and fro, screws clanging and slamming doors – up the metal staircase towards my cell on Landing One.

Another screw's at the top waiting to take the day's applications. If you want to apply for sick or a visit or send some letters, that's when you do it. If you don't, that's it until tomorrow. I'm feeling all right, haven't got any letters and I applied yesterday for a visit, so apart from saying, "Morning, Mr Fellowes," and him saying back, "Peters," – he doesn't say, "Morning, Peters," just "Peters," – I walk on. Other screws don't even say that.

I pick up my towel, flannel and soap and go back down to the washroom where another screw is waiting. He sees me, goes into his canvas bag, pulls out my shaving-kit and hands it over. It's got the number of my cell on it in black, No 7. I go to a sink and mirror and get washing and shaving. I'm careful who I stand next to 'cos these are steel and, if you upset anyone, you're in hospital with a slashed face. Job done, I hand the gear to the screw and go back to my cell.

I've got about half an hour to clean and tidy the cell. I fold my sheets so each sheet is a perfect square. I fold the blankets the same way. I stack them sheet, blanket, sheet, blanket, box-shaped at the head of my bed. The pillow goes on top. You can put a ruler down the side of it and see how straight it is. I check my locker's upright against the wall, bright and clean. No dirt. No posters or pull-outs from girlie mags on the walls. I inspect the floor that has to be polished by hand. It's wooden with little tiles.

Inspection is every Saturday. That's tomorrow. Two screws, probably the Senior Officer, the SO, and another come round and inspect your cell and if it's dirty, they nick ya. If you get nicked, you lose privileges. So it has to be bang on.

Us lot on One take pride in our cells. Mine is the dog's bollocks, o' course. The fella with the best cell is awarded an extra privilege for the week. I've won it a couple of times and I get a bit miffed when I don't win. But I know there's always next week. That's the way the screws run it so that's the way you have to do it. Simple as that.

Then it's time for breakfast. No different from slopping out except instead of throwing it down the sink, you close your eyes, shove it in your mouth, swallow and hope for the best. You get a slice of toast and a dollop of porridge which is real pigswill.

Nine times out of ten, while you're waiting to get your pigswill, one of the trays ends up over some other geezer's head in the queue 'cos there'll be a punch-up across the hot-plate. It'll be one of the kitchen staff arguing with one of the cons. Someone'll hit someone with a ladle and all hell breaks lose. The alarms go off and fifty thousand screws come running in from every angle, pile on whoever's fighting and bash his bollocks in. And if you're the idiot who started it, you ain't gonna win. No way. 'Cos if you try it on, the screws'll kill ya. Most of the screws wear them great big army boots with steel toe-caps which means they're always ready to pounce and kick your head in.

I get my breakfast, sit at a table and shovel it in before I throw up.

* * * * *

It's my job to clean the landing where my cell is, the annexe, the washroom and the slush room. And it's not just about dragging a mop everywhere and walking away to let it dry.

I get down on my hands and knees, scrub the landing from top to bottom and then the annexe. I polish it – it takes hours – and when that's finally done, I go into the washroom. There are two rows of sinks, one each side with mirrors. These aren't your normal mirrors. They're stainless steel mirrors plunged into the wall so you can't cut yourself or anyone else in a fight. So my job's cleaning the sinks and they have to be proper spotless. If they aren't, there's big trouble.

Then there's the pipework. All solid brass. It goes under the sinks and the length of the washroom on both sides. Every sink has brass tubing coming down and branching off to the main brass unit that takes the water away. And, yeah, I have to clean that. It's a nightmare, a real bastard. I have to put metal polish on it and have to get it off quick 'cos if I don't, it sets and I can't get it off. So I have to polish that and it has to gleam, no green bits, no snidey bits. It has to be pukka.

Once I've done that, I tackle the recess floor. It's made of deep wine-red tiles. I have to scrub 'em, clean 'em up, get the old polish off, wait for the tiles to dry, put the new polish down, wait for that to dry and then use the buffer. The buffer is like a massive great brush with weights on it like a big box about eighteen inches long and ten inches wide. On the bottom is brushes and out the top of it comes a great handle about four and a half feet long. I push it straight along the tiles and make the shine come up. Then I put a rag on the end of the buffer and go over it so I can see my face in the tiles.

Once a week, I have to polish my part of the stairs going up to the next landing. Because it's black with metal strips, I put boot polish down and buff it up to make it shine.

Also, I give the clothes out when they come round – pants, shirts, socks, whatever.

Don't speak to a soul throughout, unless one of the screws is bored or got nothing much to do. Then he might say, "Get on with it, Peters, can't have you slacking, can we?" If I've missed a bit and he sees it, he nicks me and I lose my earnings, my pay and privileges. I need my wages to buy smokes and stamps for letters home.

* * * * *

Twice a week, all the cleaners from the wings – that's six of us – scrub out the dining-hall.

First, we put the tables up on end on top of one another, then clear the whole hall. We make a line right the way across with our mops, buckets, blocks of soap, scrubbing brushes, green cloths and kneeling-pads. Then we scrub the floor, starting at one end and work together along to the other end.

As you can imagine, a helluva lot o' water gets splashed about. But around the sides of the dining-hall are little water grids. That's when, 'cos of the water, the mice run out at a hundred miles an hour. They try to get across the floor but, obviously, they run into the water, soap and God knows what.

There's always about twenty or thirty, all running at different angles. So everybody gets their mops and chases 'em around the floor, smashing and splattering 'em with the end of their mops. We do that for half an hour, then collect 'em up and drop 'em in the bin.

When Mr Fellowes is on duty, he gives me a bit o' slack. He knows how boring the work is and, when no-one else is about, he lets me go on to the other landings to see who's there.

Outside each cell door is a card. On the card is the con's name and how long he's doing. On my landing, it goes three years, three years, five years, five years, seven years.

The first time I look I realise, doing a three is the lowest sentence. And I think, 'cos I'm doing a three, "Well, I ain't got it that bad."

I carry on walking along the landing. Then I go upstairs on to the second and third landings and it goes life, life, fifteen, ten, life, HMP, HMP, HMP. All the way along. HMP stands for "Her Majesty's Pleasure" and means no release date. That's it. You're stuffed.

This time, when I'm going along, taking a look, I notice there's a new con on Landing Three. Alfred Ward. HMP.

When I get back down, I say to Mr Fellowes, "Who's this Alfred Ward, then?"

"Oh, lad," he says, "a bad 'un."

"What's he do?"

"You don't want to know."

"Yes, I do."

"He breaks into an old lady's house to rob her. She tries to stop him so he strangles her with his bare hands. Then he has sex with her dead body. He pulls up the floorboards and shoves her in and puts the floorboards back. Then he robs the house. With the cash he finds, he trips off to Calais for the day. When he gets back, he goes back to her house, pulls up the floorboards and has sex with her again."

"How'd he get caught?"

"Back to work now," he says, "there's a good lad."

"Yes, Mr Fellowes."

That's my job. Every day. Day in, day out. Seven days a week.

* * * * *

Every Sunday morning, we sit in the gym for an hour and listen to the vicar spout his mouth off. One Sunday, he tells us to be friends with everyone. Does he mean the screws? Only if you wanna get your head bashed in. Next time, it's, "Love your enemy." Yeah, I can just see me getting off with the judge who put me in here.

This time, he comes out with, "Do unto others as you would have them do unto you."

Someone at the front says, "Hallelujah." Someone else says, "Amen."

That's the Jesus Brigade, the vicar's cronies, goonies, call 'em what you like. Guys doing a lot of bird who think by crawling around the vicar, 'cos he sits on the Parole Board, he's gonna put a good word in for 'em. So they creep around him. Everybody but the simple-minded vicar knows they don't mean a word of it.

A big Jamaican fella, Winston Masters, built like a brick shithouse, in for double murder, sitting behind me, says something to his mate. I can't make it out but little Eric Dobbs, who's next to me, always up for bashing someone's head in, does.

He jumps up, turns round. "What did you say?"

"Hey, cool it, bro," Winston says, smiling, nodding, friendly-like.

But Eric's having none of it. He picks up his red plastic chair and throws it at him.

Winston and his mates are on their feet, clenching their fists, ready to do little Eric in. But as fast as it flares up, it's over 'cos four screws are there like a flash, pinning Eric down and dragging him off, each screw holding on to an arm or a leg while Eric's screaming and struggling. The vicar stands at the front, carrying on as if nothing's happening. Me and a few others have edged out the way pretty pronto. We don't wanna be anywhere near things like that.

The last thing I want to do is have a row with someone because, if I keep my nose clean, I might get parole. Parole means I do only one year out of my three. Home in twelve months. If I don't get parole, it's two years. The last thing I want is to have fighting on my record. 'Specially as I'm already inside for hitting one geezer across the head and another in the back with a club hammer. If I start throwing my fists about in the nick, I'm done for. The Board'll laugh at me.

Let's get this straight.

I'm a normal lad.

All right, I got a bit out of hand. I know that. I'm a thief. That's all. I might have had a bit of a tear-up with a few blokes at a party but that don't make me violent. And I'm not a lunatic. And I'm not a nonce. I'm not a kiddy fiddler. I don't rape old grannies and bury 'em under floorboards. I shouldn't be locked up with these pyschos. Look at 'em and they'll take your eyes out. Cut you wide open. They're already doing HMP, what difference does it make to them?

So, early on, I decided to behave. Adapt, learn how to read people quick and keep on everyone's right side.

* * * * *

Anyway, what with cleaning on my own all day and trying to keep to myself so I don't upset anyone or get in a fight, I don't have many friends inside. But I have a few. One of 'em's Danny Chatteris. Extremely nice lad. To me.

But to the screws, he's a nightmare. To the other cons, he's a nightmare. 'Cos if he gets upset with any of 'em, he smacks 'em in the mouth. He don't give a monkey's.

He's out of Hull, a bit of a half-caste, can throw a good right-hander and a year younger than me. That makes him eighteen. He killed someone, is doing HMP, and I don't wonder. He's got a violent temper on him. Every other day, he fights with screws. All of 'em. At the same time. It's a regular sight, ten screws grabbing him, kicking him, holding him, gripping his head. But, as I say, Danny don't give a shit. If he went into an empty room, he'd pick a fight with the wallpaper. He doesn't know when to stop.

We're in the TV room. There's me, Danny, Barry Henshaw – an old school mate o' mine – and a bunch of Jamaicans. We're watching *Blue Peter*. Lesley Judd and John Noakes are showing us how to make a spaceship out of two Fairy bottles, a bog-roll, some sticky-backed plastic and three squares of Fuzzy Felt.

Campbell, the Jamaican crew's head honcho, says, "Where's the cricket?" He gets up, goes to the TV, switches it over to the England-New Zealand Test, sits down.

But Danny's watching Lesley and John getting Shep the dog ready to fly to Mars. So up he jumps, goes to the TV, which is on a stand high-up, stretches, switches it back and sits down.

Campbell's in a spot now. He's lost face. His crew's watching, expecting him to do something – anything. So he gets up, goes over to the TV, switches it over to the bloody cricket and goes to sit down.

The rest of us don't move. Don't make a noise. This can go on all night. We don't really care what we watch, we're just glad to be out of our cells for a while. *Blue Peter*, cricket, who gives a toss? But we can see what's coming.

Now you gotta understand, Campbell is six foot two with muscles in places I'm not sure it's possible to have muscles. And, mind you, the strength to match.

Danny's, what, maybe, five foot four and what he don't have in muscles and strength, he more than makes up for in persistence and bloody-mindedness.

He gets up, goes over to Campbell, who hasn't sat down yet, and thumps him in the bollocks. Campbell screams out in pain – course he does, who wouldn't – and bends forwards in shock. Danny smashes him in the face. As Campbell is flung back, Danny wraps his hands around Campbell's neck, lifts him off his feet and hurls him over a few metal chairs. Campbell hits the wall, slithers down to the floor and he's out for the count, eyes closed to the world, tongue hanging out his mouth.

Next thing – talk about the cavalry arriving too late – a dozen screws run in, order the rest of us back to our cells, grab Danny, take him away and Campbell to the hospital.

Danny gets 28 days in the isolation block. Bread and water, three days on, three days off.

138

Two months after he gets out of isolation, Danny's at it again, this time 'cos he says someone spat in his minestrone soup. A few of us ask how he knows, soup in Aylesbury being what it is. I mean, when the cook serves up, it's already like a cat's pissed in it. Or it's who's stolen his soap. Or who's giving him the evil eye. Or who's stepped on his foot. Or who's nudged him. Let's face it, the lad's off his head.

After he comes out of yet another two weeks in isolation, I say to him, "Danny, you gotta turn it in, you gotta behave yourself 'cos you'll never get out."

"Look, Frank," he says, "I've got... I'm in here for the next ten, twenty, years, or whatever, and, um... I cope on the wing for, say, a month, two months, even three. Then I get fed up with the regime and the routine and one thing and another and I need a break.

"No disrespect, mate," he says, "but you're doing three years, you can see daylight at the end of your tunnel. I've got no daylight in this concrete box. So – so – my – my method – I'll smack a screw straight in the mouth – or I'll find a nonce or some moron I don't like and smack 'em one. Then they cart me off down to the isolation block.

"I know, like, it's a punch-up and all that getting down with screws but then I'm left alone in a cell. On me own. And I know it's bread and water and all that bollocks. But it's a different, different atmosphere, different regime, different, different, different.

"Basically, Frank," he says, "it's like going for a little holiday away from the main wing and the stress and everything. Time out. I re-generate in isolation. I come alive again. When I come back, I'm good for another three months."

And I think, Jesus, God almighty, Danny ain't off his head, after all. I'm wrong and he's right. He's getting by the best way he can. 'Cos everybody needs time out. 'Specially in this place where you don't get no time out. Danny creates his own by sentencing himself to isolation.

Another good mate is Stevie Carver. He's a quiet lad, can't be more than seventeen, don't say much. But we have a good laugh. Sometimes we're put on kitchen duty together, which means we do the washing-up once the cons have had their meals, calmed down, gone off for gym and left us in peace and quiet.

It takes me a while to get out of him why he's doing HMP but, bit by bit, he lets it out.

One night, when he was fifteen or so, him and a couple of young fellas are out for an evening. There's a murder in the area and the Old Bill put it on the boys.

Then one day, Stevie's gone. He ain't in Aylesbury no more.

"Where is he, Mr Fellowes?" I ask.

"Gone, lad," he says.

"Yeah, I can see that. But where's he gone?"

"Back to work now," he says, "there's a good lad."

That's all Mr Fellowes ever says to anything I ask. Back to work, there's a good lad.

And that's the last anyone hears of Stevie until about three months later, when we're in the TV room and *Panorama* comes on.

"Hey!" someone shouts, "it's Stevie Carver. Well, bugger me, Stevie Carver's on the telly!"

And sure enough, there's his photo and everything.

It turns out that the Old Bill fitted young Stevie and the two lads up and because one of the lads was a bit divvy, the police got him to sign statements he knew nothing about. It all comes out and they totally exonerate the three of 'em. They give 'em pardons.

I can't believe it.

Me and Stevie spent hours together, hours washing up and cleaning the dining-hall and one thing and another and, you know, and – huh! – he never says, "Frank, they fitted me up," or "I never done it, mate." Never once did he grumble, say a word against the Old Bill – or the screws

– or anyone, come to that.

And when I realise that's what they done to Stevie and the other two lads, I really feel for him because that must've been hard. Being in a place like Aylesbury, knowing you never done a bloody thing, doing your bird and never talking about it. How did he manage that?

* * * * *

Then there's the screws. The odd one's okay, like Mr Fellowes, but he's an exception.

Worst of the lot is Mr Lawson. He's a big bloke, about six five, maybe even six eight. 'Cos I'm on the short side, I don't find it easy to measure heights. He shaves his head bald and he's got a jaw like a mastodon, only he hasn't got the tusks to go with it. He wears big army boots, loves kicking cons up the arse with 'em. Sometimes, the way he struts about the place, he thinks he's an army sergeant major with a swagger stick. Only he ain't got a swagger stick.

Usually, we only see him at shower time.

"C'm' on, lads," he barks like he's got us square-bashing, "we ain't got all day."

Eight of us – me, Danny Chatteris, Barry Henshaw, Eric Dobbs, others – pile into the shower room, put our stuff on the benches, hang our towels on the hooks and get our kit off. Ten cubicles, so plenty room for everyone. Two new ones come in only yesterday so they're quiet enough and get on with it. They wrap towels round themselves, pick up their gear and head for the cubicles.

Mr Lawson's watching us. He likes doing that. He likes watching a load of lads strip off. Christ knows why. It's the most uninteresting thing to happen in Aylesbury. For most of us, sex is a lonely wank after lights out. The few queers there tend to bunch together and we leave 'em to it. They don't bother us. We don't bother them.

Anyway, when the two new lads are in cubicles – one in the first one you come to, the other in the furthest, showering away, Mr Lawson says, "Right!"

We watch as he turns his head with a grin. Well, his version of a grin. The ugly bastard's like a hyena with a migraine. He wanders over to one of the cubicles one of these lads is in, nods and wanders back to the rest of us.

"Right!" he says again. "I'm going for a cup of tea. I'll lock you in. I'll be back in fifteen minutes."

This is the routine he goes through every time we have a shower with a new kid on the block. That's his signal that the lad in the cubicle is a perv, a nonce, a kiddy fiddler. Out he goes and, like he says, locks us in. No supervision, nothing.

Now these cubicles don't have doors you bolt but shower curtains to pull across, so it's easy to get to the nonce. We leave our gear and towels where they are and make our way over. Someone pulls the curtain back and he's there, back to us, scrubbing his arse like he needs it clean for later. He turns, sees us – all his dreams come true, six naked lads staring at him – but he don't stand a chance.

Barry and someone else dive into the cubicle and pull him out. Two of us buckle him at the back of his legs and down he goes, squealing like an hysterical woman. "No!" he screams. "No! No! No!" That's the only word the perv knows. There he goes again. "No! No! No!"

The lad in the end cubicle pops his head from behind the curtain, sees what's going on and goes back in. This is only his second day and he wants none of it. Once he's been here a month, he'll join in. Like we all do. I was the same. At first, I wanted nothing to do with it. But I don't like nonces. No-one likes nonces. For Chrissake, even nonces don't like other nonces.

Then we kick him, punch him, jump on his face, pound his bollocks into the end of next week, scratch him raw from his tits to his pubes. Razors find their way out of the washrooms and a couple are in here today. We turn the nonce over and wet, bloody razors etch two long, thick, blood-pissing lines from his shoulder blades, slicing through his bum cheeks down to his ankles, along the soles of his feet and through the balls of his big toes.

I don't do blades myself. Too messy. I don't like mess. Never have done. You can get the same result without spilling blood all over the place. And, speaking as one of the prison's cleaners, someone's gonna have to clear this lot up. I bet you a week's baccy, it's me. On the other hand, you gotta hand it to the cutters, they know what they're doing: fast, efficient, precise, accurate.

We stand back, get our towels and washing kit, go in the cubicles and shower. The lad at the end's still there, waiting for the all-clear.

A couple of minutes later, a key turns in the lock, the door opens. Seven spurting showers and six raucous lads singing at the tops of their voices drown out any sounds Mr Lawson's making. But everyone knows what's going on.

He's found the geezer drenched in claret, no longer screaming his head off. Mr Lawson stands still for a minute or two. Then he presses the button. We hear the bell clanging throughout the place, stop singing and come out of the cubicles.

"Get yourselves dried and dressed, boys," Mr Lawson says. "Back to your cells."

While we're doing that, half a dozen screws come running in and see what's gone down. They call the doctor who gets the bloke to the prison hospital. Once he's patched up, they transfer him to Grendon Underwood on the grounds that he can't protect himself and there he'll stay.

Grendon Underwood is what they call a psychiatric hospital but to you and me it's a prison for the criminally insane, a nuthouse, a loony bin. If the nonce ain't already off his chump when he goes in, he will be after a few months.

When the fuss dies down, I'm told to mop up the mess.

* * * * *

The only time I share a cell is when Terry Bowyer turns up.

He's four years older than me and has a wife and little boy in Harlow. Like me, he's playing the game – keeping his nose out of trouble – but he's a big lad with a bad temper and almost every day when he's in the cell, he's fuming about someone, saying he's gonna kill 'em. But he don't. He calms down as quick as he flares up. Which is as well. He's in for robbery. Violence on his sheet won't do him any good when he applies for parole.

I'm up for jam roll November '73, a year after my trial. Terry, a month later.

One morning, I'm working on the landing and one of the screws comes along.

"Put that mop down," he says, "and get to the office. Governor wants to see you."

The Governor's waiting for me. "Peters, your parole result's here."

I look straight at his desk. If you get parole, the paper is a big piece saying you've got it, along with all the conditions. A little piece, then you haven't. It just says you ain't got it, nothing more.

It's a little piece.

"Peters," he says, "you ain't got it."

"Why not?" I say. "I've behaved myself, ain't I?"

"No reasons given," he says. "You know that. Back to work, lad."

"I'm not one o' your nonces, I'm a thief, that's all, a thief. Why ain't I got it?"

"Peters," he says, as calm as can be, "You attacked two people with a four-pound club hammer. One of 'em, you bashed his head in and the other lost vital organs. You're a danger to the public."

"It was self-defence, mate!" I holler.

"I'm not your mate," he says. "You pleaded guilty. If it'd been self-defence, you'd have gone not guilty, wouldn't you? But you didn't, you pleaded guilty – "

"I took my brief's advice, didn't I?"

144

"Well, maybe next time, you'll choose your brief a bit more carefully, won't you? You're a thug, Peters. Less backchat, get out of my office or I'll put you on report."

As I go back to the landing and my bucket and mop, all I can think is, "For Chrissake, not another year in this shithole." And I'm so angry, I attack that landing like a homicidal charlady, all the time thinking he's right. I should've gone not guilty. Any brief worth his grubby wig would've got me off. By the time I've finished, that floor is so bloody clean, I can see my scowling fizzog in the reflection.

A couple of hours later, I've calmed down enough to ask Mr Donaldson if I can see Social Services. My family are visiting on Sunday, that's four days away, and I don't want it spoilt with crying and tears and stuff when I tell 'em I bin turned down. So I figure, better they know before they come, then we can have a decent time together, no fuss.

"Leave it with me, Peters," says the woman in the Social office. "I'll call them this afternoon."

"That's a load off my mind," I say to Mr Donaldson as he escorts me back. "I don't wanna see my mum or Linda – "

"That's your bint, is it?" he says.

"Yeah," I say, although I don't like him calling her a bint. "It's bad enough having to come all that way without having them blubbing their eyes out on me."

"You're right there, son," he says. "Now zip your mouth up and get on with your work."

"Yes, Mr Donaldson."

He's a good bloke is Mr Donaldson, so I'm happy enough – for once – to get back to cleaning the toilets. And I'm happy enough for the next three days, eight hours a day cleaning on my own, no-one to talk to. After all, I'm gonna see my dad, my mum and my girlfriend on Sunday and we'll have a nice time together.

Sunday's soon here and my mum, dad and Linda come into the meeting-room.

Linda's the best thing that's ever happened to me and

she's bloody gorgeous as well. She could be a Swedish model. A pink dress that more or less covers what it should, a black coat that finishes just past the hem of the dress, undone so I can see her jugs juggle when she walks towards me, black leather boots up to her knees, beige suede shoulder bag.

And the icing on the cake, long blonde hair down to her bum, straight and shining like she's stepped out of a shampoo advert. She's a royal picture, I tell ya, a sight for very sore eyes. Everyone stops talking as she walks by. I'm proud she's made the effort.

"So," I say, when they've sat down and I've taken a deep breath, "they called up about my parole, eh?"

Mum says, her eyes lighting up, "Oh, you got it! When you coming home?"

"I'm not coming home. They turned me down. Didn't they tell you?"

"No, Frank," Dad says. "They didn't tell us."

By now, Mum's bawling her eyes out, Linda's bawling her eyes out and Dad's clenching his fists, ready to bop someone.

"Come on," I say. "Don't be like that."

"Another year, Frank," Linda blubs through her hanky. "If I didn't love you so much, I don't think I could stand it another week."

"Yeah." I turn away. I can't bear to see the two best women in the world crying. And it's all my fault. The governor's right. I should've gone not guilty on self-defence. That bloody brief. I make my mind up. I turn back to them. "I'm putting in for a transfer to get out of this shit-hole. I'm going back to the Scrubs. At least it'll be nearer for you. I'm gonna put in to be starred up."

Next day, Monday, I go into the office and tell Donaldson I wanna go back to the Scrubs.

"Yeah," he says, "you'll go all right. I'll see to it. Don't you worry about that."

A week later, Terry gets word he's got parole. He goes home Christmas Eve.

146

We get up, he shakes my hand, he gives me a quick hug and shakes my hand again.

"Look after yourself, Frank," he says, standing there as happy as a bunny in shining purple clover.

"And you, mate," I say, smiling. We're good mates, it's Christmas Eve, he's going home to his wife and little boy and I'm happy for him.

That night, I'm on my own in the cell. I've done a day's work, Donaldson tries to talk to me, I tell him to fuck off and I speak to no-one else all day. I'm sitting on the top bunk, listening to Radio Luxembourg doing a countdown of the year's number one hits. On comes Gary Glitter, "I Love You Love Me Love". As I hum along, I look out the window – that's what they call the little hole high up in the ceiling – the window – and, to complete the Christmas Eve, it's snowing.

Terry's out. I've no-one to talk to. If my transfer application doesn't work out, I'm stuck in this lunatic asylum for another year. Linda's probably crying her mince pies out.

Merry Christmas.

Chapter 8. Spring Hill, 98 Block

Been here in the Scrubs coming up to six months now and I love it. First day, I'm put into the main kitchens and still here. Absolutely love it. What's not to like? Great job, great team, lots of food and – I never thought I'd say this – but a great screw in charge.

It's hard work, though. Every morning, I'm up at six to do breakfast. Well, my part of it. It's my job is to make the porridge for everyone. Fifteen hundred men. We have these gigantic pots, we call 'em coppers, and I mix everything in that. Pounds and pounds of oatmeal and gallons and gallons of milk.

Once that's over, I have to clean the coppers out, ready for dinner. I have to climb in to clean 'em properly. 'Cos I'm on the small side, I can get in. Bit difficult getting out but once I get the knack, it ain't so bad. I think that's why they gave me that job. Dinner, I make the soup. More pounds and gallons and more cleaning out afterwards.

We do suppers in the evenings. That's where we go round and take cups of tea to the cells, and a bun or a cake or whatever's on the menu that particular night. But we have to go in to prepare it all.

The screw, the cookery screw, is a great guy called Bert. Sometimes he says, "Right, lads, get the jobs done, get 'em done, get it cleaned up. If you do a good job, you can have a fry-up."

That's what he's like, a blinding screw. So, once we're done, if Bert's happy, we sit down. The great thing about this is we have pigs, a whole pig in the butchery part of the kitchen, and the butcher lads carve whole steaks off 'em. So us on kitchen duty have steaks, eggs, sausages, everything, a proper good meal. Not like them in the cells. Bert calls them "our customers". That's how respectful he is.

What's more, being in the kitchens gives me leverage elsewhere. I get my clothes tailored by the tailor shop lads, so I have the best jeans and the best jackets and I give 'em grub for doing it. I serve up nice bits of food, I get nice clothes and everyone's happy. I've got a really good little number going.

The governor calls me in his office. "Look, young Peters, you've been in that kitchen for six months."

"That's right and I love it."

"That's the problem, young man," he says. "You love it. Trouble is, what with Aylesbury and here, you're institutionalised. And that's wrong. I'm sending you to an open prison."

Wide-eyed, I stare at him. I can't believe what I'm hearing. "But I don't want to go to an open prison. I love it here. I've got some good mates, love my work. I'll stay here, if you don't mind."

He says, "No, Peters, you're going. You got six months left. You've been locked up in a cell for eighteen months. That's not good. You're going to an open prison. You've got to get used to the outside again."

News travels fast. When I get back, the lads come at me from all angles, grab me in the middle of the kitchen and plonk me in one of the coppers, which they've thoughtfully filled to the brim with freezing cold water. The screws, they don't give a damn, they stand back, laughing their heads off.

That kind of friendly gesture tells me I'm well liked in the Scrubs.

* * * * *

Along with the other three cons, I climb out of the prison bus.

"Right, lads," Noodle, the SO, says, "you see that over there? That's Spring Hill Reception. Wander over, will you? Take your time. No hurry." He leans against the bus and lights up a fag. "Have a smoke before you get there, if you like."

The four of us stand there, watching him. Then we look

at each other. One, his eyes bulging, lets his mouth drop open. "What?" he says.

And he's right. *What?*

We're supposed to be in a prison. Wander over? Have a smoke before you get there if you like? No walls, fields everywhere you look, bright blue sky, sun shining.

"No hurry, boys," the SO says. "Too hot to hurry."

He's got a point. They said on the radio coming up that today will be the hottest day of the year. 15th of June 1974 – that's today – is going to reach 77°F.

"Blimey," one of the others says, "doing a runner here is gonna be cat's piss."

"Don't be stupid," I tell him. "What's the point? I've done eighteen months, only six to go."

But, when the SO's finished his fag and we saunter over to Reception, I'm thinking, while I won't do a runner, I am going to do all I can to get myself nicked. Then they'll send me back to the Scrubs. I miss it already. Being in London, of course, it's so much better for Mum, Dad and Linda to visit. When I'm released, they can pick me up and I'm home in an hour.

"It's huts," another SO says as we're walking over after the admin. "22 to a hut. This place was the base for the SOE – that's the Special Operations Executive to you lot. It's really interesting."

I don't take long to settle in. Some of the time, it's like being in a Butlin's holiday camp. About once a week, after lights out, some of the lads go out into the fields and collect parcels their girlfriends have dropped off. Then we have a stinker of a party. Whisky, beer, gin, vodka, cigarettes, grub. You name it, we got it.

Next morning, of course, we're a bit worse for wear.

"Come on, up, up, up!" the medical screw shouts one morning, striding up and down the hut, screaming his head off, banging a frying-pan against the beds. "Get exercising, you lazy louts!" Dr Sardine is his name – I've never come across a sillier name – and he's short, fat and bald. His shirt's a size too small and even this early in the morning, it's out over the top of his trousers. And *he's* telling *us* to get exercising.

I look at the clock hanging high up on the wall. It's a few minutes past seven and I don't wanna get up. Another half hour will suit me fine.

"Come on, you," Sardine says, jiggling the bottom of my bed.

Turning over, I say nothing.

He grabs the sheets and pulls them off my bed. "I said get moving!"

So there I am, in my jockeys, curled up on an uncovered bed. But I don't move. Don't wanna move. Don't see why I should. "Fuck off."

He says, "Watch it, lad. You're treading on eggs."

"So nick me."

"What's your name?" he says, getting out his notebook and pencil.

I don't answer him.

"What's his name?" he hollers down the hut.

"Jack the fucking Ripper."

"Peters," someone pipes up. "That's Frank Peters."

There's a short silence while Sardine stands staring at me. Then he says, "Don't do it again, Peters." And he walks away.

As soon as he's out the hut, the lads burst into laughter and applause. "You nailed him, Frank, you nailed him!"

A few days later, they put me on gardening duties in Grendon Underwood, the prison next door. Now, Grendon Underwood is the nuthouse for the criminally insane. We're not allowed in there, of course. There's a great big prison fence around it. But outside of that is a compound of gardens. In the mornings, me and three others water the plants. Then, after dinner, two of us build polytunnels and the other two carry on watering. The SO in charge is called Squash.

Noodle. Sardine. Squash. I think you're not allowed to be a prison officer in Spring Hill if you ain't got a funny name.

151

"What's your name, Officer?"

"Blenkinsop-Sopworth-Dingbat."

"You're not an officer. You ain't got a funny name. You're nicked."

Squash says, "I've got more than four thousand peppers, aubergines and chillies in here. Today, they need to be fed as well as watered. So, you and you – " pointing to me and Jibby – "I'm going to show you how to feed them. You and you – " pointing to the other two " – carry on with the watering."

So, while the other two get their watering-cans, Squash takes me and Jibby over to the greenhouse sink and draining-board where he's got the feed, a couple of pots of little plants and some spoons.

"Now, Frank, Jibby," he says, "I want you to pay close attention. These are seedlings. It's very important you do this correctly. If you don't, you'll kill them. Do you understand?"

"Yes, Mr Squash."

"Jibby?"

"Yes, Mr Squash."

"Good lads. This is high potash liquid fertiliser. You fill your watering-can. Like so." He fills his watering-can. "Then you put this amount of the fertiliser in the water." He lobs a spoon or so in. "Swirl it about a bit so it mixes." He gives it a good swirl. "Then you water lightly." He waters lightly. "Don't overwater, Jibby, or you'll kill the plants… Good lad. Well done, Frank."

We put the cans down.

"Okay," he says, "you know what to do. I've got a meeting. Get them all fed before dinner, then afterwards get on with the tunnels."

Jibby and me get watering with what's left in the cans, like Squash showed us. But then we have to mix some more.

"How much of this stuff shall I put in?" Jibby says once he's filled his can with water.

"Dunno, mate," I say. "I wasn't watching."

"Me neither," he says. He picks up the spoon and looks at me.

"Put the lot in," I say. I'm hungry. "Let's get this over with."

Soon we're tripping up and down the place, watering everything in sight. Squash has left enough fertiliser to go round and after we finish, we clear off for dinner. It's good grub here. We have a hot hot hot burning chicken chilli curry and rice, followed by peaches, ice cream and coffee. Then we go for a slash and have a fag.

When we get back, Squash is waiting for us, like always. But he is not a happy Squash. "What did you do?" he screams down the greenhouse as soon as we're at the door. "You've killed 'em! I showed you how to do it!" He's on the point of crying his eyes out, poor bugger. "I don't understand it. What the hell did you do?" His elbows drop on to one of the benches, his chin cupped in his hands.

We walk up to him. "We did what you said," Jibby says. "Honest, Mr Squash. It ain't our fault."

"Look," he sobs, "my seedlings, my babies. You've murdered them."

I spot an opportunity. "It's my fault, Mr Squash. Jibby had nothing to with it. I did it. I plastered 'em with the stuff."

"Why?" he says, drying his eyes. "Why would you want to do that?"

"I hate chillies," I say. "I hate anything that burns my mouth."

He puts his handkerchief away, rubs his eyes with his hands and turns to Jibby. "You're nicked. Now both of you – "

"What about me?" I say. "You've gotta nick me. It was me that murdered your precious seedlings."

"Sorry, Mr Squash," Jibby says. "We'll do better next time."

"Next time?" he screams, standing up, getting so close our chests are touching. "There won't be a next time. As for you, Peters, you miserable little wanker, get out my greenhouse!"

* * * * *

"So, Peters," the Governor says the next day in his office, "I hear you're banned from the greenhouse."

I don't know whether to grin or pretend to be serious. "Yes, sir," I say with as straight a face as I can manage. "Are you gonna nick me?"

"You had a nice little number there – "

"Yes, sir."

" – and you blew it."

"Yes, sir."

"Stupid boy."

"Yes, sir."

"I'm not going to nick you," he says. "I'm giving you another chance."

"I don't want another chance."

"You're getting one whether you want it or not," he says. "The officers' gardens need attention. I'm appointing you the officers' gardener. And, seeing as I and my wife hate gardening, you're also our personal gardener."

"I hate gardening."

"Wrong answer, son. From now on, you love gardening more than you love your cock."

"If you say so."

"And don't go spreading Mr Squash's magic potion everywhere."

"No, sir."

"Mr Florizel will supervise you. Off you go."

Mr Florizel is waiting for me next to the Governor's front lawn. I haven't come across him before. He's young, slim and smart. Unlike some of the other officers, his tie is precisely in place and shiny golden curls poke out from under his cap.

We nod briefly and he says, "Let's get the tools."

We go round the back to the shed. A dustbin stands

154

nearby, chock-a-block with wine bottles and a couple of White Horse whisky bottles. I think I see a Gordon's gin bottle somewhere there as well. "Someone likes a drink."

"Shut your face," Florizel says. "Get the kit."

I go into the shed and pull the lawn mower out. Florizel takes it.

"You'll need the shears," he says.

I take them off a shelf. By the time I get out, he's taken the mower back round to the front and come back.

"Deckchair," he says, pointing.

While I take the shears, he carries the chair. Round the front, he sets it up, plonks himself down. As it's a steaming hot day, I take my shirt off and I'm thinking this might not be so bad, after all. I grab hold of the mower handle.

"Right, you scrawny toe-rag," he says, "get mowing."

He's slouching in the deckchair, grinning. He's only a couple of years older than me, the toffee-nosed bastard, and I'm not having him talk to me like that.

I drop the mower handle. "Bollocks."

He doesn't move. "What do you mean?"

"I ain't doing it."

He gets up. "I'll nick you."

"Do what you like, mate. I ain't doing it."

He take a step towards me.

I don't move an inch.

"Do you know what that'll mean?" he says. "You'll go back to the Scrubs."

"Suits me, mate. Nick me all you like."

"All right, have it your own way," he says. "You're nicked."

"Good."

"And I'm not your mate."

I put my shirt on, we put the stuff back in the shed and he marches me back to my hut where he grounds me for the rest of the day.

Next morning, I'm summoned to the Governor's office and he's sitting there, a screw standing either side of him.

155

Florizel stands next to me and reads out the charge. Insubordination. He tells the Governor what happened.

"Is that what happened?" the Governor asks me.

"No, sir," I say. "When Mr Florizel says he told me to mow the lawn, what he actually said was, '"Right, you scrawny toe-rag, get mowing.'"

"Is Peters right, Mr Florizel?"

"Can't remember, sir."

"Mmm," the Governor mutters, shaking his head.

"That's why I refused," I say. "There's a way of asking and a way of asking. When he sits there in his deckchair – "

"Were you sitting in my deckchair, Mr Florizel?"

"Too right he was," I say, not giving the snobby git a chance. "When he comes over, giving it large about I'll do this and I'll do that, he can go and get fucked. 'Cos I ain't having it. I'm not having it. There's a way of talking to me and that ain't it. You done the prisons, Guv, and you well know there's a way o' talking and there's a way o' talking. He got right up my 'ooter the way he told me to mow that lawn. And the minute he said that, there's no way I would've backed down. So do what you like, I don't give a fuck."

The Governor doesn't say a word. He leans back, looks at me for a while and then at Florizel. The screws either side of him don't move a muscle or utter a word. They're like them statues in Parliament Square.

Eventually, after I thought they'd all fallen asleep, the Governor says, "Mr Florizel, you should know better. You've got a lot to learn about these men. You, Peters, get out."

Next day, I'm doing the Governor's garden, only now I'm on my own, no-one supervising me. I never see Florizel again.

* * * * *

"How long before you're out, Frank?" Evan says as he sets up the board. He's teaching me chess.

We're up a corner in the social area.

"Three months, two days."

"Do you know what I did before I landed up here?" I shake my head. I've no idea. I don't ask. Not a good idea to ask. You never know what you're gonna get involved in. I always wait for people to say.

He carries on placing the pieces.

Evan Phillips is one of the good guys. In fact, I'd say he's one of the best I've ever met. Works in the prison library. Very clever, very polite, never a bad word to say about anyone. Always neat and tidy, always spick and span. Carefully manicured fingernails, slicked back hair – and you never see him in dirty or grubby clothes. With his face, he could've bin a film star. I'd say mid-thirties. Public school, obviously.

After he's put down the final pawn, he leans forward.

In almost a whisper, he says, "About seven years ago, I made my first porn film. *Like Mother, Like Daughter*. Took me nearly an hour to write the script." He laughs. "A flimsy story, I must confess, Frank, but it provided many cinematographic opportunities." He laughs again.

"Our young, handsome hero is trying to escape the underworld and hides out with a woman he fancies. But, of course, she has a glamorous daughter, doesn't she? They invite some friends for a party. Queers, lesbians, chocolate, vanilla. The lot. Cue sex scenes in many permutations. To my complete astonishment, the actors, if we may loosely call them that, come up with some I hadn't thought of.

"It took a whole day to film. That's how complex it was. But also, rough and ready, I must confess. Used my house for the location. Cost me £200 to make. Sold at £15 a copy. I made more than two grand profit. As word spread, my film-making career developed. Same budgets, similar locations. Soon I was selling at £100 a copy.

"Before long, I was approached by one of the, shall we say, major players in the business who, er, persuaded me to deal exclusively with him. Suited me, old sport, suited

157

me. Increased the production values and was able to sell, through my partner's powers of persuasion, at £1,000 a copy. We split the profits 50-50. Had no choice, really, did I?"

I smile, impressed. I'm finally talking to a real operator. None of your small-time drumming, or your failed jewellery thieving or pointless garden mash-ups. No, here he was, telling me his life story. Evan Phillips. The real McCoy. The genuine article.

I understand now why he wants us to sit in the corner. We can't be disturbed. At the same time, I am wondering why he's telling me all this. If I keep schtum long enough, I'll find out.

"Soon," he says, "I'm a millionaire. Mansion outside Reading, house in Spain, one in Scotland and a yacht. I also own a block of flats in the East End, which accrues useful revenue and I'm paying appropriately selected personnel in the Clubs and Vice Squad to warn us when we were going to be paid a visit."

"So what happened?"

"'Twas quite simple, old sport," he says. "One night, we didn't get the tip-off. Me, my partner and our staff. We had ten shops. All our staff were nicked. Everyone was nicked."

"We follow different paths," I chuckle, "and end up in the same place." I'm still puzzling over why he's telling me all this.

He leans forward. "You're wondering why I'm telling you all this, aren't you?"

"Well, Evan," I say, "it did sort of cross my mind, you know?"

"What you got lined up when you get out?"

"Dunno," I say. "Haven't thought about it."

"You need to know all of this," he says, "because of what I'm going to say next." He looks about, making sure no-one can hear. "Frank," he says, "I've been watching you. The way you're learning chess. The way you conduct yourself. How you get on with everyone. You're a very impressive young man... I'm gonna make you an offer."

Now is not the time to show my excitement. "An offer?"

"When I get out," he says, clasping his hands behind his head as he leans back, "I intend to re-build my film business. It doesn't matter how many there are doing it, there's always room for another. Besides, I was one of the first. I've been jotting down ideas for scripts. Even started one. I shall need an assistant."

"You want me?" I say. "What do I know about film production? Evan, I'm just a – "

"When I get out," he says, "I want you by my side. I want to teach you the industry. I want you to learn the porn game, the ins and outs of everything."

"What?"

"And while I explore other opportunities, I want you to run that side of my business interests."

"Evan, you are joking, ain't ya?"

"First of all," he says, "all you'll do is drive me about. I've got a Roller. Are your legs long enough to reach the pedals?" He smiles.

"Course they are," I say, not smiling at all. "I can drive anything."

"What do you say?"

If I'm completely honest, I don't know what to say. One thing niggles me straightaway. "Why are you making *me* this offer? What do you get out of it? I ain't gonna be your nancyboy. If that's what you're after, you're wrong."

"Frank," he says, "I'm a businessman. If I'd wanted your cock, I'd've had it long before now. Simple fact is, everyone who's worked for me is locked up in a cell. Every day I'm in here, I'm losing thousands. But I know that once you've earned this kind of money, you can go right back up." He looks me straight in the eye. "Won't take me long." Then he looks at the wall-clock, stands up, comes round and grips my shoulder. "Tell me tomorrow. Visiting time approaches. My sweetheart awaits."

"Oh, that's – "

"Astrid, the sweetest girl who ever lived," he says, smiling. "She's been in the Canaries on a photo shoot for the last week. She has kindly agreed to be my wife when I get out. Only six months to go. I love her, Frank. I can't describe how much I love her. Fear not, old sport, I'm not after your arse. Only your quick-witted brain and your willingness to learn."

After he leaves, I stay still and stare at the chess pieces.

Next day, I tell him I'm in. We shake hands.

"Good boy," he says. "First thing I want you to do. When you get out, keep out of trouble. Don't drop a piece of litter. Don't frighten next-door's cat. Don't even fart without written permission. I'll be out three months after you. We'll meet and agree details. Then we're in business."

Pleased with ourselves, we shake hands again.

* * * * *

14 December 1974, I'm out after two years of a three-year stretch.

Mum and Dad are now living in a beautiful flat in Enfield. Even before I've taken my coat off, I tell them about Evan.

Dad says, "I know him. Good bloke."

"How do you know Evan Phillips?" Mum says.

"That associate of his," he says, "was Harry Whetstone."

"You mean," she says, "that slimy creep you worked for when we was living in Oak Tree Avenue?"

"The same."

"Oh, Frank," she says, alarmed. "Don't get involved. Not with Harry Whetstone. Please!"

"Frank'll be all right," Dad says. "Harry did a runner and cleared off abroad, didn't he?"

"Right!" I say, getting up. "I'm off out."

"Going to see Linda?" Mum says.

"Plenty of time for that. I need a drink."

I've arranged to meet a mate for a pint or two. It'll be good to see him after all this time. Gordon France, an old drummer pal who I haven't seen for years, has heard I'm out. There was a time when we talked about teaming up but I didn't like the idea of breaking into people's homes, even if they were them big country houses and not your threepenny ha'penny council two-up two-down places.

He brings along a mate of his, Dennis Flowers, and we spend a couple of hours having a good time, sharing experiences and the like. I tell them about Evan and they're pleased for me.

"Going straight at last, eh, Frank?" Gordon says.

"Sort of," I say. "It's a great opportunity."

"Good luck to ya," Dennis says, shaking my hand.

After that, while I'm waiting for Evan to get out, I decorate the bedroom Mum and Dad have let me have in their flat, see Linda a good bit, go to the pub a lot. Evan and I have agreed I won't visit him. Best, he said, to keep our relationship on the QT until everything's set up. I'd like to see him but he's the boss so I don't argue. He knows best.

And, before you know it, he's out and on the phone.

"Good to hear your voice, Frank," he says.

"Ready to meet?"

"I've got a few things to sort out," he says. "A few business contacts to re-establish, Astrid to see, get myself settled. After that."

We agree a time, date and place, two weeks away. Lubbly Jubbly. At last – something proper to get my teeth into. I can hardly wait.

'Cos we're meeting on a Monday, the Saturday before I invite Gordon and Dennis to go on a bit of a bender to celebrate my upcoming career. Then I'll sleep and rest on the Sunday and get ready for Evan. I want to be bright-eyed and bushy-tailed. Nice suit, white shirt, proper good tie. I intend to present myself as Evan's apprentice businessman. Show him from the off that I'm serious.

Gordon, Dennis and me have a real good time. Great

meal, solid drinking session, long laughs. I crash at Gordon's, 'cos I'm not fit to drive, get to Mum and Dad's mid-Sunday morning. Mum's in the kitchen, peeling some spuds, cooking a joint, making some gravy.

As I'm getting myself a coffee, she says, "Better look at the papers, Frank."

"Why?"

"There's something you ought to see."

I go into the living-room, pick 'em up. *Sunday People. News of the World.*

Soho porn king kills himself.

Seems Evan gets out of Spring Hill only to find Astrid's gone and married some world-famous photographer. His suicide note says everything he lived for was wrapped up in his future with her and now there's no point to anything. So he does himself in. The papers don't say how. But me, knowing how he liked to pop the pills when he was in Spring Hill, it don't take much working out.

I go to the funeral. Hardly anyone there. Six, including me and the vicar. That's all. No Astrid. No world-famous photographer. And them who used to party on his yacht and in his houses or mansion? Nowhere to be seen. They didn't mind his parties, they didn't mind snorting his stuff. So where are they now? Going around saying they never heard of him, I'll bet. Scumbags, the lot of 'em.

Poor old geezer.

One o' the best fellas I ever met.

Gone.

And taken my future career with him.

* * * * *

"Frank," Dad says on the 'phone about a year later, "what's going on?"

"What dya mean?"

"We got the Regional Crime Squad all over the house."

"You're joking," I say, trying to work out what they'll

find. Can't think of a thing.

"Can you hear me laughing?" he says, "Get it sorted, son."

Straightaway, I ring the local nick. "I hear you're looking for me."

One of the sergeants, who I know, says, "Hold on a minute." There's some muttering in the background and then he says, "Look, Frank, are you going to hand yourself in?"

"What for?" I say. "I ain't done nothing."

"Frank," he says, lowering his voice to a whisper, "we got Regional swarming all over the nick. They're nothing to do with us, we got no control over 'em. If you don't get yourself down here sharpish, they'll turn over everybody you ever talked to, including your old granny."

"All right," I say. "I'll be there."

"Good lad," he says. "It's not a big deal."

He's a bloody liar, for a kick-off. I mean, if you can't trust the Old Bill, who can you trust?

When I get there, some big knob from Regional is waiting for me. He don't mince his words. Soon as I get in Reception, he says, "Francis Wilfred Peters, I'm arresting you on suspicion of burglary." He cautions me, grabs hold of my arm and frogmarches me down to the cells. No clearing it with Custody, no asking if I want a solicitor. Straight to the cells.

After three or four hours of sitting there, I'm hauled up for interview. They don't let me walk on my own, though. Two gorillas gripping my arms like they're squeezing lemons drag me along.

"This yours?" the head honcho says. The two gorillas are now standing about the room, leaning against the walls like the building might collapse if they walk away. He bends down, picks up a large polythene bag and throws it on the table. In it is a large, ornate silver candelabra.

I'm thinking about what I'm gonna say. This is a bit of the gear Gordon and me got from the drum of that TV sports commentator a while back. We weren't able to shift it straightaway so I stashed it in the wardrobe of Mum and Dad's spare room. Then went and forgot about it.

"And this?" he says, plonking a rather nice eighteenth-century inlaid tea-caddy next to it.

"And this?" A beautiful cloisonné jewellery box.

"Answer the Chief!" one of the gorillas thunders, thumping me in the back.

"Forgot how to squeal, have you, you flea-bitten weasel?" shouts the other, grabbing my hair and pulling my head back.

"C'm' on," whispers the first as he slaps me about.

"We've got France, your old mate, in the next room," Chief says, "coughing up. Do the honourable thing, Peters. Don't let's be wasting the taxpayers' money. We got you bang to rights."

I can't help but laugh. Except on *Z Cars*, I've never heard any copper say "bang to rights". While I'm sitting there, wondering whether TV cop shows inspire the Old Bill or the other way round, Chief stands up.

"We don't need your confession," he says. "We've got enough evidence to charge you with thirty-four counts of burglary. Do you want the duty solicitor?"

"Don't legal procedures mean anything to you?" I say.

As he picks up the gear, he nods to his henchmen and goes out.

They charge me with the thirty-four counts. Turns out they charge Gordon and Dennis Flowers and Mack, some mate of Dennis who I've never heard of, with the same. Which ain't right. Some of the jobs Gordon and me done, well, okay, but some of 'em I don't know nothing about. They're down to Gordon or Dennis or Mack or Gordon and Dennis or Mack and Dennis – or any other combination of our names I can't work out. Regional have lumped us together and we and our solicitors can't do a damn thing about it.

February, '76, the four of us are in the dock together at St Albans, like targets set up in a human coconut shy.

The judge gives Mack and Dennis eighteen months

each.

"France," he says, "I want you to read this before I sentence you." A geezer in a wig hands him a bunch of papers which he makes out he's reading. I'm standing next to him and I can see he's not even looking at 'em.

"Yeah, all right," he says.

"What you mean, 'Yeah, all right'?" the judge says. "Have you read the documents or not?"

"S'pose so."

I lean over. "Don't wind him up, Gordy."

Gordy nods at me and says, "Well, I suppose I – "

"No, no, no, no, no," says the judge. "If you're not interested in the eighteen months I'm offering you, France, then neither am I. Two and a half years."

That's what you get for insulting a judge.

"Peters – "

My turn.

" – in your case, as you've just finished a three-year sentence, we can now talk about a suspended sentence."

Gordy knocks my foot as if to say, "You've got it."

"I've gone into it very thoroughly," the judge says.

"Thank you, my lord," I pipe up. After what's he done to Gordy, I reckon a bit of arse-licking won't go amiss.

"Shut up," he says. "As I say, I've gone into it very thoroughly and I, I, I feel I can't give you the suspended sentence after all. Peters, you're going to prison for eighteen months with the rest of them. Take them down."

I look at Gordy. "What?" I say. I mean, why give it to me with one hand, then take it away with the other?

"He's on something," Gordy says. "Gotta be."

When we get underneath, I'm cuffed too tight. I kick one of the warders and headbutt another. Right now, at this precise moment, I don't care what I do. I really don't give a monkey's. By the time we get to the Scrubs, I'm really worked up. In Reception, eleven screws – count 'em, nine, ten, eleven – stand with an SO seated at a table.

He says, "Name?"

"Bollocks."

He looks up. "What?"

One of the screws behind me, another gorilla, says, "Say *sir*."

"Bollocks."

The SO says, "Date of birth?"

"Ain't you already got that written down?"

"Say *sir*."

"Fuck off."

The screw behind comes up. "You piece of shit." And he punches me straight in the back. Feels like he's hit me in the kidney.

I look at the SO, head down, pretending to write. "Do you see what he done to me?" I say. "He give me a right fucking dig."

Without looking up, the SO says, "Date of birth?"

"Fuck off."

The SO looks up, his unshaven, tired face a picture of bored resignation. "Look, sonny," he says, "I'm here for another ten hours. While I'm sitting here waiting for you to co-operate, I'm not doing something else, like supervising my officers here to piss in every next meal you'll eat. I can sit here all day and all night, if that's what you want. But while you're telling my officers and me to fuck off, you're not getting any grub or sleep or telly time. So it's up to you. Which is it going to be?"

Finally, they take us to C Wing. After a few days, while I'm still settling in, they call me down with Penney, another con. They're transferring us to 98 Block, Standford Hill, on the Isle of Sheppey.

* * * * *

What a bloody awful journey. It's February so it's cold, no heating in the bus, and it's pissing down with rain. And it ain't called the Isle of Sheppey 'cos they like the sound of the word "isle". It really is an island. The bus drives over a bridge, through a great big gate in a high fence. When we reach the prison itself, we get out. We can hardly see, what with the rain and the mist coming in from the North Sea.

"Cheerful, ain't it?" the driver says. "And don't even think about escaping. They lift the bridge and you're trapped."

We go into Reception, answer their questions and then they take me to the wing. It's like no other prison I've ever seen. Down a long corridor, like a hospital with rooms going off either side. Four to a room. We get to the last room, I'm put in there where three men are laying on their beds. Loony, Windom and Pete.

Loony's laying there in his boxers, resting his hands behind his head. He sits up straight and says, "I'd like to thank you for watching me and my little show here tonight. If you've enjoyed it then it's all been worthwhile. So until we meet again, goodnight, and I love you all!" He drops back, closes his eyes and doesn't speak for the rest of the evening.

Windom and Pete come over, shake my hand.

Windom says, "We're from – "

"Dagenham," Pete says.

"We don't always – "

"Finish each – "

"Other's sentences," Windom says.

Both burst into laughter and slap my back so much I end up face down on my bed, laughing my head off. This is gonna be all right, I think. They're good blokes. Even Loony.

I've got the next day to find my way around the place while they decide what to do with me. It don't take long to figure out what's going on. It's obvious everybody in this prison is here 'cos they're either anti-social or they won't do as they're told or they keep getting nicked – or all three.

Basically, nobody gives a toss. Everyone does as they're told and all that 'cos it's clear the screws run the place. No volunteering, no cheerful friendliness between the cons and the screws, it's them and us, a constant campaign by them to keep us down and a series of skirmishes by us to let 'em know we ain't gonna let 'em and that we don't give a bollocks.

A couple of nights later, we're in the TV room, watching *Love Story*.

The bell goes. Everyone gets up and starts to leave, except me.

"C'm' on," Windom says. "Dining-hall. They're gonna count us."

So up I get and follow, *Love Story* still playing.

We sit at the tables while the screws march up and down. First one of 'em counts us, then another and then they stand at the end checking their numbers. We're muttering to ourselves, munching on granite-hard rock cakes they've put out for us and we've got the bad needle 'cos we're missing *Love Story*.

They count us again. For Chrissake, how difficult is this? The thick-headed morons.

"Do you want some help, mate?" someone shouts out. He pushes back his chair and stands up. "One, two, three – " he says, randomly pointing.

"Carter, sit down!" one of the screws shouts back. He's a big, burly bloke with a mophead of bright ginger hair and wearing a long, black prison cape. As he rushes over, his cape opens up like he's got wings, swiping every con in the face as he passes.

He gets to Carter. "Sit down!" he bawls, his arms waving about like he's gonna take off.

But Carter's having none of it. He picks up a rock cake and smashes it into the screw's ear, knocking him over sideways, bashing him against another con sitting in a red plastic chair. The con doesn't move. Nor does anyone else.

The screw lays there, head leaning over, shouting, "Bang 'em up! Bang 'em all up! Get 'em out of my sight!"

We're confined to our rooms, we don't get the rest of *Love Story* and that's an end to it.

But not for Carter.

He spends the next day making a smoke bomb.

It's not difficult. What you do is sneak into the Games Room and lift two or three ping-pong balls. Then you get

168

the half ounce of baccy you've been saving for just such an occasion. Take the baccy out the packet and put it to one side. You won't need it. Smooth out the silver packing 'til it's flat. Take the ping-pong balls, gently smash them up into little pieces and place them on the silver wrapping. Roll the package up and twist each end so the whole thing looks like a Christmas cracker.

Now for the next stage.

When no-one's looking, creep on all fours to Reception, making sure the on-duty screw is sitting at his desk, sifting through some paperwork. Quietly, so he can't hear, open the door wide enough to get your arm through. Then, light both ends of the Christmas cracker, sling it into the office, close the door, run back to your room and wait.

It don't take long before all we can hear is coughing, spluttering, choking, yelling, bells ringing and doors are opening and slamming all over the place. Then loud cackling, laughing and guffawing from us cons. Carter don't make a sound. He sits in his room, reading a book, as if nothing's going off.

By the time they've cleared up and the screw's bin checked out by the medic that he's okay, it's time for our evening meal. Then straight back to our room, 'cos TV and recreation are banned for the next three nights.

We don't mind. Carter did what he had to do and nobody blames him.

But a few weeks later, we still ain't got revenge for not being allowed to watch *Love Story*. So Loony comes up with a plan. Typical of him, it's very playground, so naturally everybody thinks it's great.

Every night, we have to stand by our beds while they go up and down the hallways, counting us in. Loony, Windom, Pete, me. That's us in. Then the next room, one, two, three, four. And so on. There's five wings, six rooms a wing, that's a hundred and twenty all told. All in.

The screws march down the corridors like bad actors in a film about Nazi soldiers on patrol, all the way down, go out, turn and close the big wooden doors at the end. We hear the thick, heavy bars being dropped in place. We can't get out now until the morning when they lift the bars and open up.

Only what they don't know is we've used massive tins of boot polish to cake-hole the door handles and bars with the stuff. Everyone on every wing's done the same.

Five minutes later, the tannoy goes on.

"Oh, nice one, lads. We're smothered in shit up here. Hands, shirts, faces. Who d'ya think you are? Make-up girls for the Black and White Minstrels? You ain't heard the last o' this, we'll sort this out, you'll see."

We get into our beds, sniggering like kids, congratulating Loony.

"That's the way – " Windom says.

"To do it," Pete says.

A few hours later, maybe four o'clock, on comes the tannoy, blasting out some foreign radio station with all its crap Euro trash. Everyone is soon awake, shouting for it to be turned off.

"Sorry, lads."

And it goes off.

Twenty minutes later, on it comes again, playing full volume for about fifteen minutes.

"Oh, my mistake. Pressed the wrong button, didn't I?"

Thirty minutes go by and then, here we go again, more foreign muck screeching all round the place.

"Whoops! Silly me! Sorry!"

On, off, on, off, right up to breakfast. By the time we're shovelling back our eggs, bacon, sausages and fried bread, we're shattered, the screws are delighted and I never want to hear Métal Urbain, Stinky Toys or any other French punk music ever again.

* * * * *

"I'm proud and honoured," I say to the other four seated around the table, "to be elected Chairman of the Inmates Support Committee and I hope I live up to your expectations."

"Are you sure this is all right?"

"Is what all right, Allan?"

"Sitting here in the dining-hall having this meeting? With screws eavesdropping?

"I spoke to the Governor," I say. "He said we could meet for two hours a week here with no listening in. It's all okay. I cleared it."

"Sorry," Allan says. "I only asked."

"We are here," I say, "to voice the concerns of all inmates on a variety of subjects. The Governor's said he'll listen to my report. Anything that makes the lives of our fellow inmates better has gotta be good, ain't it? James, got your pad and pen ready for notes?"

"Yes, Mr Chairman," James says. He's the rep from A Wing and our secretary. Likes a bit of structure, does our James. He's an accountant who went a bit wrong when he bashed a client over the head when the client didn't agree with his innovative approach to his financial arrangements.

Nick, from B Wing, has been inside more times than he's got fingers and toes. 'Though that ain't saying much 'cos he's only got one arm. Got into a barney with a doorman at a night-club, didn't he, and ended up – he won't tell us how – losing his left arm. It's left him a cynical bastard who won't put up with anyone's bullshit. Best to have him on your side, is all I can say. The opposite don't bear thinking about.

Patsy's from C Wing. Nobody laughs at his name. Not if you value your body parts. But he's okay. I mean, *okay*. Don't know why he's in 98 Block. He won't say. All anyone knows is he's Frankie Fraser's boy. Yeah, that's "Mad" Frankie Fraser, of the Richardson Gang. But, as far as I'm concerned, couldn't wish for a nicer bloke. Almost as nice as Evan.

Allan, D Wing, is the softie on our Committee. A big black lad who says he hates everyone but underneath he'll never say yah boo sucks to a lame snail. Spent the last few years in the car import/export trade. Shipping, he calls it.

I'm E Wing and Chairman, o' course. Don't know how it happened but shows I'm a respected member of the 98 Block community.

"Right," I say, "let's get down to business. First item. Travel arrangements. James?"

"I am pleased to report," he says, "that in the last month, we have assisted nine customers. Fowley, Haversham, Cheadle, Kowslowski, Burden, Shave, Inglenook –"

"Who's Inglenook?" Nick says.

"Young lad," I say, "keep fit fanatic. Drummer. You remember. Came from up north, Leicester way."

"Oh yeah," Nick says, nodding.

"Ollerenshaw – "

"Ah, Ollerenshaw," Patsy smiles. "I liked him."

"Everyone liked Ollerenshaw," Nick says.

"You liked Ollerenshaw?" I say, surprised.

"Yeah."

"But you don't like nobody."

"I liked Ollerenshaw," Nick says. "You wanna make something of it?"

"No, no, no," I say. "You liked Ollerenshaw."

"And Tompkinson," James finishes.

"Thank you, James," I say. "Resources. Allan."

"Pete in E Wing, your roomie, Frank, what he's doing is getting a pair of boots and some screws – "

"We ain't having any screws in this," Nick snaps.

"Not them screws, you idiot," Allan says.

Nick goes to get up, his only fist clenched.

I touch him lightly on the shoulder and ease him down. "No cause for alarm, mate. He means them metal things you hang pictures on."

"Course I do," Allan says. "He shoves the ends of the *screws* through the inside so they stick out the bottom and you've got a pair o' mountain boots. He's also bending some strips of metal and *screwing* 'em in pieces of wood."

"So how's it all work, Al?" I ask, leading the meeting in the direction of valuable discussion. That's what a

172

chairman does. "You getting this, James?"

James nods, writing like his life depends on it.

"The date is fixed for the customer's departure," Al says. "He puts on his climbing boots. When the screw has passed by the start of the travel route, we tell him go, go go. The customer climbs out the window, crosses to the fence. He uses the bits o' wood to lever himself up and over and, dum dum dum – he's away!"

"When will the gear be ready, Al?"

"Couple o' days, mate."

"Next item," I say. "Subscriptions. James?"

"As you know," he says, "the fee has been one ounce of baccy per customer per journey. As we're upping the equipment we provide, I propose we increase it to two ounces for each unit trip. Our customers can afford it and of course, once they're travelling, they won't need it."

I look round the table. "All agreed?"

"What happens to the baccy?" Nick says. "No good charging 'em if we ain't getting any."

"The fees for travelling aren't for the Committee to share among themselves," I tell him. "You know that, Nick. I don't know why you're asking – "

"Checking, that's all. I gotta right to ask, ain't I?"

"Course you have," I say. "It goes into the kitty to donate to less fortunate inmates. Every one of us has living expenses. The Committee helps those who can't always make ends meet. Are we agreed?"

Patsy nods so everyone nods.

"But," I continue, "we've also had some unlucky customers. Nick, you wanna start with your B Wing report?"

"Yeah, well," he says. "The Aussie, can't remember his stupid name. What a cock-up. 'Cos he spent a year living on Bondi Beach, thinks he can swim, don't he? Gets out and instead o' leggin' it over the fields, tries to evade the dogs by swimming the River Swale. Reckons without all the shit in it and the English weather. Nearly drowns."

"James? A Wing?"

"Aaron Landisman gets out, over the fence, then loses his way. Hides under a big lump of cardboard in a field. They find him five days later, starving and twelve hours away from having a meet with The Grim Reaper."

"And Billy and Benny," I say.

"Who the hell are Billy and Benny?" Nick asks.

I don't know why he asks all these questions. He knows the answers. But, as I say, he's a bloody-minded bastard who likes arguing. The only surprise to me is he's still got an arm.

"Billy the Barrel," I tell him, "and Benny the Beanpole. They're the ones who made that aluminium ladder."

"Where'd they get the aluminium?" James asks, always interested in finance and sourcing.

"How the fuck do I know?" I say. "Last Thursday night, they get the ladder and smash the doors at the bottom of E Wing. They run across the lawn to the fence. When they get there, they shove the ladder up against it. Then Billy the Barrel scrambles up it with Benny the Beanpole holding it steady at the bottom. Only thing is, when they was making the ladder, they didn't check it for strength and weight, did they? I mean, Billy the Barrel ain't called that 'cos he wears metal hoops round his fat arse. He gets halfway up and the ladder snaps in two. He tumbles down, bang on top of Benny the Beanpole. Benny don't see him coming 'cos it's night. Billy screams his head off 'cos he's falling. Benny screams *his* head off 'cos Billy's crashed his twenty stone on him. The screws run out and haul 'em back inside. I mean – "

"Laurel and Hardy don't even begin to cover it," Patsy says.

"Now, gentlemen," I say, leaning forward, "the Aussie, Aaron Landisman and Billy and Benny tried to get out without the approval or support of this Committee. It's clear to me we're failing to get it through to our customers that they gotta come to us if they want their travel plans to succeed. If they cough up their subscriptions, they get out. Simple as that. We gotta put the word about. At the next

174

meeting, I want full reports of your marketing efforts."

Everyone mutters, "Sure thing," "Will do" "Yes, Frank." Nick goes, "Hah!"

"Now then," I say, leaning back. "Grub. James has something to say on the subject of parsnips."

Chapter 9. Great Yarmouth

"Mum, Dad," I say, six weeks after I get out of 98 Block, "Linda and me are getting married."

As Mum purses her lips, she looks at Dad.

"What?" I say.

"Nothing, son," Dad says. "As long as you're sure that's what you want."

"Why shouldn't it be?"

"She's an interesting girl," Dad says.

"I hope you'll be very happy," Mum says as she brushes down her apron. She gets up from the breakfast table and leaves the room.

"What's up?" I say. "Is there something you're not telling me?"

Dad reaches for his No 6 ciggies and lights up. "Linda's a very loving girl. We, er, were surprised when she moved in next door."

"Yeah," I say, helping myself to a smoke. "That came as a surprise to me, too. After all," I add, putting my lighter down, "she didn't tell me, you know, 'til I turned up and found her there."

"No," he says. "She didn't tell us either."

"I've done two stretches and she waited for me through the lot, visited me, wrote to me."

"But do you love her?"

"What's love got to do with it? She wants to marry me. She's earned it."

"You know she's jealous of your mum, don't you?"

"Jealous?"

"They don't get on," he says. "She doesn't like the affection you show for your mum."

"That's stupid."

"Well," he says, "I'm telling you, that's all. Best to know these things."

A couple of months later, we marry at Enfield Register Office. Everyone comes. Must be a hundred altogether.

My family and mates, her girlfriends and family. I didn't know she had so many relatives.

Linda's a picture, a real beauty. Long blonde hair, smashing outfit, can't stop smiling. When we get out, man and wife, she stands in the street for the photos and even people passing by stop and stare at her, they can't believe how stunning she is.

The Maloneys, Linda's family, are a bunch of East End market traders and while a few get drunk at the reception and Linda ends up a bit worse for wear, I don't mind. Everyone has a cracking good time, that's all that matters.

As everyone's finally leaving, Pat, one of her brothers, pissed out of his head, grabs hold of me and says, "What did an ugly fucker like you do to deserve her?" He cackles. "Must be your cock. You got nothing else goin' for ya."

I think of decking him but out the corner of my eye, I see Mum watching – she must've heard what the Irish git said – so I pat him on the back, laugh too much and shove him out into the car park.

We've got us a flat a few streets away from Mum and Dad. We spend the next few days sorting it out before going away to Great Yarmouth. Lovely place, the hotel's good, the food's the same and we have a fine old time walking up and down the seafront like an old married couple.

When we get back, Linda fusses around the place, ironing curtains and fluffing about in the bathroom. She spends hours in British Home Stores, choosing lampshades, photo frames and cushions – and even longer choosing one o' them toilet-roll covers shaped like a pink doll. I let her get on with it.

* * * * *

A few months later, Gordy gets out so we meet in the Horse and Cart to discuss some possibilities. When I tell him me and Linda are married, he goes like Mum did.

"If you're happy, mate," he says, sipping his beer,

"then congratulations."

"We're very happy."

"That's all right, then."

"Couldn't wish for a nicer girl."

"Pleased for you, mate," Gordy says.

We go through his list of drums and my list of other places, agree what we're gonna look at, have another chat, fix a date to meet again and then it's time for the off.

It's drizzling a bit when we get into the street but it's warm enough, so we don't mind.

Gordy looks down the street. "Oh, blimey," he says, "it's Linda. See ya, mate." He hitches up his jeans and before I can say, "See ya," he's round the corner and Linda's marching up, carrying a green rolled-up telescope umbrella.

"Where you bin?" she hollers. "I bin looking for ya!"

I hold up my hands like Wyatt Earp's taking me in. "For a drink with Gordy," I say. "I told ya."

"You did no such bloody thing!" she screams from here to Catford.

"I had a bit o' business to attend to."

"I won't have it, Frank," she shouts, biffing me over the head with her brolly. "I won't have you leaving me alone like that." And she biffs me again.

"Hey, watch it, you," I shout back, trying to grab hold of her. "Fighting in the street like this. Shut it, Linda."

But she won't stay still. She's writhing and wriggling all over the place with her long blonde hair swishing everywhere, swiping me in the face. She's like an octopus on speed. I swear, if she don't calm down soon, I'll slap her one.

She gets an arm free, grabs my hair and tugs. Christ, that girl's got some strength. I yell out, trying to push her away. At last, she edges back and holds up her fist, a prize pug escaping with a trophy. She gets her trophy, all right. A clump o' my hair.

I shoot my hand up at the pain above my earhole. I'm bald. For Chrissake, she's pulled so much hair out, I'm bald!

* * * * *

The Shamrock Arms is an old Irish pub Dad introduced me to when I first got home. Full of Irish blokes, as you'd expect, sloshing back Guinness. But they're good blokes. Good for a laugh, a game o' darts or snooker or whatever and, most of all – o' course – good at talking. And that's what I like most about 'em. They don't treat you like you're stupid, you can have a good old barney, disagree like crazy and come out of it still the mates you were before it all kicked off.

Linda's decided she wants to tag along.

"You'll hate it," I tell her. "It's not your kind o' place."

But she don't listen. She never listens. Once she's got something into her head, there's no talkin' to her.

"I'm coming," she says.

"All right," I say. "But don't blame me if anything happens."

"What's gonna happen?"

"Friday night?" I say. "Irish pub? What do you think?"

"So?"

I shake my head and go and get ready while she dabbles about with her make-up. I dunno – when I get back, she looks the same as she was before. But what do I know? Anyway, she seems pleased with her handiwork so I keep my mouth shut.

When we get there, she sees some girl she knows, Tracey somebody. I get them both drinks, they sit down for a natter. They don't want me with 'em, so I lean up against the bar, looking around to see if there's anyone I know. Don't really matter. The place is packed, it's buzzing like an overcrowded wasps' nest, it's just nice to be standing there with my pint, taking it all in. Linda's happy. Everyone else is happy. So I'm happy.

A bloke comes up to the bar, stands next to me and waves for the barman. He glances my way. Nods.

He's a big fella, make no mistake. Tattoos on both arms, shaved head, dainty silver ring through one of his earlobes. Must be a navvy, I reckon. I noticed his green rugger shirt. Could be a rugger bugger. Could be both, for all I know.

I nod.

"What do you say, old sport?" he says. "T-G-I-F, eh?"

Old sport. *Old sport*. I thought Evan was the only one who said that.

"'Ere," I say, pulling out my wallet and a tenner. "Let me get that for ya."

I catch the barman's eye and order.

"Much appreesh- " the fella says in his soft Irish lilt, like he's come down from his castle to mingle with us spud-pickin' peasants. "Much appreesh- " He grabs hold of the bar and gives a rough shake of the head. "Much… Grateful." He looks up and smiles.

"Frank," I say, holding out my hand.

"Brendan," he says and goes to shake my hand. But he misses and falls against the bar.

"Steady, Brendan," I say, trying to prop him up. As I say, he's a large lump and it takes a bit of effort.

The jars arrive.

"So," he says, "what line are you in?"

"Oh – er – "

"Me?" he says. "Import, export."

"Yeah," I say, "you could say that's my line. In a manner of speaking." I chuckle, liking my new job title. Import, export. I'm gonna use that next time someone asks.

He picks up his Guinness, takes a long, hard drink and slaps it down. He stands up straight, stretches so he's a good bit taller than me.

I give him one o' my best smiles. He's a whopper of a bloke, I don't even come up to his shoulders. Best to keep him sweet, I reckon.

"I can beat you up," he says.

Linda's by my side now, clutching on to my arm. I turn

and nod to her. "This is Brendan."

"I can beat him in a fight," Brendan says to her.

"Course you can," I say.

But Linda's gotta have her say, ain't she. She can't keep her nose out of anything. "No, you can't," she says. "Frank can lay you out in two minutes."

"Shut your mouth," I hiss at her. "I'm gonna get mullahed if you don't keep quiet."

"But you can!" the stupid cow blurts out.

"No, no, no," she shouts, so half the pub can hear. "I'm not having an Irishman talking to us like that. Go on, Frank, give him one."

"I'm sorry about this," I say to Brendan, trying to back away with as much grace as I can.

He picks up his jar, takes another slurp, carefully puts it down again and turns so he's facing her. By now, everyone around us has gone quiet.

I don't like the way this is going.

"I know you," he says to her. "You're one of the Maloneys, aren't ya?"

"You making something of it?" she says.

"Oh, I don't want no trouble with that family," he says like he's talking to the Queen. He looks at me. "They're mad, they're completely insane. I don't want no trouble with 'em." He looks at his watch. "Time I was off."

And he slips into the crowd, leaving me and Linda standing there and everyone else picking up from where they left off before my bitch of a wife tried to get me duffed up.

* * * * *

It's a hot summer's night and I'm driving Linda and me in my new red Triumph TR7 Automatic to a party in Roydon, a couple of miles from Harlow. As usual, she's moaning her mouth off. No idea what about 'cos I've put the radio on full blast. "Hotel California", the Eagles. I love this track but she keeps on and on.

181

We get to the place, lovely bungalow with a big garden front and back. Yeah, well, the last time I went into a lovely bungalow with a big garden front and back, I bashed someone over the head with a hammer, didn't I, and ended up in Aylesbury. The way Linda's squawking her head off, I don't think we'll get to the garden, we'll have the fight here and now.

We get out the car. We're walking up the pathway.

"These fucking shoes are killing me," she says.

"What d'ya want me to do?"

"This dress is sticking up my arse. And this bra's pinching right into my tits."

She's coming to a posh party with cultured people and here she is, not thirty seconds away from meeting 'em and she's talkin' like a bint who failed the entrance exam to the Institute of Homeless Prostitutes.

I look at her. Whatever did I see in her? Her long blonde hair, her great body, her big blue eyes. That's what. Now I understand what "All that glitters is not gold" means. Her, gold? She ain't even tin plate.

"I'm not gonna row with you," I tell her. "I've come 'ere to enjoy myself and if you keep on moanin', I'm off."

"For fuck's sake, I've brought the wrong bag."

She ain't heard a word I said. I might as well've not been there. So I do an about-turn and walk back down the path to the motor. As I'm getting in and starting the engine, she comes running down towards me.

"Don't you leave me here, you snivellin' coward!" Tears running down her face, she's waving her arms about in crazed semaphore signals.

I've got the engine running. But I don't pull away 'cos, to be honest, I don't know what to do for the best. She's my wife, after all, and I've got a responsibility to make sure she's safe.

She stands in front of the car so I can't move, anyway. I put my foot on the accelerator a touch and nudge forwards. She still don't move. I try a few inches more.

She lets out a wail and leaps on to the bonnet, her arms

and legs in a star, her hands clutching the windscreen wipers, her face pressed against the glass. The silly bitch don't even looked scared.

I wind down the window. "Get off my car!"

"Fuck off!"

Then I think, what the hell, I've had enough of this. I put my foot back on the pedal and drive up the road, not too fast, mind, but enough for any sane person to want to get off. Not her. She clings on to them wipers like her life depends on it. Well, I suppose it does really. I mean, if I take a quick swerve, she'll be off, probably fall under the motor. That's another body on a slab and I'm up for murder.

But, you know what, I don't care. I just wanna be shot of her. I speed up a bit and then brake hard, expecting her to slip off and maybe break an arm or something. But not her. She's gripping them wipers, her ashen face staring at me through the windscreen, crying her eyes out.

Poor bird. Poor, poor little bird.

I get out and walk round the front. "C'm' on, babe," I say, lifting her down. "I'll take you home."

She throws her arms around me and hugs me so tight I lose my breath for a second or two.

"Frank," she whispers in my ear, "when we get there, let's go to bed."

We get on to the B194 to Nazeing. By now it's pitch black outside and, as there's a boggy ditch by the side of the road, I'm driving slower than usual.

Then, in the middle of the road, the engine cuts out and the car stops.

I reach down to put the gear back into drive. She's only gone and tried to shove it in reverse, ain't she? She's probably wrecked the gears, if not the engine.

"What you done?" I say.

"You're driving, not me," she says.

"Whadya do that for?"

"Felt like it, didn't I?"

For a second or two, I slump over the steering-wheel.

That's it. She's gone too far. We coulda bin killed. Now I *really* don't care. I take the key out the ignition, get out, walk round to her door and open it.

"Get out," I say. "You're not coming near me or the motor ever again."

"Fuck off."

"All right," I say. "Have it your way."

I lean in, get hold of her arm, pull her out and let her fall to the ground.

She don't say a word. She gets up, reaches in for her bag – the one she didn't like – jumps down into the ditch, crawls through it, up the other side into a field and off she goes. It gets darker and darker the further she goes away from the headlights, the more she scrambles through the grass and nettles.

I don't believe it. Once again, she calls my bluff. Once again, I can't leave her like this.

So I slip into the ditch, get myself covered in sludge, shit and Christ knows what, climb up the other side and chase after her.

"C'm' on, babe," I shout. "Don't be a prat. Let's go home, eh?"

"Like bollocks I will."

"Linda!"

"Leave me alone!"

"Hallo!" A man's voice, deep, throaty. "Everything okay?"

Foreign. From the direction of the road. I turn round.

A great big artic's parked in front of and across the Triumph with its headlights aimed over the field and at us. As far as I can make out the silhouettes, two geezers, one of 'em fat.

"You want help?"

"Nah!" I call back. "Family argument."

They have a talk, then the other shouts, "We come."

"We're all right!" I holler.

"We come!"

They disappear for a few seconds while they get

184

through the ditch and, after a couple of minutes, they're standing next to me.

My eyes have got used to the headlights. The older one must be in his fifties. He's going bald, has four double chins and a massive beer gut. The other's in his mid-twenties, massive shoulders, broad chest, slim waist. Hair cut like a squaddie's.

The older one stares at Linda, who, by now, has sat down in the grass and arranged her hair so she looks like some beauty in one o' them Victorian paintings. The young 'un keeps his eyes on me.

"This man hurt you?" the older one asks Linda.

"He rape you?" says Soldier Boy, still looking at me, clenching his fists.

"Linda!" I yelp, shit-scared he's gonna beat me up. "Tell 'em I'm your husband! Tell 'em we're having a domestic."

"Like bollocks I will."

For a good while, none of us moves. The older guy's giving Linda the visuals, she's fluttering her eyelids at him, Soldier Boy's getting ready to thump the daylights out o' me and I'm standing there like a useless pillock, not knowing what the hell to do.

So, for want of anything better, I get my fags out and light up. "Want one?" I say to Soldier Boy.

He steps forward and takes one. "*Danke.*" He pulls out a lighter. "My friend smoke also," he says, lighting up.

The older guy takes one. He takes another, crouches down, hands it to Linda, lights it and then his own.

"Hey," he says to her, letting out a cloud o' smoke, "you okay?"

"Course she is," I say, staring at Soldier Boy, not daring to move a muscle.

"I speak to the lady," the older one says.

The two talk in their own lingo. They nod a lot. Finally, the older one gets up, both smile and nod at me, turn and start to walk back to the artic.

"Wait for me!" I call, trotting after them, catching 'em

185

up.

"Men!" Linda screams into the night. "You're all the bloody same!"

Soldier Boy says, "You leave Bo Derek in field?"

"Yeah," I tell him. "She can make her own way home."

As we near the ditch, I hear the thud of running feet behind us.

"Wait for me! Wait for me!"

We turn round and there she is, panting to catch us, her boobs jumping up, down, all over the place. She must've taken off that bra that was pinching her so much.

By now, the three of us are on the road.

"I help," Soldier Boy says, going back through the ditch and picking her up. She puts her arms tightly round his neck and, smiling, pushes her face up close to his. Another few seconds and she'll have her hands inside his shirt.

"He is good boy," the other says.

Soldier Boy carries her up on to the road and puts her down. He's coated in mud. He don't care.

Then it's hugs, handshakes and thanks all round. Linda gives Soldier Boy a plump kiss on his mouth. The two men get in the artic, reverse into the road and drive off, pipping their hooter as they go.

Linda and me get in the car. I fiddle about with the gear stick to make sure no damage is done, say a little prayer the engine'll start, turn the ignition and, thank God, we're okay.

"Frank," Linda says, rubbing her hand up and down my thigh, "let's hurry home, eh?"

"Nah," I yawn, putting my foot down and moving off. "I'm cream-crackered. When we get back to the pope, it's Bo-Peep time."

"Okay," she says. "Anything you say, babes."

* * * * *

A couple of days later, Pat, Linda's brother, comes up to

me as I'm placing a bet and says he'll pump my eyes out if I ever do that to his sister again. Do what? I tell him I've no idea what he's talking about and he should keep his nose out of things that don't concern him. I don't even bother to ask Linda what she told him. Or why.

Two weeks after that, our landlord puts up the rent. I tell him we ain't paying until he fixes the damp patch in the spare bedroom. He says that's my responsibility. I remind him what the tenancy agreement says. He gives us a month's notice to quit.

We can't move in with Mum and Dad 'cos they've bought a guest house in Great Yarmouth, where Linda and me went after our wedding, so we get a couple of rooms with my Nan in Hoddesdon. We haven't been there a week and Linda's saying Nan stole some money. I believe her. After all, my Nan was done for thieving that giro all those years ago. But when I come home one evening and find 'em getting ready to have a scrap... My wife fighting my nan over fifty quid?

Nah.

I call Mum. "The whole family's the same. Her dad's a nutcase, mother's a nutcase, the brother's off his head. All the uncles are round the twist."

"Come and stay with us," she says. "But only you, mind. I'm not having that woman in the house."

"Don't worry about that, Mum. I ain't ever going near her again."

* * * * *

I get to Yarmouth with a bit of dough in my pocket but no job, o' course. Mum and Dad let me have a room in their guest house. First week free, they say, but after that –

"We're running a business here, son," Dad says. "If you have a room, that's a percentage decrease in our profits."

So after the first week, I have to pay my way. Fair enough from their point of view, but not so great from mine.

"You married that girl, we didn't," Dad goes on, "so now you've got to live with the consequences."

"Yeah," I say. "S'pose so."

"No suppose about it," he says. "Fact."

So happens they're short-staffed for a couple of weeks, so I pay my rent by doing the washing-up, waiting the tables, that sort o' thing, until I can find something else and somewhere of my own to live.

"Frank," Dad says a month or so later, "I've got an opening for you. Go and see Bill Wilby."

"Who's he?"

He looks at me as if I'm soft in the head. "Bill owns Aspreys – "

"The night-club?"

" – and Stella's – "

"The disco?"

Mum comes in. "Doesn't he own the pier as well, Sid?"

"He *owns* Yarmouth Pier?"

"No," Dad says. "His pier is up the coast. He's got a couple of casinos as well. Loaded, son, loaded."

"How do you come to know him?"

"Grew up together," Dad says. "Used the same outside bog, didn't we."

"Is there anyone you don't know, Dad?"

Dad thinks for a minute. Then he says, "Trevor Francis and me, we're like *that*."

Trouble is, I don't know if he's kiddin'.

* * * * *

I go along on the day, the time Dad's fixed up.

Mr Wilby's on the short side, a tad taller than me. Unlike me, though, he's a chubby chap with long grey sideburns and not much hair on top. What there is is just as grey.

Sitting behind an enormous desk, he waves to a chair. He don't even say hello or shake my hand. "You bin inside, ain't ya?"

"Just a bit."

"From what Sid tells me, you're a seasoned ex-con, ain't ya?"

I nod. I think I'll go now.

"What did ya learn from your experiences inside?"

"Not a lot."

"You're not very good at this crime lark, are ya?"

I shrug.

"Well, son," he says, "if you were any good, you wouldn't a bin locked up all those times, would ya?"

"S'pose not."

"Sid says you're a good lad. Why should I believe him?"

"When you share a bog with someone, you get to know if you can believe what they say," I say. It's all I can think of.

He stares at me for a minute or so, then bursts out laughing, slapping the desk, laughing again. Next thing, he's offering me a job. "Start at the bottom and you can work your way up fast," he says.

"Yes, Mr Wilby."

"Call me Bill."

"Yes, Bill."

He puts me behind the bar at Stella's. Turns out it's named after his wife. "The staff are working a bundle of fiddles, Frank. I want you to find out how they're doing it and how much they're raking off. That's my profits they're stashing away. I pay 'em more than enough. I won't have 'em taking advantage. Bad for business. Bad for my reputation."

Within a couple o' months, I've sussed it and report back. Four get the push and I'm promoted to bar manager, him being one o' those who's pushed.

I advertise and interview for new staff. Soon takings are going through the roof 'cos everyone knows I'm keeping an eye on everything. Once they see I treat 'em fairly, everyone getting equal shares of tips and bonuses –

and me not taking any shares – they brighten up. Soon they're as happy as Larry and can't do enough for me. Maybe I did learn something inside. I find myself thinking a lot about Florizel and the Governor's garden. Treat everyone fairly and be seen to treat everyone fairly. That's what Florizel didn't do. It's taken me all this time to realise it.

Once a year at the end of the season, Bill has a party at his home for all the staff. Them from Aspreys, Stella's, the casinos and the pier. His friends and family, too – and the stars playing in Bill's places. We're all there together. The guy next door opens up his house and garden as well and has a party. He's got a swimming-pool. So everyone goes from party to party. It's bloody brilliant.

I'm sitting in Bill's front room with Wayne, his son, watching *Dallas*. In comes a top act from one of Bill's shows with his manager. Wayne and them sit down for a chat. I don't give 'em a second glance. I tell ya, once you seen one of the most famous comedians in the country standing in his filthy underpants in his dressing-room, knocking back a bottle of booze after a brilliant, sell-out show, you don't get star struck just 'cos you're sitting next to him in Bill Wilby's front room.

Through the French windows, I can see Shirley strolling across the lawn with a glass of champagne.

I met Shirl about eight months ago, a couple of months after I came up to Yarmouth. We hit it off straightaway. Yep. That thing I didn't believe in. Love at first sight.

She's Scottish, comes from Coventry, got the reddest hair I've ever seen, calm, level-headed, don't get worked up over the slightest thing and is never violent. Thank God. When she got pregnant, we found a flat, moved in together. No problem that – we'd been planning to set up home, anyway.

We're really happy and now she's showing, I'm even happier. Who'd've thought it? Me, going straight. Can't believe how good it makes me feel. A woman who loves me – how great is that? And a kid on the way. Me, a dad!

Mum and Dad are proud of me, can't wait to be grandparents. They're amazed I've done all this without getting myself locked up in the process.

This has gotta be the best time ever.

I can't stop smiling.

Dad's leaning up against the bar on the patio, chatting with –

But my happiness is interrupted by what's going on in the hallway. Bill has a baby grand there – it's that big a house – and Mum's standing, listening to Sean, part of an Irish group who's also headlining one of Bill's outfits.

Mum's saying, "Sing the famous one, the one you made famous. 'Joanne, I love you, Joanne'."

Sean stops playing and gives her the evil eye. "'Joanne'?" he says. "I hate that song. 'Joanne'? Fuck 'Joanne'!"

She says, "Fuck 'Joanne'? That song made you a very, very rich man. How dare you talk to me like that."

With that, Sean slams down the piano lid, gets up and staggers into the kitchen.

I quickly lose interest in *Dallas*, where my Shirl is or who Dad's talking to. I get up and go into the kitchen.

Sean's as rat-arsed as a cat drowning in a barrel of Newcastle Brown. A lump of bread crust dangles out his mouth.

"Your time's up, mate," I say. "You gotta go."

"You're not telling me what to do," he manages to say. "Don't you know who I am?"

"Well, if you don't know, I ain't gonna tell ya," I say. "C'm' on."

"Get your hands off me, you little squirt," he says, the bits of crust falling down his chin.

"You may think you're the big 'I am', chum," I tell him, "but I'm one of Bill's managers, so shut your bleedin' mouth." I get hold of him and drag him out to the front drive. "What car you in?"

He points to a white Merc. I get his keys from his pocket, shove him in the driver's seat, put the ignition key in, slam the car door and go back in the house.

"Will he be all right?" Mum says.

"Who cares?" I say. "Up to him whether he drives himself home or sleeps it off there. Nobody talks to you like that and gets away with it."

* * * * *

Three months later, my Shirl has a beautiful baby girl, seven pounds four ounces. She wants to call her Bernice. Who calls a baby Bernice? I'm not having that. Anyway, we agreed. If it's a boy, she names him. If it's a girl, I name her. So my daughter's name is Eve Valerie. After Evan Phillips, because I never want to forget him, and Valerie, after my mum. Eve Valerie Peters. That is so good.

A year later, it's still good. Eve's talking and taking her first steps. Shirl's happy and keeps a good home, cooks beautifully and everyone loves her.

"Frank," Bill says one day in his office, "It's about time you went on some proper training. How about it?"

"Sure." I really like this idea, it'll be good for me.

"I'm thinking of buying a few hotels. That's the direction I want you to take. You up for that?"

"Anything you say, Bill."

"Stella's found some likely prospects. There's a week's course in hotel management in Mayfair she likes the look of. And one in Madrid – "

"I don't speak Spanish."

"You won't need to. It's for English speakers managing hotels in Spain. You can go there. Broaden your horizon. Learn all about that foreign stuff. Customers like that. Makes 'em think they're classy."

"Thanks, Bill."

"We're thinking you'd do well to get some cooking under your belt as well. And wine, of course. Then some accountancy, personnel, how to train people and all that malarkey."

"Bloody hell."

"It'll take two to three years. You okay with that?"

"Yeah. Thanks."

"My idea. You can thank me for that," he says. "But Stella's done all the graft. She found the courses."

Couple of weeks later, Bill and me goes to my dad's for a late Saturday night drink after we've closed up the clubs.

"Stella's booked you on those courses," Bill says.

"This calls for a toast," Dad says. "I'll open a bottle of vino."

"Make sure it's good stuff," Bill says, "or Frank'll be after you."

The three of us have a good laugh over that, we toast my future and settle down for a chat.

Soon, it's five in the morning and Bill stands up.

"Gotta go," he says. "Stella'll be thinking I'm dead or something."

He shouldn't't've said that, 'cos two hours later he is. Proper dead.

He'd got home with a terrible pain in his chest, fallen face down on to the kitchen floor and died ten minutes later from a massive heart attack.

Within a month of the funeral, Stella sells everything off – Aspreys, Stella's, the casinos, the pier and all the other property they've got. My courses are cancelled. Everyone's thrown out, no jobs, no money, no nothing, not even a month's pay to help us on our way.

So I can't pay the rent. Then I reckon I'll not even try. The council have got to give us a place. They can't let a man, his wife and baby girl go homeless. Couple of weeks later, they ring me up. "We've got a place for you. You can have the keys on Monday."

Monday, I go for the keys.

"You're not gonna believe this," the council bloke says, "but we've been inundated from London with boat people. They take priority. Your house is gone."

When I tell Shirl, she says, "Ah cannae tek this. This place is nae big enough."

And there was me, thinking how nice it was.

"Ah'm off back tae Coventry," she says, "Ah can get a hoose up there easy enough."

Three days later, the divorce from Linda comes through.

Chapter 10. Coventry

Three or four months after skulking around Yarmouth, trying to get something together – and not doing it – I make my way to Coventry to be with Shirl and Eve. Shirl's got a house on an estate outside of Nuneaton. It's a mining estate full of Glaswegians and families from the north-east. It's rough. I mean, *rough*.

I thought the East End of London was hard but it ain't like this. The thing about the East End is, while you always have to have your brain switched on, ready to go, the place itself is clean and everyone's proud of who they are, where they live and what they do. Here, it's dirty, nobody's got no respect for nothing or no-one and it don't take long for me to realise they don't like Londoners, either. And here I am, a Londoner living in the middle of an estate full of Geordies, beards, yelling kids and fatty cutties.

Worse than that, half the time I can't understand a word they're saying. Just when I think they're clearing their throats and spitting out their smoker's coughs for the day, I realise they've been telling me something. What's worse, they don't understand half of what I say. Down in London and even in Yarmouth, I was at home, with my own kind, but this… I don't know how I'm gonna survive, I tell ya.

Shirl's okay with it. Course she is. She's Scottish, like the rest of 'em. She knows their ways, knows the lingo – speaks it herself, don't she – and she's shocked when I tell her, "Shirl, I've lived in better prisons than this place you've brought me to."

The place is crammed full of miners. But being a miner don't give you the excuse to behave like they do. At least in prison they give you a chance before they stick a knife in you. Here, they stick a knife in you and walk away without a word. At least in prison they wash once a day and eat off clean plates. Here, they don't know what that means. But here I am and here I'm gonna stay.

I'm not leaving Eve to grow up in this pile o' pus festering on the arsehole of the universe. Not without my protection. I'm already shuddering at the thought of what she'll turn out like if she's left to her own devices – and she's only six months old. What about when she's in her teens? They'll shove her in some shop and she'll end up pregnant, surrounded by booze, soot, swearing, swagger and thuggery. 'Cos the way things are going at the moment with Thatcher and Scargill, Eve won't have a proper life, not like I had when my dad set me up in the safecracking business. She'll be pushing a pram around by the time she's eighteen.

So how do I support my family? There's no work here other than the pit and there's no way I'm going down the pit. Not even for Eve.

I spend a few weeks spying out the area, seeing what's going on, and the only thing I latch on to is, everybody's dabbling in drugs. But having a hard time getting 'em. That's my way in. I put myself about in Coventry, Nuneaton, finding out who the firms are, who to talk to and who not to talk to and, 'cos o' the type of bloke I am, it's easy to meet up with them that's running the place.

Like everything in this life, it's who you know that counts. A couple of mates down the Smoke put me in touch with the right people and, with their help and some local persuasion, within six months I'm running Coventry, Nuneaton, Bedworth, parts of Leicester, and parts of Birmingham.

Every morning, I commute down on the train with all the other office workers. I have a drink on the train, have a drink at Euston, nip over to the East End, do my business, store the product in my briefcase and have another drink on the train on the way back.

Once I'm back, I meet my people in the boozer. It's protected by villains. No Old Bill dare go in. I know I'm safe. Every day. Every night. Never slow down, sometimes taking speed to keep me going.

* * * * *

Pavel is my minder. Polish. Does a bit of wrestling and when he's not doing that or working for me, he's on the doors at The Roundabout, a night-club for all the Coventry low-life you ever want to meet. And then some. It allows him to keep his hand in. When they see Pavel, they behave.

Because of who he is and 'cos they know what he can do, I don't need anybody else. I pay him well. He does as he's told.

"Pavel," I say, "we got a customer who ain't payin' up. He owes for a kilo. Let's go and chat him."

"Okay, boss," he says.

He calls me "boss". I try a couple of times to get him to call me Frank but it's no use. I give up. Then I realise if he calls me "boss" in front of everybody, we don't have to work at persuading them to keep in line. Besides, I like "boss". Gives me a warm feeling inside.

"Good morning, Mrs O'Callaghan," I say when she comes to the door with a tiny sprog gripping her thigh.

"Mr Peters," she says. "I know what you want. You're looking for Mike, ain't ya?"

"That's right. Is he in?"

"No," she says. "He's on the piss somewhere. I don't know where he is."

"Know when he'll be back?"

She looks at the kid playing with the hem of her apron, bends down and picks it up. "Will you wait here?"

"Of course."

She takes the kid back into the house and after a few minutes comes back without it. "Here," she says, stretching out her hand. "Here's my giro and my family allowance book. That's all I've got."

I stare down at what she's offering me. Then I put my hands in my pockets. "You gotta be joking. The debt is with me and your husband, not with you and the kids, darling."

She doesn't move, keeps offering them.

"You hold on to them," I tell her. "Don't you worry. I'll sort it out with Mike."

She takes 'em back and smiles. She's so pale and thin. That kid didn't look much better, either.

"Struggling, are ya?" I say. "This strike doin' you in?"

She nods. "Bloody Thatcher," she says. "Bloody pigs. Bloody miners. I'd like to knock all their heads together. Can't any of 'em see what it's doin' to us?"

Pavel and I go away. Later, we go to Tesco's, buy up two weeks' groceries and I get him to take 'em round.

A month later, there's a knock on the door. Pavel answers it and brings Mike in.

"Here," he says, holding out an envelope.

The cash is there. One hundred in fivers.

"Where d'ya get this?" I say. "Hit the gee-gees, have ya?"

"Nah," he says. "Family had a whip-round. Sorry."

"Okay. Debt cleared. All forgotten."

He turns to go. Then, "Er, you ain't got some you can let me have?"

"No, Mike," I tell him. "You keep what little money you got for your family. What good are you to them, pissin' it up against the wall? When the strike's over and you got a bit stashed away, then we'll see."

"Yeah," he says. "Thanks, Frank." He nods at Pavel and goes.

"Pavel."

"Yes, boss?"

"Keep your eye on him. If you find out he's using, let me know."

"Yes, boss."

* * * * *

By the time the Miners' Strike ends, I'm piling up the notes like they're dirty money no-one wants to touch. Sometimes, more than three grand a week. Can't put it into a bank account, of course, so it's in heaps across the living-room floor. As we have to keep Eve's sticky fingers off it, I buy another playpen and stash it in there.

What's even better is, London can't sell me enough of the stuff, either. I'm shifting it that quick. Still commuting and now on friendly terms with the others in the buffet car. I tell 'em I run a dozen secondhand shops so I have to go down every morning to buy up stock. They're amazed I can move furniture and everything so fast.

I smile, pat my briefcase. "Business is boomin'."

"If you ever need a partner," one of 'em says every time he sees me, every time giving me his card, "talk to me first."

One particular day when I'm in London visiting my associates, loading up my case with the drugs, Courtney says to me, "Come and look at my latest project."

He grabs my arm and nudges into a back room.

Despite his posh name, Courtney is a mucky bugger. I don't think I've ever seen him in a clean shirt. Within five minutes of him putting one on, it's covered in tomato ketchup from a pizza or burger or something. So is his long, straggly beard. Most times I've met him, it's full of dried egg or milk. But he's a fair-minded businessman, gets good stuff and I've known him God knows how long.

Six geezers, none of 'em older than nineteen, are clustered around a large table, heads down, not talking, working hard. On the table are printing machines and, on chairs lining the walls, stacks of twenty-pound notes held together by coloured elastic bands.

"How much are you payin' 'em?" I say, waving at the lads.

"Enough," he says. "Plus all the free samples they want."

"Fair enough."

"Help yourself, why don't you," he says.

I go to the nearest chair and put down my case. I pick up a bundle and give a quick count. Two grand. "Thanks, Courtney." I bend down, open my case and shove the notes in between the bags of merchandise.

Shirl and Eve are out when I get home, so after I've changed, I put half the notes in a Tesco carrier bag and stash it at the back of the airing-cupboard. As I need some new slippers and Shirl's birthday's coming up soon, I decide to pop into Nuneaton for a bit o' shopping and have a go with the notes.

I get in the motor and reach in my pocket for my fags and lighter. Ain't got 'em. Left them on the side where I put them while changing. Can't be bothered to go back. I'll get some in town with one of the notes.

After I've parked the motor, I drop into the nearest newsagent and buy a couple of packs of ciggies and a lighter, hand over one of the twenties. She gives me fourteen pound fifty change and I walk out without a problem. That's a nice margin. Looks like I'm on to a good thing. Thanks once again, Courtney.

Haven't decided yet what to get Shirl so, while I'm thinking about it, I reckon I'll get the slippers. They're easy to buy, after all. Don't have to hang about trying 'em on and all that malarkey. Then I'll wander around Debenhams, see what's on offer. Might get something for Eve while I'm at it.

I go into the high street, find a small shoe shop with a sign in the window. "Slippers £2 a pair" in black felt-tip on a shiny orange card. That looks all right. I go in.

An Indian fella sits behind a counter near the door. An Indian woman is tidying things up towards the back. She's so tiny she can hardly reach the top shelves. Has to stand on one of those footstools you find in a library. She's wobbling a bit but he doesn't go and help her. He's more interested in the fact that someone has come in and wants to buy something.

"Yes, sir," he says. "And how can I help you this fine day?"

"I want some slippers," I say, seeing them on a rack halfway down.

He follows me over. I find a pair in my size. Bright

orange. Not my colour but they'll do.

"You try them on?" he says.

"Nah," I say, walking back to the counter. "Can you change a twenty?"

"Of course I can, sir," he says, following me. "I can do anything."

I hand it over.

He takes it, opens his till, counts out a tenner, a fiver and three pound coins, hands 'em over, wraps the slippers and hands them over as well.

"Thanks, mate."

"Pleasure to do business, sir. You come again?"

"Next time I want some slippers that light up in the dark," I say, "this is the place I'll come."

As I'm walking down the street towards Debenhams, I hear a voice calling out. "Sir! Sir! You stop, please! You stop!"

I turn round and it's him, the Indian from the shoe shop. I wait for him to get to me.

"Please, you come back to the shop for a minute, please," he says, out of breath. "I have a question for you."

As we walk back, I chuckle, "What's the matter, mate? You want me to buy you out?"

"I tell you when we are in my shop."

When we get back, he goes behind his counter, opens the till, pulls out a twenty-pound note and, with both hands, holds it up to the light. "There is something wrong. These words, 'Bank of England'" – he runs a finger over the note – "they are not raised. They should be raised. This is wrong. Where did you get it?"

"Dunno, mate," I shrug.

Fuck this. If I ain't careful, I'll be down the cop shop before you can sing "Double your money, and try to get rich".

"Tell you what," I say, "You give me that, I'll give you another and we'll say no more about it."

"Oh no, no, no," he screams, losing control. "Once I give you that, I never see you again. I'm calling the

201

police." He picks up the receiver of the phone standing on the counter and starts dialling.

"Oh yeah?" I say. Like I'm gonna wait around while the rozzers climb into their sweet little panda car and drive over to see what he's yelling his head off about. "See ya, mate," I say, throwing the bag of slippers in his face, making a quick exit.

I do a left turn, canter down a few streets 'til I get out on to Coton Road. I need some time to think. I mean, I can dump the nine hundred and sixty quid o' notes but then someone'll find 'em and they've got my dabs all over 'em. And then what? No, I gotta find somewhere safe to sit and think. Riversley Park's a short walk from here, through the underpass, far enough away from the shops. They won't find me there.

When I get to a bench, I need a fag. I sit down, take the wrapping off one of the packets I bought at the newsagents and light up with my new lighter. Aah, yeah, that's better. You can't beat a Dunhill. I needed that. Now, thinking cap on.

I figure my best bet is to get home and torch the notes. Courtney was good enough to let me have the notes for nothing, as a favour, if you like, and I appreciate it. 'E's a good bloke, but it hasn't worked out. Still, what you don't try, you don't know about. That's always been my motto. Well, it has been since I thought of it. Which was when I lit a Dunhill a couple of minutes ago.

I'll call for a taxi and get out of here.

I reach in my pocket for my phone. Wrong pocket. I go into my other pocket. Not there. I search all my pockets. It ain't there. Where is it? *Where the fuck is my phone?* I take a long drag and let the smoke out in a long, long sigh. It's on the side with my fags and lighter, ain't it? I took it out my suit pocket when I changed and didn't pick it up, did I?

I've got some change from the newsagents, so if I can find a phone box, I'll get a taxi that way. I'm safe enough now, got a plan. It's a beautiful day, daffodils stretching up to the sun, a few girls pushing prams about so I decide to linger a bit. I have another fag. These Dunhills are all right, reckon I'll switch to 'em.

An hour or so later, I get up and there it is. Just outside the park is a roundabout. On the other side is a phone box.

I'm standing on the kerb, waiting to cross the road when, would you believe, the Indian geezer from the shoe shop and a copper are going round the roundabout in a panda car and they spot me. I mean, *come on*! I bin in the park well over an hour and they're still out looking for me. What are the chances of that?

Anyway, before they can stop, I dart across the road, dash between the signs, over the roundabout itself and shut myself in the phone box. I pull out the wad o' notes and shove it down the back of my Fred Flintstone boxers and up the cheeks of my arse. I have to. I can't eat 'em, I can't dump 'em, I can't hand 'em over. There's nowhere else to put them. Up my arse they go. Bloody uncomfortable. Walking naturally ain't easy either, as I discover when I come out the phone box and face the hopping mad shoe shop keeper and a rosy red apple-cheeked copper.

"Come on, you," the uniform says. "Get in the car."

Reg Harding, the copper who interviews me with the uniform at his side, is from the old school. Like Ron Chantrell, my old mate, from my hard-earned youth. Polite. Considerate, even. Knows how the game's played. I've not met him before but he knows all about me.

"Hallo, Frank," he says like we're standing next to each other at snot-infested urinals in some grotty pub up the backend of Bethnal Green. "How you doing?"

"Mr Harding," I say, nodding, trying to seem comfortable. 'Cept I ain't, of course, 'cos I'm sitting there with all them banknotes up my arse and they're digging into me something awful.

"Tell me," he says, "why did you throw those slippers at Mr Dutta and run from his shop?"

"I was scared," I say. Even I don't believe that.

"Oh, Frank," he says. "I'm sorry to hear that. Why were you scared?"

"You'd arrest me, look at my record and automatically think I'd done it."

"Done what, Frank?"

"Whatever it was you arrested me for."

"This twenty," he says, laying it on the table, smoothing it out, looking at me all the time, "where'd you get it?"

"Dunno," I say. "Must've got it in change from a shop somewhere."

"Got it in change?" he says, his voice keeping even, his eyebrows rising. "Change from what? What sort of cash do you carry around for you to get twenty-pound notes in change?"

"You think I got that sort of money to flash about?"

"Well, Frank, you must have if you get twenty-pound notes *in change*, mustn't you? Who gave it you?"

"Maybe I got it from the bank. I dunno, do I?" I tell him. "I'm not in the habit of keeping a record of everyone who gives me notes."

"I appreciate that, Frank," he says. "PC Smith," – nodding at the uniform sitting next to him, the copper from the panda car – "says when you saw him and Mr Dutta, you ran and hid in a telephone box – "

"That ain't true," I say. "I ran to avoid the traffic when crossing the road. I went into the phone box to call for a taxi. I didn't run and hide in a telephone box because I saw them. That ain't true."

"You see," he says, "I think there's more of this funny money and I think you've got some of it. Furthermore, I think you know where it came from."

"Mr Harding," I say, "you're entitled to your opinion. It's wrong but if that's your opinion, well, I hope you'll have many happy years together."

"*Have* you got some more of it, Frank?"

"'Course I ain't," I say.

Both of 'em, silent, grim-faced, stare at me.

"What?" I say. "What?" I stare back. "You wanna search me or something?"

"What's the point of that?" Harding says. "You're hardly like to have it on you, are you?"

"Unless he's got it stuck up his arse," PC Smith laughs.

"Knowing Frank," Harding says, looking straight at me, "I wouldn't be surprised."

"As if," I say.

"So where'd you get this, Frank?" he says, tapping the note on the table.

"Am I under arrest?" I say.

"You're helping us with our enquiries."

"So I can go?"

"Only if you don't want to help us with our enquiries."

"Well, I don't," I say, pushing the chair back with my bum and standing up.

But my bum pushed the chair too hard. I feel my boxers slip down a notch. The notes come loose. I get hold of the belt around my trousers and hitch myself up. But that don't do the trick. Instead, it shakes the notes even more and I feel a couple slither down so they're caught against the bottom hem of my Fred Flintstones.

"Can I use your toilet?" I say. If I get in there, everything'll be okay.

"Of course," Harding says. "Darren, show Mr Peters the way."

Darren stands up as I carefully edge out from behind the table. I make my way to the door.

"Er, Frank," Harding says.

I turn to see him and Darren staring down at the floor.

Harding peers up at me. "Carry your own toilet paper, do you?"

A trail of twenty pound notes decorates my walk from the chair to the door.

Darren bursts out laughing.

* * * * *

I get six months in Winson Green Prison for the funny money. But I'm out in four, thank God. Pavel's looked

205

after the business while I was away. He's a good bloke. First thing I do when I get out is give him a honking pay rise.

But a couple of years on, I'm driving a beautiful car, wearing the best suits, drinking the finest wines and me, Shirl and Eve have moved into a lovely house. Pavel's now got a family of his own and is doing well. We're over my little blip with the funny money, back in business like before and profits are three grand a week and rising.

If I'm honest, I'm not in this for the money but the wheeling and dealing. Definitely not the drugs. Don't touch 'em. Maybe the odd popper now and again to keep me awake. But that's all. There's nothing on God's earth that compares to setting up a meet, talking to suppliers, shaking hands on a deal well done, taking delivery, chatting up customers, collecting payments, counting it all up.

Sometimes, when I'm negotiating a good deal, it's better than me and Shirl having it off. I mean, I love her and all that, don't get me wrong – course I do – she gave me Eve, didn't she? – but that's nothing like having to think quick while you're on your feet, that great feeling you get when you shake hands, the buzz, the success, the authority. The feeling you've somehow climbed to the top of Everest.

What's best, though, is knowing I've licked them Broxbourne snotty snobs that used to look down their noses at me. To think, I wanted to be like them. Wanted to *be* them. Now they don't come close.

I'm respected by everyone who knows me. Feared, even. Nothing compares. Thomas Ellwood School, Lee Valley Comp, Broxbourne. Up yours.

I don't hang on to much cash. Shirl and me spend it. I've been in situations where everything good has collapsed overnight. Thanks to Bobby Crick, Ron Chantrell, Leroy Maypole, Evan Phillips, Gordy France, Bill Wilby and his missus. If I've learnt anything, it's that you can't rely on anyone except yourself. Let me down, every one of 'em.

* * * * *

One morning, early April, 1988, I'm running late. Shirl's under the weather so I drop Eve off at nursery school. I miss my usual train.

Using my flash new mobile phone, I call the safe house where they store about a ton of cannabis, speed, ecstasy and who knows what else. They can't accommodate me later so fix it for me to meet one o' their guys, Melv, in his motor in Doric Way, round Euston. I can walk there, do the business and get the next train back in time to pick Eve up.

Melv's waiting in his white Escort. I've met him before. He's a nice enough guy but not what you'd call turned out. He don't make any effort. He's not combed his hair, he's in a pair of jeans I wouldn't wear if I was gonna dig a ditch, the interior of his Escort is smothered in fag ash. He always looks as if he's slept in his car all night.

We're sitting there having a chat but suddenly I get that feeling. You get them sometimes. You know something's wrong. I twist the rear view mirror round and take a gander.

"Hold up, Melv," I say. "Asshole Bill behind us. Standing in the road. Plain clothes."

He swings the mirror back and looks. "No, it's not."

"It bloody is."

"Anyway," he says, "I got ten kilos in the back for you."

"I don't want ten kilos," I say, "not with him eying us. Gimme two and I'll come down for the other eight tomorrow."

We get out, go round to the boot, he gets the stuff, I put it in my briefcase, give him the cash and we part. I leg it back to Euston sharpish, get on the train and sit down in the buffet car with the rest of 'em. I treat myself to a couple of ham rolls, a packet of crisps and a large brandy.

Melv's wrong. I know it. It don't matter how they dress, who they are, I can smell the Old Bill a mile off. They can dress like City gents or old lags, poncy duchesses or hard-thighed tarts. But it's the way they set their jaws like they're Mel Gibson in *Lethal Weapon*. Even the women. Their eyes are always half-shut, squinting half-cocked at the world through a peep-hole in them What The Butler Saw machines that used to be on Southend sea front.

A couple of hours later, we get into Coventry. I'm walking along the platform with everyone else. And there they are. Everywhere. You can't move for rozzers.

As I come through the turnstile, the biggest of 'em steps forward and puts his hand on my shoulder. "You're nicked."

I am. I've got the gear on me. Can't go back, can't go forward, no way out.

He pushes me up against a glass partition, takes my briefcase, shoves my arms up and says, "Search him."

Commuters are hurrying past, a railway official watches, I'm surrounded. Can't move. A pair of hands run up one leg, then the other. They pat my bum a couple o' times, then feel their way up my back. I'm turned round, shoved against the partition and I see whose hands they are. A middle-aged ferret with hardly any hair poring his mitts up my arms, into my pits, over my chest and down, over my thighs again, to my feet. He's enjoying this.

The one who's got the briefcase opens it and finds – of course he does – the two kilos. All I can think is, thank Christ I didn't take the ten.

"Oh, Frank, my son," he says, "you are well and truly nicked."

They bundle me out of the station into their car and take me to Nuneaton. I write out a confession. What choice do I have? They got me with the goods, didn't they?

Still, I reckon, I've had four good years, earned untold dough. That's a good enough whack.

I'm bailed to appear at Warwick Crown Court.

When I finally get home, Shirl's sitting in the front room, crying her eyes out. The room's a wreck.

"Where d'ya think you've bin?" she hollers.

"Where's Eve?"

"Never mind the bloody bairn!" she screams. "The polis have bin. Look at the place."

As quick as a scared hamster, I go into the living-room. The playpen and the notes haven't been touched. I go back. "The dough's still there. Where's Eve?"

"They turned everythin' over," she sobs. "Couldnae be arsed to put everythin' back, could they? It'll tek days to sort oot."

"I'll help."

"Damn right ye will. This is doon tae you. I told ye what would happen if ye started peddlin' swedgers."

"No, you didn't, you stupid bitch!" I bark back. "And you didn't have no problem living off the proceeds, did ya? Why didn't they touch the dough? Where's Eve?"

"They couldnae find nothin'," she says, calming down. "No a trace. 'Cos o' that, they couldnae tek the dough. Nae proof." She turns away. "Eve's at a birthday party." She gets up. "I'll go fetch her."

"I'll go," I say. "You stay here and start clearin' up."

"*I'll go*," she says. "You can crack on wi' clearin' up. I'm no having you swannin' aboot wi' ma daughter."

"She's my daughter as well."

"Frank, get it into yon fat heed o' yours, will ye? You're no Mr Big nae more," she says. "You're gonna be thrown in the clink. Is that the da you want for Eve? The man you want her wee pals to see?"

"Shirl," I say, "you knew what you was gettin' involved with. I never hid anything from you."

"Nah," she says. "Sounds to me like you never hid nothin' frae the polis, either. What sort of eejit are ye?"

"What sort of idiot do ya want me to be?" I say, trying to make her laugh.

She glares at me, then leaves the room. A minute later,

the front door opens and slams shut.

It ain't long before Pavel catches up with me. He wants out, he says, before the Old Bill haul him in as well. I pay him off with a hefty fistful of notes out of the playpen. Within the month, he takes his wife and kid to Poland. I open a bank account with the rest of the dosh. I'm gonna need it for legal fees and to provide for Shirl and Eve while I'm away.

To keep myself clean, I team up with a good mate I've made in Coventry, Sean Boughton. He won't have anything to do with drugs, bless him. He's a down-to-earth honest market-trader. He reckons if I supply – my London connections will do us some good, he says – and he looks after sales, we should make a nice little packet between us. Sounds good to me.

Before long, we're well set up. I ship stuff in from the Smoke and he moves it out at a good margin round the markets in Coventry, Nuneaton, Bedworth, parts of Leicester, and parts of Birmingham. The same areas, in fact, where I was dealing.

Shirl's not convinced. "You cannae leave it alone, can ye?" she says one night as we're getting into bed. "Hoo many backs o' lorries have ye bin on in the last month?"

"It's not like that, Shirl," I tell her. "This is clean cash. No fiddlin' about. Sean's as straight as they come."

"Aye," she says, "and ma fanny's the Archbishop o' friggin' Canterbury."

"Oh, c'm' on, sweetheart," I coo as we get under the covers and I reach for her, "don't be like that."

"Ha!" she says, turning over.

"Shirl," I try again, curling my legs round her.

"Frank," she says, her back to me, her feet kicking me away, "you're gonna be a few years inside. On yer own. Sooner ye get used tae it, the better aff we'll all be."

Chapter 11. Seven Sisters

"Frank," Biff, a pal from Seven Sisters, says when he calls me a couple of weeks later – I'm out on bail – "I hear you're market trading."

"What you got, mate?"

"It's like this, innit," he says. "Got some tee-shirts coming over from Thailand. Interested?"

"What they like, Biff?" He's called Biff 'cos he's a champion amateur boxer.

"They're all right, mate," he says. "None o' your backstreet tat. Good sellers, too. I've shifted a few thousand before. Got crocodiles all over 'em. The kids love 'em, dunt they?"

"What you asking?"

"I'll be straight with you, Frank. I'm buying in at two pound fifty a unit. I'll let you have 'em for five. I sell 'em at fifteen. You'll turn 'em out for eighteen, twenty, easy. How many do you want?"

"I'll wanna take a butcher's first. We'll come down and if they're all right, line me up for five hundred. That suit ya?"

We arrange a date, time and place to view. Sean and me'll go down and, if the samples are kosher, Sean'll drive his Transit down next day to pick them up. He'll take them to his warehouse round the back of Spon Street in Coventry.

So, a week later, Sean and me get down to Euston. I've got my bag with the two and a half grand in notes. I've made sure it's big enough to load a dozen or so samples for me to take there and then. First thing we do is nip upstairs to the bar for a drink. The place is crowded but we find a cubicle, have a drink and smoke while we finalise details for shipping them back. Providing the deal comes off, of course – and we've no reason to doubt it.

We take the Victoria Line, come out of Seven Sisters and walk a few yards along the West Green Road to the

West Green Tavern. We go to the bar, order, sit down. I call Biff and he says he's on his way. They do a good plate of grub in here and we enjoy tucking in. About thirty minutes later, Biff calls. He's parked up Beaconsfield Road.

"Right-o, mate," I tell him. "We'll find you."

As we come out the pub, Sean remembers he's gotta go for a piss. Great lumbering idiot. He coulda gone while we was in there.

"I'll catch you up," he says, diving back inside.

"Okay, mate."

I walk along West Green Road, bag in hand. A geezer in a shabby serge suit and a blonde bird are coming towards me, so I step aside to let them pass.

But as they get close, he puts his arm around my shoulder. "Hello, Frank," he says. "You're nicked."

"What?" I blurt out. "Who the fuck are you?"

"Drugs Squad, mate," he says. "Where's the drugs?"

"I ain't got no drugs," I say.

The blonde bint says, "Open the bag, Frank."

I drop it on to the pavement and unzip it. Two and a half grand in assorted notes. "See?" I say. "I ain't got no drugs."

The geezer bends down, rifles through the notes, lifts 'em up, looks underneath, can't find no drugs. He looks up at me. "Son, you're still nicked."

We turn as we hear footsteps. Sean's running to catch me up. When he sees what's going down, he stops, backs off and turns to walk away.

But the scruffy geezer says to the girl, "Go after him, Tamsin. He's nicked."

She's too fast for Sean. He might be a good lad but he never knew how to keep in shape. She brings him back, they cuff us and take us and the bag to their car. In no time at all, we're at Tottenham police station.

As we walk into Reception, a fella's sitting on one of the chairs, putting some files together.

"You a lawyer?" I say.

He stands up, nodding.

"Do me a favour," I say. "Represent me. They're taking me down to the cells. I need a brief now 'cos otherwise they'll hang me out to dry."

He nods again. "What about your friend?" he says.

"Sean?" I call out – they're booking him in. "You wanna brief?"

"Might as well," he says, emptying his pockets, plonking his lighter, wallet, some change and a grubby hanky on the counter. "This lot are ready to pin Jack the Ripper on me."

Then it's my turn. Lighter, wallet, some change, keys, a clean folded hanky, my phone. The sergeant starts writing out a receipt.

"And the two and a half grand," I say. "If you don't mind."

"That's evidence," says the plod who arrested me in the street.

"Not yet," my brief says. "Not until you've cautioned my client."

The sergeant looks at the detective, who nods once. As the sergeant finishes the receipt, my brief snatches it out of his hands, reads it, folds it into four and puts it in his briefcase.

"What's your name?" I ask him.

"Gideon Stumpf."

I turn to the sergeant. "This is – "

"We know who he is," the sergeant says, shaking his head.

He takes Stumpf and me into an interview room. When he's gone, we sit down.

"Now, Mr Peters," Stumpf says, "tell me your story."

I tell him what happened.

"And why," he says, putting on his specs, "would these fine upstanding officers of the law get it into their shiny bright heads that you were carrying illegal substances?"

He's short, dumpy, probably in his fifties with a bald patch surrounded by a thick circle of black curly hair. It's

213

as if someone held him upside-down and used his head as a floor mop so many times the middle has worn away.

I tell him about my drugs arrest.

"I see."

He's a snappy dresser, though, I'll give him that. Anyone can see he has his suits and shirts made in Savile Row. Gold silk tie and cufflinks to match. If anyone needs a fast-thinking lawyer in a hurry, Gideon Stumpf is the man to call. He's the business, all right. I shall recommend him to all my friends.

"But this time," he says, "it really was for five hundred tee-shirts?"

"Talk to Biff!" I tell him. "He'll tell you. Straight as Big Ben."

"I will," he murmurs. "Although, Mr Peters, as you know, Big Ben is far from straight. It's rectangular at the bottom with an isosceles triangle at the top. It has many squares in between, of course, and, would you believe, a trapezoid?"

"Really?" I say. I haven't got a clue what he's on about.

He's blushing now. "Geometry is a hobby of mine. Mmm," he says, reading his notes. "If what you say is the truth, the whole truth and nothing but the truth, Mr Peters, then we should have you out of here very soon."

I give him my biggest smile. "Good man, Gideon."

"Nice of you to remember," he says.

"What?"

"Gideon Goodman. Great-uncle of mine. Perished in Treblinka."

"I'm sorry."

"Don't be," he says. "He always did mix with the wrong crowd."

* * * * *

At last, the Old Bill comes in. It's the bastard and the bird who arrested me and Biff in Seven Sisters. He introduces himself as Detective Inspector Tony Harrow, Area 1,

Drugs Squad. She's Detective Sergeant Tamsin Keyes.

He opens his notepad, pulls a pencil out his breast pocket and writes something. He looks up at me and says, "Why did you have all that money?"

I say, "No comment."

"Where were you going?"

"No comment."

"You don't live in Seven Sisters, do you?"

"No comment."

"Where do you live?"

"No comment."

"What's your mate's name?"

"No comment."

"What's your name?"

"No comment."

"Am I interviewing you?"

"No comment."

"Are you breathing?"

"No comment."

Harrow takes a deep sigh, looks at the bird, then Gideon, then back at me. "Are you," he says, trying to control his temper, "just gonna fucking sit there and go 'No comment' all day?"

"No comment."

"Three police divisions have invested a lot of money today nicking you."

Gideon smiles. "Well, I hope you can still afford the damages the court will award my client when he brings his suit for wrongful arrest."

"Look, matey," Harrow carries on, ignoring Gideon, staring straight at me. "We had West Midlands Police follow you from your home on to the train at Coventry. They stood behind you when you ordered your drinks at Euston. We had a unit in the next cubicle, listening to every word you and your pal were saying. They followed you to Seven Sisters. We had you eyeballed from the moment you came out the tube. We know what you're up to. What do you say to that?"

"No comment."

He jumps up, knocking his chair backwards on to the floor. "Peters," he says, jabbing his pencil at me, "I've not having this! We fucking got you and you fucking know it!"

Gideon puts a hand on my shoulder, keeping me in *my* chair. "Detective Inspector Harrow," he says, leaning back, "I do hope you're not threatening my client with unprovoked violence. Especially with all these witnesses present, one of them a fellow police officer."

Harrow freezes for a second, throws down his pencil and dashes out. Tamsin picks up his pencil and the pad and follows.

"Well done," Gideon says, patting me on the back.

"What now?"

"They'll keep you overnight," he says, doodling on his pad, "and we'll resume in the morning. Remember, Frank, my boy, keep shtum."

They keep us waiting nearly two hours. Then, Gideon's right, they put me in a cell for the night. It ain't easy sleeping in a cell when all you've got is a hard plank for a bed. I'm nodding off, it's about midnight, when the door opens and the sergeant waves in this bloke.

He's about my age, hasn't shaved for a week, his black hair is wringing wet, his shirt's hanging out of his trousers – which are caked in mud – his trainers are as wet as his hair and he's wearing odd socks, one black and one blue.

If that ain't enough, he's in my cell. Now, they don't do that, put two in a cell. When they keep you down at night, that's it, the cell's yours. They don't put another body in there.

"Get in there," the copper says, "and sleep it off."

He slams the door shut and the geezer stumbles over to the chair and flops down.

"Where am I gonna kip?" he says, slurring his words.

"Had too much?" I say.

"A few pints, that's all," he says.

Ha! He's as pissed as I am – and I'm as sober as the

beak I'm coming up in front of tomorrow morning. Thing is, he can say as much as he likes that he's had a few pints but he don't smell of booze. I've never met a drunk who don't smell. And he don't smell.

I decide I'm not gonna even try to get some zees while he's there. Who knows? I might talk in my sleep. So I lay there, eyes wide open, and he sits there, pretending to sleep it off. I can hear some mutterings outside but, apart from that, we don't move, we don't speak. It's like dossing in a morgue.

After what must a bin an hour – but probably ain't – he pretends to come to.

"Where am I?" he says, getting up and walking up and down.

"Tottenham nick."

"That ain't right," he says. Now his speech ain't slurred, now he ain't pissed, now he's walking in a straight line. "I gotta get outa here."

He goes to the door and bangs on it with his fist. "Let me out! I'm not supposed to be in here! Hey, you, let me out!"

It don't take long for the Old Bill to come and undo the door. "All right," the copper says, "you can go."

So he's bin in here couple of hours tops and they're answering his banging and shouting straightaway *and* letting him out. Better than room service in some swanky hotel.

And just as he's going, he turns and says to me, "You got anyone you want me to phone for you?"

So that's their game. They're trying to get a name and number from me.

I keep shtum.

* * * * *

Next morning, Wednesday, I'm in the magistrates' court and the police are applying to keep me on remand "while our investigations continue". Gideon's there. Applies for bail, of course, but don't get it.

"Wilfred Peter Franks," the magistrate says, "you are remanded in custody for – "

Gideon gets to his feet. "Sir – "

"Yes, Mr Stumpf? Can't it wait?"

"My client's name is Frank Wilfred Peters, not Wilfred Peter Franks."

The magistrate looks down, reads and then says, "Oh, sorry." He coughs and then says, "Peter Frank Wilfred – "

Gideon and the police inspector look at each other and shake their heads.

Gideon gets up again. "I'm sorry to interrupt you again, sir – "

"Have I got it wrong again?" He looks down and reads again. "Frank Wilfred Peters, you are remanded – "

Gideon gets up *again*.

"That was right, wasn't it?" the magistrate says.

"Yes, sir, it was," Gideon says. "For which I thank you. But I am impelled to remind you, as I said earlier, that Mr Peters is due to appear at Warwick Crown Court on Friday, the day after tomorrow. If you remand him in custody, he will miss that hearing through no fault of his own."

Now the beak don't know what to do. He looks over his bench and down at the Clerk of the Court, who stands up so his head's level with the top of the bench. They whisper for a bit, the Clerk sits down, the old beak remands me in custody. Gideon tries to get them to understand what's going off at Warwick on Friday but the Old Bill don't care so, of course, the magistrate don't. I'm put in a Black Maria and taken to the Scrubs.

As soon as I get there, I tell them about Friday's Crown Court but they don't listen. I tell the screw who puts me in the cell. He shrugs and shuts the door. I tell the screw who unlocks me Thursday morning. But he shrugs. I tell the screw in the dining-hall. He shrugs. I'm fast getting the feeling the Governor's organised classes in upper body aerobics.

Friday, I ask to see the chief screw. "I'm supposed to be at Warwick Crown Court today. The judge will do his nut if you don't get me there."

"Piss off."

After that, I give up. What's the point? I'm trying to help them out and they don't wanna know.

On Monday, this is Bank Holiday Monday, one of the screws comes to me. "C'm' on."

"Where we goin'?"

"Shut your mouth."

They shove me in a Securicor van and drive up to Winson Green, where I'd stayed for a few months 'cos of handling funny money.

Next day, Tuesday, I'm in Warwick Crown Court.

Turns out I was wrong about the judge doing his nut. Better than that. Seems he went up the fucking wall, shouting at everybody within shouting distance, telling the Old Bill if they don't have me in court on the Tuesday, he'll do 'em all for something or other. He didn't know yet what he'd do 'em for but he'd find something.

First, he apologises to me. Somehow he had got to know that Gideon had told the magistrate and that I'd tried to tell the Scrubs screws.

Second, he thanks me.

Third, he gives me two years for the two kilos.

* * * * *

I've been in Winson Green before, o' course, and it's the same shithole now as it was then. The screws haven't changed, either. Their idea of keeping order, if you get on the wrong side of them, is bashing the fuck out of you. I should have been shipped out weeks ago. But I'm still here.

One day, the Governor pulls me to one side and says, "Why have you been here so long? What's going on?"

"I'll tell you what's going on," I say. "The court's making requests for me to attend Snaresbrook in London on three counts for what Area 1 done to me and they're refusing to take me down to the hearing. I'm nicked for conspiracy to supply drugs for having a couple of grand on me. It's ridiculous."

"I'm not having this," he says. "I'm transferring you to Ashwell."

I dunno what difference that makes. If Area 1 can fetch me from a prison in Rutland, they can fetch me from a prison in Birmingham. But if that's what the SO wants, it's up to him. Seeing as how Ashwell's a Category C, maybe he reckons I'll be more comfortable there. And, of course, I'll be out of his way, so he's not storing himself up any likely trouble.

When I get to Ashwell, I meet a screw I've known for years. Des Turner. Lovely bloke. Now he's the Governor. Wouldn't strangle a fluffy white kitten even if it had a Kalashnikov aimed straight at his balls.

"Bloody hell, Peters," he says, "what you doin' here?"

"That's the way it goes, Des."

He says, "What's going on?"

"I'll tell you what's going on," I say. "They're screwing me up for my parole on the sentence. I'm doing a two. Due for parole in eight months, ain't I, and they're trying to do me in. Like Area 1 are. So when I go up for parole, they'll think I'm on more charges. And that ain't fair, Des.

"Originally, I should've been taken back to court and dealt with all on the same day as the puff. That way I get a better chance with the judge. But they took that away from me. They're out to get me, Des. The only thing they ain't done yet is hide dog turds in my grub."

For a good minute, Des says nothing. "Well, fuck the Old Bill. I run this prison, not them. I decide who gets parole and who doesn't." He looks me up and down. "Tell you what, lad," he says. "Keep your nose clean and you'll get parole on your date."

He puts me to work on the hospital wing. I stick to my side of the bargain by keeping my nose clean and, true to his word, I get parole. What a decent bloke! I always did like him.

Two weeks after I'm home, I get a letter from Snaresbrook Crown Court. They want me for what they call an Old Style Hearing. The letter explains this is where the court hears the evidence to decide whether there is a case to answer. I call Sean Boughton. He's had the same letter, so we agree to go down together.

When we get there, I meet up with my barrister, a beautiful bird called Claudette Harmon.

"No need to worry, Mr Peters," she says.

Mr Peters, eh? I like that. Makes me feel important. I'd shag her here and now given half the chance.

"This is a preliminary hearing," she carries on while I'm dreaming about what could be. "The case should have been dealt with while you were serving your sentence and you're now on parole. The prosecution's case is replete with falsehoods. Their evidence is flimsy. Even if the judge finds a case to answer, you have no reason to be concerned."

We go in.

The prosecution geezer stands up. "Your Honour," he says, "I want Peters and Boughton remanded in custody."

I look at Claudette. She's gone bright red. She stands.

"Thank you, Miss Harmon," the judge says. "Allow Mr Quigley to speak."

"But Your Honour – "

The judge looks at Quigley.

Quigley's a tall, thin geezer. His wig keeps sliding forward over his eyebrows. He's got no hair on top, you see. As bald as a billiard ball with alopecia. So his wig's got no grip. Every time he looks down at his papers, he has to hold his wig up. Then his hand's blocking his eyes so he can't see what he's trying to read.

"Mr Quigley?" the judge says.

"Thank you, Your Honour," he says, "I request that Peters, particularly, is remanded. He is involved in organised crime all over London. Consequently, we are not convinced he will appear in court to answer his bail. Also," – looks down, pushes wig up, looks up – "the police are confident he will commit other offences if bailed. It is clear to us that he would also attempt to interfere with prosecution witnesses. We want him out of the way, Your Honour. Off the streets."

"Your Honour," Claudette says as she stands, "my client has been serving a two-year sentence, for which he has recently been put on parole. This means the prosecution have had nearly two years to prepare their case. Which they have clearly failed to do. Are they telling the court they need even more time? What do they still have to do that they couldn't do in the last two years? I submit that they have had plenty of time to prepare their case.

"Therefore I further submit, Your Honour, they should proceed with their case today or withdraw it. The defence has been ready for two years. Why hasn't the Prosecution?

"Your Honour, the Prosecution says my client will not answer his bail when his trial begins. This is a simple matter for Your Honour to resolve. Set the conditions of bail to include daily reporting to a nominated police station, along with a fixed address at which my client must reside so the police can monitor his movements, together with the surrender of my client's passport.

"Also, Your Honour has the power to set the amount for bail at such a level it will not be in my client's interests to consider absconding. Which I may assure you, Your Honour, he does not consider doing in any event. Your Honour is aware that my client will plead not guilty. He is eager to face the charges set before him and wholeheartedly refute them.

"Finally, my learned friend, Mr Quigley, says Mr Peters may attempt to interfere with the prosecution's witnesses. As all the prosecution witnesses are police officers, I am compelled to ask, Your Honour, what is Mr Quigley implying about the integrity of those police officers?"

But after everything Claudette throws at the judge, he's having none of it. For Chrissake, the old fart doesn't even pretend to think about it.

"Peters," he barks like an arthritic sheepdog rounding up an exhausted ram, "you are remanded in custody. Boughton, you will be released on bail on a surety of ten thousand pounds."

Quigley, pushing back his wig again, smirks at Claudette. As Sean and me are hauled down, she, bless her, apologises. I'm speechless. Whatever happened to justice in this country? It ain't at Snaresbrook that day, I tell ya.

We're shipped off to Brixton. We get there about half five and no sooner are we put in a cell when a screw opens the door and says, "Boughton, you're going home." Somehow, and don't ask me how, he's made bail. Either he or someone he knows – and who's that? – has got ten grand to put up for him.

Me, I'm stuck here while Quigley, his gang and their scruffy wigs sit on their fat arses playing with themselves until someone reminds them I'm here. And, although Brixton ain't so bad, I'm in for six months. Six months!

When we finally get a date to go to court, Quigley's wig turns round and says their people are on holiday so, he tells the judge, I'll have to wait another three months until they can get another date. I mean, who totally empties an office for three months so everyone can go on holiday all at the same time? What the hell are they up to?

I get law books out of the prison library. Mainly *Archbold*, of course. That's *Archbold Criminal Pleading, Evidence and Practice* to you and me, *Archbold* to the legal beagles. The 42nd edition. Can you believe that? Someone's sat down and written this book 42 times. Why couldn't they get it right the first time? Every day I go through it to get points of law or anything I can find for Claudette to use against 'em.

Me and Claudette meet quite a few times, too, to discuss my case and she thanks me every time for the things I show her in *Archbold*. I don't think she really needs my help but she makes out she does. That's good enough for me. She makes me feel as if I'm a human being with rights and not some pile of shit the Old Bill are trying to shove down a drain. She's a helluva good barrister. Not only that but given half the chance, I'd still shag her into the middle of next week. But she's a professional, ain't she, so pretends she don't notice. But I bet she does.

Finally. *Finally.* April the tenth, 1989. First day of the trial. There we are, me and Sean in the dock. Claudette, that Quigley bloke and his wig in their places in the well of the court. The judge high up behind his bench. Any Old Bill who ain't giving evidence sit where they like.

The jury are sworn in. Now, the good thing about Snaresbrook Crown Court is all the jurors – or most of 'em, anyway – are East End people who know the Old Bill tell fibs. So I've already got half a chance before we start. 'Cos, when all's said and done, Claudette's gonna accuse the Old Bill of out and out lying. Which, o' course, they was. How, I dunno, but she is.

First up is a copper called Detective Sergeant Toby Witherenshaw. From King's Cross. He says, "I followed Peters and Boughton from the Euston bar all through the underground. I went on the same train as they did and they went all the way over to Seven Sisters."

When it's Claudette's turn, she stands up, tugs at her gown and says, "Detective Sergeant Witherenshaw, what line did you take?"

"Line?"

"Yes," she says, "line. What line did you take?"

Looking at his feet, Witherenshaw mumbles, "Don't know, Miss. I just got on the train Peters and Boughton got on."

"Sorry, Detective Sergeant, I didn't catch that. Will you repeat it more loudly?"

Witherenshaw looks up and says so people in the Pacific Isles can hear, "Don't know, Miss. I followed Peters and Boughton and got on whatever train they did."

"How long have you been a police officer?"

"Sixteen years."

"So with your sixteen years' experience as a police officer, you didn't think it important to note such details? I repeat my question. What line did my client – Mr Peters – Mr Boughton and you take? Was it the Northern Line," she says, "the District Line, the Circle Line, the Piccadilly Line? What was the line?"

"Oh, er, um – the Piccadilly Line."

"The Piccadilly Line. Are you sure?"

"Yes, ma'am. It was definitely the Piccadilly Line."

She shuffles among some documents and produces a piece of paper. "Will you look at this, please?" She hands it to the court usher who strolls over and gives it to Witherenshaw. "A map of the London Underground, Your Honour."

Witherenshaw studies it.

"You say my client went from Euston to Seven Sisters?"

"Yes, Miss."

"Please study the map, Detective Sergeant. If you were directing a commuter who wanted to travel from Euston to Seven Sisters by the most direct route, which line would you recommend?"

He stares at the map for a full, dead silent minute. The court is so quiet you could hear a woodlouse sneeze. Then he looks up and says, "Victoria."

"Yes, Detective Sergeant Witherenshaw," Claudette says. "The Victoria Line." She looks at the jury. "Not the Piccadilly Line."

Witherenshaw says, "They could have taken the Piccadilly, changed at Finsbury Park and got to Seven Sisters that way."

"Indeed they could," she says. "But in your original evidence, you said, 'I went on the same train as they did and they went all the way over to Seven Sisters.'" She looks at the jury again. "'All the way to Seven Sisters'. No mention of changing at Finsbury Park."

225

His jaw hits the floor, his eyes jumping out like ping-pong balls on tightly coiled springs. He looks to the back of the court for help from his seniors.

"Don't look for help with something you've just made up," Claudette says. "You're lying, aren't you?"

He went, "I'm not lying."

"Yes, you are."

Next up is some geezer calling himself Detective Constable Stephen Margerison. He says, "I followed Peters and Boughton into the West Green Tavern in the West Green Road. I sat in the next cubicle to them as a result of which I was able to watch their every move during the course of which I overheard Peters make a phone call during which he arranged to make a pick-up of a load of puff."

Claudette gets up. "What is puff, Detective Constable Margerison?"

"Grass, weed, cannabis, marijuana."

"So the jury can understand exactly what was going on," she says, "you followed my client and Mr Boughton into the West Green Tavern, which is on West Green Road, Seven Sisters. They sat in a cubicle. You sat in the adjacent cubicle. Have I understood you correctly?"

"Yes, Miss."

"And you were near enough to be able to hear everything they were saying?"

"Yes, Miss."

"And you heard my client, Mr Peters, make a phone call in which he arranged, as you put it, 'to make a pick-up of a load of puff'?"

"Yes, Miss."

"Did you make verbatim notes of the conversation at the time or did you write it up later?"

"I wrote it up later."

"Thank you, Detective Constable," Claudette says. "I think members of the jury can picture it in their minds. But just to make sure, so there's no confusion, I'm handing you a photograph of the interior of the West Green Tavern.

226

Copies for Your Honour, my learned friends and the jury, please."

There's a few minutes shuffling and coughing as she hands them to the usher who strides around giving them out. I don't get one. There again, as long as Claudette knows what she's doing, I don't need one.

"Your Honour, the publican of the West Green Tavern is available if the court wishes to confirm this is a photograph of the interior of his premises."

"Thank you, Miss Harmon."

"Detective Constable Margerison," she says, turning to the witness box, "do you recognise this as the interior of the West Green Tavern?"

He doesn't answer.

"I'll take your silence as agreement, shall I?" she says. "Please describe what you see."

"Er," Margerison says. "Around the walls are benches with tables in between. In the centre, there's a large circular bench with stools around it."

"And this is the only room in the West Green Tavern, is it?"

"Don't know, Miss."

"Your Honour, the publican is available, should you require it, to testify it is the only room within the premises." She turns back to Margerison. "As you can see, there are no cubicles. *There are no cubicles, Detective Constable Margerison.* So please explain to us how you sat in an adjacent cubicle and overheard a conversation between my client and Mr Boughton and then heard my client make a telephone call?"

He doesn't say a word. He doesn't say a fucking word. How can he? The bastard, like the one before him, is lying from the bottom of his rotting molars.

"Thank you, Detective Constable, for clearing that up." She sits down. Quigley lets his wig fall over his closed eyes.

That's the end of the second day. When the jury gets up to go home, they have to walk by the dock with me and

227

Sean still sitting there. As they pass, three of 'em put their thumbs up and smile. We smile back.

Next day, it's the turn of Area 1, the Drug Squad.

"Why," Claudette asks Detective Inspector Harrow, "did you arrest my client?"

"We had good reason to suspect him of dealing in drugs."

"When you stopped and searched him, did he have any drugs on him?"

"No, Miss."

"When you searched his home, did you find any drugs?"

"No, Miss."

"At any time since then, has my client admitted to dealing in drugs or having drugs on his person, in his home or anywhere else?"

"No, Miss."

"In fact," Claudette says, "the Prosecution's charges against my client of conspiracy to deal in drugs is based on the evidence that at no time did you find any drugs on him. Isn't that so, Detective Inspector Harrow?"

He doesn't say a word. He's as silent as the dead body Gaffer finds in the first chapter of *Our Mutual Friend* by Charles Dickens.

It don't take the brains of a jug of left-over custard to work out that, when the jury comes back after twenty minutes, they're full of not guilties for me and Sean.

We're taken down to the cells to sign out, Sean in one room, me in another. As I'm standing there, Harrow walks in. He picks up the wodge of notes laying on the screw's table – 'cos, strictly speaking, I'm in the screw's custody until I've signed the release papers – and says, "Here y'are, sunshine, all yours."

I ain't having that. What do they think I am? I throw my hands up like I'm ready to jump on to a trapeze bar, swing about and do a Backend Batman and Robin with him. "Don't give me that!" I shout, so everyone in Winson Green can hear. "I'm not touching that."

Still with my hands in the air, I say, "Number one, for a kick-off. How you and your crooked cronies didn't get nicked upstairs in the court, I don't know. I lost count of the lies you lot told. If that'd bin me, I'd a bin locked up and they'd've shoved the key up a gorilla's arse.

"And number two," I said, lowering my hands, making sure they see me put them firmly in my trouser pockets, "that money, I don't know where it's bin, do I? Don't know who's had their mucky mitts on it, do I? How do I know you ain't dipped your filthy fingers in it, eh, and helped yourself to a few quid?"

"Are you suggesting I'm bent?" he says, steam, smoke and white-hot lava coming out his ears.

"After the lies you lot just told?" I say. "Well, what do you think? What do you fucking think? Eh? Eh? You can fucking sit down there and count out every fucking note. If it's all there, I'll sign for it and be away. Then you can fuck off back into that rat-filled sewer of shit they dredged you up from."

Harrow looks at the screw. He's smirking his head off and backed away from the table, leaving the notes and Harrow to argue it out. Harrow's got no choice. He sits down and counts out the lot.

If I'm honest, I'm disappointed when he's counted out the two grand. It's all there. Damn. I'd've loved it if it had been short. I can't help laughing at the thought of what would've happened then. I'd've had him. I would've well and truly had him, the lying toad.

But, as I say, it's all there. I pick it up, shove it in the envelope the screw kindly hands me, sign the release papers, turn and get out of there.

Sean's waiting for me on the steps outside. As we shake hands, he says, "Let's go for a drink."

We cross the road to the pub. It's jam-packed. Near the back are the jury. When they see us, they stand up, cheer and applaud like we're Morecambe and Wise doing an encore.

"I tell you what," I shout, "I'm buying the drinks. The

229

lot o' ya. Drinks all round!" After all, I've got two grand in cash on me, haven't I? Might as well make good use of it.

Another round of applause. Even the barmaid joins in, 'though she's no idea why. Then the publican joins in. And he does know why. You can see the pound signs rolling up his eyes like a one-armed bandit.

While I'm standing at the bar, counting out the dosh 'cos suddenly everyone's drinking double malt whisky, one of the jurors – I think it's the foreman, the bloke what announced the not guilties – comes up to me.

"Look," he says, grabbing hold of my elbow so I have to stop counting, "the reason we give you not guilties was… Well, whether you was or whether you wasn't, that's not here nor there. The thing is, all you had was money on you and the other bloke didn't have nothing on him. We wasn't prepared to put you away for only having money. We knew from the start they was lying. And then, when your brief caught 'em all lying, it was obvious they was stitching you up. Bleedin' obvious, innit. We weren't prepared to do it."

He picks up his double malt whisky and throws it back in one go. "Cheers, mate."

If I had ever had any doubts, I knew it then. The lengths the Old Bill will go to, to fuck you about or nick you. I should've realised it before but I suppose I never thought they'd do it to me. Those with the power will stitch you up if it suits their purpose. They'll do whatever it takes to put you away.

Chapter 12. Norwich

Shirl's waiting for me when I get back from Snaresbrook. We take Eve out to the park and enjoy being a family again – although, I must say, Shirl ain't too pleased about what happened.

"I got a not guilty."

"You shouldnae bin there anyways," she says. "Ah cannae take it, Frank. You got tae shape up. You're really tryin' ma patience."

While we're out, my mobile rings. It's Denny Blacklock, one of my business associates.

"Wotcha, mate," he says. "The drinks are on me. Celebrate your freedom, eh? See you in The Grenadier in an hour."

"That was Denny," I say. "He's buying me a drink. He wants to celebrate my freedom."

"Aye, ah bet." Shirl says. She's giving me one of her looks.

"Well, it's more than you've done since – "

"Since what, Frank? Freedom? Ha!" she snorts. "Yer only just oot and yer back to yer auld ways."

I've had enough of this. All I want to do is settle back into my old life, do a bit of wheeling and dealing, make some money, be with my family. I mean, that's what it's all about, ain't it? What's anyone ever want out of this life except a family, a lovin' bird, a beautiful daughter and keep 'em all comfortable and safe. For Chrissake, I was gonna suggest to Shirl we had another kid, but if that's her attitude –

Denny and me have been mates for a few years. Since I came up to the West Midlands, in fact. He was the first contact I made when I set up my drugs empire. He's about fifteen years older than me, been at it longer than me and should be more successful than me. But what he's got in contacts and muscle, he don't have in reliability.

He can be talking to you one minute like a vicar

offering comfort and prayers at a funeral and then the next minute, he's ripped his shirt off, clenched his fists and announced he's ready for a ten-round bare-knuckle fight with anyone who'll take him on. And very often, he's the one who chooses who's gonna take him on. So you have to be friendly with him. Always. 'Cos you never know what stunt he's gonna pull next.

His boy, Ryan, is the exact opposite: intelligent, a bit of a bookworm, anything for a quiet life. He's probably the prettiest boy I've ever met – that thick black hair makes him look like one of those Greeks you see in *Jason and the Argonauts*. Works out at the gym every day, but he ain't bulging in the wrong places always ready for a punch-up, unlike his dad.

He works out 'cos he loves the birds and, fair dues, the birds love him. Every time I see him with a bird on his arm, it's a different one. He could really make something of himself if it weren't for the fact that, even though he's well into his twenties, he's still doing everything his old man tells him to.

They're waiting for me in The Grenadier bar, along with four or five others who work for Denny on and off. The Grenadier's our local. You can't walk in if you're a nobody 'cos they won't have it. The Old Bill won't try anything in there either 'cos if they do, their bollocks get kicked to fuck. When you're in there, you're safe.

"What you having, Frank?" Denny says. Then, turning to the barman, "He'll have a pint o' Tennents."

"Will I?"

"You like Tennents, doncha?" he says.

"Looks like it."

"Y'all right, Frank?" Ryan says, shaking his head.

"Course I am," I say. "Got a not guilty, didn't I? You?"

"Yeah," Ryan says. "S'pose so."

"Married yet?"

"On yer bike," he chortles.

"Who is it now?"

"Sonia," he says. "Swedish. Yoga teacher."

Then it's time for another pint.

Then another. I get my wallet out – I've still got most o' that two grand left – but Ged, one of Denny's men, buys this time. I ain't allowed to buy, Denny shouts across, the drinks are on them.

Then it's time for another.

And another.

And before we know where we are, it's chucking-out time.

"Better make my way back to Shirl," I say as we stand in the gents, all eight of us in a row, having a slash.

"You going back to her in that state?" one of 'em says. "After what you just told us?"

"No choice, have I?"

"You're coming back with us," Denny says. "You can doss at mine. See her when you've sobered up."

Next morning, I've hardly woken up and Denny's passing round the cans. Tennents on corn flakes for breakfast, Tennents for mid-morning snack, Tennents and pizza for dinner, Tennents and Tesco ham and pickle sandwiches for afternoon tea and then back to The Grenadier.

This goes on for two days. Might be three. I'm not sure. Drinking, snacking, sleeping it off, doing it all over again.

Next day, it's about time I turned it in.

"Gotta go, Denny," I say, munching on some toast and Rose's lime marmalade. I look round the place. After the time we've just had, his gaffe is a rubbish tip – empty cans, greasy pizza boxes, ashtrays overflowin' with dog-ends, open poly bags of poppers. "You need a bird to clear up after you," I add. I don't like untidiness. Never have done.

"I've got one," he says. "At her bloody sister's. She'll clean up when she gets back."

I get home in one piece – just – and I'm standing there, getting the key out my pocket, when the door opens. It's Shirl. Who did I expect? Samantha Fox?

"Hello, my darlings," I say in my best Charlie Drake

voice. We ain't had a shag in God knows how long and I'm in the mood for it.

"Frank," she says, not letting me in.

"Whassup? Is Eve all right?"

She don't say a word, don't move a muscle.

I look down. "What's that you got?"

She holds it up. It's a kitchen knife.

"Yeah," I say. "Let's have a sandwich and then get to bed."

"You're nae comin' in, Frank," she says. "Ye can piss off back to them yon druggie lager lout mates o' yours."

"That's where you're wrong. I am coming in."

"You're nae listenin'" she says. "I said you're nae comin' in."

"I am." I step forward. "What you gonna do?"

She don't say a word. Instead, she lowers the breadknife and jerks it right at my goolies. As I jump out the way, the blade goes straight into my right thigh. She pulls it out and stands, blood-soaked knife in hand, watching me.

Blood spurts through my trouser leg like a tap turned full on. As my hand tries to stop the flow, I fall to the ground, screaming blue murder. My head hits the doorstep and I roll over, not knowing what to do for the best.

Shirl now realises exactly what she's done and drops the knife, caterwauling like a strangled moggy. "Och, Frank! Och, Frank! Ah'm so sorry, och – shite!!"

"Call the fuckin' ambulance, you silly cow! For fuck's sake – " I whack my head on the doorstep again. "Aargh, oooow!!!" The blood's still streamin' everywhere, she's run inside, I'm rolling about in agony.

Greg, our neighbour who wears glasses like Michael Caine in *The Ipcress File*, opens his door to see what's going on, sees me, sees the blood, sees the knife. "Oh, sweet Jesus," he cries and falls against the door jamb. He can't stand the sight of blood, you see, and this puddle of claret does him in.

The paramedics get here, bind me up, make Greg a cup

of tea with four sugars and calm Shirl down. Then, and only then – I'm the last of their worries – do they take me to the hospital where they clean the wound, stitch and bandage me up. I've got no trousers to go home in but who cares?

A panda car's parked outside the house. If it ain't my old mate, PC Darren Smith, him from the funny money chase round the roundabout.

"Do you want to press charges, Frank?" he says, flapping his hand at Shirl, who's slumped on the settee, crying her eyes out.

"How you doin', Dazzer?"

"You don't look too bright," he says, staring at the bandages. "Aren't they the boxers you were wearing when we last met?"

I look down. Fred Flintstone. "They're a snug fit."

"What about Shirley? Shall I arrest her?"

"Leave it out, mate," I say. "Domestic. Got out o' control, didn't it?"

* * * * *

Two months later, Saturday. Shirl's out somewhere and Eve, who's eight now, is playing with some dolls or reading a book or doing something in the other room. I'm having breakfast and a smoke and reading about Harry Corbett who died a couple of days ago. The nation mourns, though relieved that Sooty, Sweep and Su are being comforted in their hour of grief.

A rumbling, like a squadron of army tanks rolling by, comes from outside. I get up and take a gander. Three beaten up cars, a bright shiny Beamer, a window-cleaner's van with a ladder on top, two brand new Transits and a pick-up truck are blocking the road. Next thing, the doorbell goes. It's Denny Blacklock.

"Frank," he says.

"Mornin'."

"We're going golfing. I want you to come."

235

I've heard about these golfing events Denny hosts but I've never been to one. This is where Denny maps out his deals, sets up new contacts and gets the low-down on what's going off.

"I can't play golf," I say.

"'S all right. You can caddy. Or come for the walk. Do you good. You shouldn't be stuck in the house on a day like this."

He's obviously desperate for me to go. Christ knows why. Maybe he's got something up his sleeve. Anyway, it'll be interesting to see who's there, what he's got coming up, who he's interested in.

"Okay," I say. "Give me a few minutes. Gotta see to Eve."

"I'll wait in the car."

He goes back to the fleet of wheels, has a word with them and all of 'em except his Beamer power up their engines, make a lot of noise not moving and then shoot off like everyone's Burt Reynolds in *The Cannonball Run*.

I knock on next door's. Not Greg, he who passed out at the sight of my blood – the other side, Anita. Polly, her little girl, and Eve are friends and each of us looks after them both if one of us is going out.

"Sorry, Frank," she says. "I was going to ask you if you'd take Polly in. I've got to pop out myself."

"Oh." Wondering what to do, I look at Denny sitting in his Beamer drumming his fingers on the steering-wheel.

"What about Colin and Norman?"

Colin and Norman are brothers living two doors up. They're friendly enough blokes without families of their own and, when they're not at work or gigging with their tribute band, The Walking Brothers, they have the neighbourhood youngsters in as an audience while they rehearse.

Neither of 'em looks a bit like Scott, John or Gary and their version of "The Sun Ain't Gonna Shine Any More" makes everyone who hears it wish it was the monsoon season. And, o' course, the fact that there's only two of

236

'em, not three, takes away half the point of a Walker Brothers tribute band. Still, they're decent enough blokes, handy to have about the place.

"Okay," I say. "Can I leave Eve with you to fix it up? I gotta go." I wave at Denny to tell him I'm coming and take Eve into Anita's.

It's a lovely place, the golf club. I'll never know why the club let Denny in. Maybe he bribed the club secretary or donated a match cup or something, I dunno. But as I pull his golf cart along, he gets his hip flask out and swigs back a mouthful. It's half ten in the morning!

When we get to the first green, there's a dozen or so blokes waiting for us. Denny does the introductions. Only every drug dealer from the area. If that's not enough, Ryan's got a brewery loaded in his cart. No golf clubs. Just the lagers, the beers, the whisky, the brandy, everything else. You name it, he's got it. I can tell he's not a very happy bunny.

I go over. "You got better things to do, eh, mate?" I say out the side of my mouth.

"Anything's better than this," he said. "Dad knows I don't like doing this."

"So why don't you tell him?"

We look over at Denny, hee-hawing like a donkey having an orgasm, backslapping his mates, swigging from his flask, the others finishing cans and throwing them on to the green and opening more.

"*You* tell him," Ryan says.

"I see what you mean," I say.

By now, a group of four men in yellow and grey diamond-patterned sweaters and white caps are standing by, waiting to get started, getting more and more annoyed.

"I say," one of 'em calls out, "are you going to be much longer? We've come here to play some golf, not watch you and your pals get drunk."

Denny puts his flask in his back pocket and strolls over to them. Everyone suddenly goes quiet. Even the birds stop singing.

"What's stopping you, mate?" he says, his face three inches away from the poor bloke's. "There's another fucking seventeen fucking holes you can fucking have a go at, ain't there, you smarmy load o' fuckers."

"Well, really, there's no need for that sort of language."

"Come on, Keith. Let's move on."

"Yeah, Keith, why don't you move on?"

"I've a good mind to report you to the secretary."

"Yeah, and when you do, tell him from me – "

"Denny," I call out. "Are we here to play golf or watch you beat up some snot-nosed wanker?"

"Fair comment," Denny says, strolling back. "Fair comment, Frank."

While the four wankers walk to the second hole, Denny turns and barks, "Ryan! Harry, Duggie and Spiro's got no drinks in their hands. What do you think I'm paying you for, you lazy git?"

Silently, as Ryan hands out the drinks, everyone falls down on to the grass and sits, lies or lollops about, lighting up their fags, chatting, doing anything except get in a round of golf. Denny and me stand over them.

"What a great bunch of fellas," he says.

By the time everyone's finished their drinks and ready to start, it's twelve o'clock. No-one's suggested they get golfing and most couldn't aim a ball straight even if they wanted to.

"Look at the time," Denny hollers. "Gotta go. Gotta be somewhere. C'm' on, Frank, I'll take you home."

"'S all right," I say. "You go on. I'll make my own way."

"I invited you here," he says. "I take you home. Least I can do."

"It's no problem, Denny," I say. "I can manage."

"You're right," he says. "No problem. I'll take you home. Ryan, pack the stuff up. Teddy, Jags, you give my nine-stone weakling of a son a hand."

The nine-stone weakling, which he ain't, is not best pleased. But everyone does what Denny says, so that's

238

that.

"So it's fixed for Wednesday," Denny says as he shakes hands with everyone and everything except the golf clubs.

"Sure thing," one of them says. "Thanks for the opportunity."

"That'll be a great haul," says another.

So, somewhere among that drunken mess, Denny and his mates worked out their next operation. I didn't hear it. Must've bin speaking in code.

Me, Ryan and Jags get in the back of the Beamer with Teddy in the front with Denny behind the wheel.

"Right, Frank," Denny says. "Home we go."

Except he decides to take us the scenic route, round the back lanes where there's only enough room for one car and one car only unless you pull up on the steep bank. I mean, the bloke is pissed out of his head and he's driving like he's cruising the motorway at ninety miles an hour. All it needs is for a combine harvester to be coming the other way and we're mincemeat.

"Denny," I say, "you ain't got your seat belt on."

"Seat belts," he says, "is for women and pooftas."

And on he goes, swerving this way and that, scratting up against the steep verges on either side, not caring a hoot. He bursts into "It ain't what you do, it's the way that you do it" like he's Terry Hall out of Fun Boy Three, except it's more like Terry Wogan singing "The Floral Dance" with a sore throat.

I tell him, "Turn it in."

"Yeah, Dad," Ryan, who's stone cold sober, says. "Why don't you let me drive?"

"For Chrissake, Denny," Teddy whimpers, "give Ryan the wheel."

But he won't. He's touching seventy-five now and moved on to "Tie a Yellow Ribbon 'round the Old Oak Tree". When we hit a bend, a red Mini decorated with the Union Jack comes round with a geezer and a bird in it.

Denny hits the Mini, it goes flying up the side of the

239

bank and we go over the other side of the road, up the bank and smash into an old oak tree. The front tyre bursts, we bounce off the tree and shunt back on to the road on three wheels. That's it, we're on three wheels.

It's true what they say. You do see your whole life flash in front of you in the seconds before you die. Dad throwing Mum across the hall, me dumping Harry Whetstone's chocolates in the dustbin, Steve Bartram challenging me to a fight, Tim and me getting yellow judo belts –

If only it were that easy. But it ain't.

He's off again on three wheels, not even pausing to see if the geezer and the bird in the Mini are alive. The Beamer scrunches along, the bust wheel's metal seers along the road surface and us in the back are bumping up and down, all over each other like one-legged jack-in-the-boxes.

Teddy's near to throwing up, Jags is gripping my arm, Ryan's turning white, I'm numb with shock. And Denny? He's happily bawling "The Long and Winding Road." Of all the songs he can torture us with, he chooses that one.

We get to the end and he takes a right. He should have gone left. But he lands slap-bang in a carnival parade.

A lorry with an ugly bint perched on a throne made out of hardboard and painted orange. A girls' pipe band marching up and down. Members of the Rotary dressed like clowns walking up and down with buckets collecting pennies. An ice cream van selling lollies to half-washed kids.

That's too much, even for Denny. He screeches to a halt, thirty yards short of mowing down a team of rugby players dressed in skimpy swimming-trunks, straggling yellow wigs, overdone women's make-up, coconut shells for boobs and dancing to Elvis Presley blaring out "Rock-a-Hula Baby".

"Frank," he says, "I think I might be a tiny bit pissed. I can't afford for the Old Bill to get me, they'll have a field day." He opens the door. "Ryan, take over."

They change seats, Ryan reverses the motor, turns round and gets us back to The Grenadier in one piece. Denny bales out, tells Teddy and Jags to change the wheel, clean the motor and get it smartened up. He goes into the pub, leaving the rest of us shattered, a pile of broken tin soldiers. I feel sick, don't wanna hang around, so Ryan takes me home in his car.

Shirl's in the kitchen. She's got her coat on.

"Going out?" I say.

"Ah'm just in."

"Where's Eve?"

"Anita's," she says, picking up the kettle. "Ye fetch her 'n' ah'll make the tea.."

"Hi, there, Frank," Anita says as I walk in. "Eve's in the other room. We're making some orange squash, aren't we, Polly?" she says to her eight-year-old. "I'll take this to Eve while you pour some for Uncle Frank."

Anita picks up a tumbler, pours from the jug and goes out.

While Polly's pouring, she says, keeping her eyes on the jug, "When we play at Colin's, is it all right for him to stroke me?"

"What do you mean, darlin'?" I say, watching her.

"Well, he – "

"Where does he stroke you?"

She puts the jug down, lifts up her dress and puts her hand in between her legs. She looks up at me.

"All right, sweetheart," I say. I go to the door and call, "Anita, come here a minute."

Anita comes in. "What is it?"

"You better listen to this." I turn back to Polly. "Tell your mum what you just told me."

Polly says, "When we play round Uncle Colin's, he strokes me here." She lifts up her dress again and puts her hand where she did before.

Anita's hands shoot up to her open mouth. "Oh, my God!"

"Does he do anything else?" I say.

"You better ask Eve," Polly says. "She knows more about it than me."

Anita looks at me. I look at Anita.

"All right, honeybunch," she says to Polly, taking her into the living-room. "Go and play with Eve."

While I'm waiting for Anita to come back, I light up. I really need a smoke.

"What we gonna do, Frank?" she says when she comes back.

"I gotta talk to Eve first," I say. "Then Shirl – then we all decide together."

After a few minutes, while I finish my fag and Anita sits at the table, arms folded, saying nothing, staring at the jug of orange squash, I get Eve and take her home.

"Shirl!" I call when we get into our living-room. "C'm' here."

"Gi's a minute, ah'm getting' the tea," she calls from the kitchen.

"Forget the tea," I shout. "C'm' here."

"What's up?" she says, coming in.

"Sit down."

She sits on the settee.

"Eve," I say, "sit next to Mummy." As she does so, I sit on the armchair. "Now then, sweetheart, what does Uncle Colin do to you when you go round and play?"

Eve looks at me, then at Shirl and her lips tremble.

"You're no in any trouble, sugar," Shirl says, putting her arm around her. "We just want tae know, that's all. Tell yer ma what happens at Uncle Colin's."

After our sweet little girl has told us what them two men do to her, Shirl looks at me, back at Eve, shakes her head. For a minute or so, nobody speaks.

"You're my brave little girl," I say at last, catching my breath, putting my arm around her. "You deserve a big dish of chocolate ice cream and nuts. Go with Mummy and she'll get you some."

When Eve is safely tucked up in bed, we're staring at *The Les Dennis Laughter Show*.

"What'll we dae, Frank?"

I fix my eyes on the telly. What do you do? Go round and shoot them? Put a knife in them? *What the fuck do you do?* I know I've had to live with 'em inside but when it comes into my own home like this, you think I'll do this or I'll do that. Do I get the Old Bill involved, let them rot in stir and have a bloody shit time?

Monday, I'm still mulling it over. I give Shirl and Anita some money to go into Coventry for a day's shopping, a meal and a film. I look after Eve and Polly, take them to the park, buy them ice creams – that sort of thing. They get excited, come the evening, 'cos Polly's staying over. So, a lovely tea of fish fingers and chips, jelly and more ice cream. Lots of laughs, terrible jokes that we all think are hilarious, non-stop giggling.

As I'm expecting the girls home about eleven, I settle down for a drink, a smoke and an hour's telly.

Just as *Come Dancing* gets going, there's sirens and flashing blue lights outside. I peep through the curtains. A couple of fire engines are speeding past and come to a stop outside Colin and Norman's house. The street's packed with nosy neighbours standing around, watching what's going on. I go out and join 'em.

The downstairs is alight. Flames everywhere, burning up the furniture. Smoke pours out of the smashed windows. Paint peels off the front door. The curtains are already cinders.

"What's happening?" I ask one of the firemen who's supervising the others.

"Petrol bomb, mate," he says. "The place has been torched."

At that moment, Norman's head pops out of one of the upstairs windows. "Get me, get me!" he's shouting. Colin is nowhere to be seen.

Two firemen hoist a ladder up. One of 'em climbs up. I'm thinking they should've left the yelling paedo there. Someone's done the rest of us a favour. The fireman reaches the top, gets in and a few minutes later, he's on his way down with Norman draped over his shoulder. As soon as they're on the ground, the other fireman makes his way up – to find Colin, I suppose.

Greg, the neighbour who faints at the sight of a drop of claret, comes up to me. "Everyone knows this is down to you, Frank," he says. "You did this, didn't you?"

"Me?" I shrug. "I've bin inside all evenin', mate."

Next morning, after attending to some business, I decide to go to The White Hart for a bite to eat and a pint. As I'm strolling across the park, I see a bloke sitting on a park bench. It's the Old Bill. I can spot 'em a mile off. It's Reg Harding.

He's watching me as I get closer. "Hello, Frank," he says. "I want to talk to you about this house being torched last night."

I sit on the bench next to him. "Oh yeah?"

"We can do this one of two ways," he says. "Either we go up to the pub or we go down to the station. Which is it to be?"

"I was just on my way for a pint."

"Good idea."

Reg gets the drinks in and we sit down.

"Frank," he says, "I don't like nonces any more than you do and I know your Eve's involved."

"Oh yeah?"

"So all I'm going to say is this," he says after a couple more sips. "We believe it was white spirit that was poured through the letter-box. Now, we can't match petrol but we can match white spirit if we find the rest of it."

"Oh yeah?"

"So I suggest," he carries on, looking me straight in the eye, "if anybody's got any white spirit laying about, they get rid of it." He stops and waits.

I gaze into my beer for a few seconds, then look straight back at him. "Mr Harding, you got all the jocks, all the Geordies up on that estate. Anyone could've done it, mate, anyone of 'em. You can't – "

"That's why you're not nicked, Frank, 'cos we know

you can say that and – "

"Well, I am saying that so let's say no more about it, eh?" I stand up. "Let me get you a pint."

"Thanks," he says, finishing off his jar, "but I've got to be on my way. By the way, seen anything of Denny Blacklock lately?"

"Not for weeks. Are you lookin' for him?"

"No… Just asking."

* * * * *

"Frank," Shirl says, "it's nae ma fault. Gaddin' off God knows where, ending up in the clink, leaving me to look after Eve on ma own. Sometimes, you're like a wee bairn. Nae thought for naebody, have ye?"

"I won't have it, Shirl," I tell her. "I won't have it. You can pack your bags."

She pulls on her fag. "How d'ya find out?"

"D'ya think I didn't notice how many shopping trips you were having? How many times I'd come home and you weren't here? Maybe if you'd not been out so much but looked after Eve, Colin and Norman would've kept away from her."

"Yeah, well," she says. "I'm sorry aboot that."

"So you should be," I snap. "For Chrissake, Shirl, he works in a laundrette."

"What's wrang wi' that? You like yer clothes to be clean, don't ye?"

"Called Alistair."

"Al."

"Alistair John Lithgow."

"How d'you ken that?"

"Anita told me," I say. "Really, Shirl, you should choose your alibis more carefully."

"And you'd ken all aboot that, wouldn't ye?" She lets out a big sigh. "Anyway, he's gone noo. Thanks to you. When ah told him who you were – "

"You'll be out by the end of the week, then."

She stands up. "Nae point hanging aboot. Ah'll go now. We'll be at my ma's. You can visit Eve any time." She picks up her fags and lighter.

"At least Linda stuck by me."

"Aye, 'n' she was a friggin' psycho."

I nod. "You're right about that."

She and Eve come back the next day for the rest of their things and by the end of the week, it's as if they've never been here. Shirl's as good as her word and I see Eve two or three times a week, take her out, buy her things, stuff like that.

Colin and Norman disappear. Nobody knows where. Everyone says good riddance. The council do the house up and a new family move in. When I say "family", I mean a woman called Trudy and her two girls, Nancy and Molly.

Like a few others, I go round to see if I can help her sort her things out. But she's managing well enough.

"The least I can do," I say, "is make us a cup of tea."

"That'd be lovely."

I watch as she finds a box and gets the cups out. She's got long black hair down over her shoulders and it falls round her face as she bends down. Her tits, the size of over-ripe melons, bulge through her pink tee-shirt as she rummages about. Underneath her jeans, I can see the outline of her panties and two luscious buns asking to be fondled.

"So where you do work?" I say, following her every gorgeous move.

"The betting-shop," she says, taking newspaper off the cups. "You know, down – "

"Yeah," I say. "I know. Use it myself a few times."

"Oh yes? I've not seen you."

"I'm sure I'd've noticed you."

We laugh, she sets up the milk, sugar and whatnot. Then we're waiting for the kettle to boil and, o' course, the more we stand there watching it, the longer it takes.

"So, um," she says, for something to say, "what do you do when you're not making cups of tea?"

"Oh, you know, a bit of this, a bit of that... Import, export," I add, using Evan's words.

"That must be very interesting."

"Ups and downs," I say, watching her all the time. "Highs and lows."

Not moving, not smiling or anything, we stare at each other.

At last, she says, "The kettle's boiled."

"What?"

"The kettle's boiled."

"So it has."

I don't move.

Neither does she.

"I like a bit of sugar," she said.

"So do I."

"Would you like to put some sugar in my cup?"

* * * * *

Three months later, I move in with Trudy. Her two girls and I get on well enough. "We're used to it," Molly says. I'm not sure what she means. A week after that, Shirl and Eve move back into the house we were in. She's entitled. The rent card's in her name.

As we're living within a few doors, it's natural we bump into each other, almost on a daily basis, you might say. But then it gets ridiculous. Shirl's standing at her front door when I leave Trudy's. Shirl pretends to do some gardening when Trudy comes home from the betting-shop. Shirl's at her window when we go to the pub. It gets so when Trudy and me are at home for an evening, we have to pull the curtains 'cos Shirl walks up and down outside, staring in.

One night, when Nancy and Molly are at their friends, I say to Trudy, "'Stead o' cooking, I'll get a takeaway from Ming's and a couple of bottles of wine, we'll have that."

I pop into Tesco's for some Jacob's Creek Chardonnay – Trudy's favourite – and a packet of fags, and from

Ming's I get some barbecued spare ribs, beef in Szechuan Toa Pan spicy sauce, sweet and sour King Prawn Balls, some stir fried mixed vegetables in black bean sauce and mushroom fried rice. Ming's is the best Chinese takeaway I think I've ever come across. This is gonna be a great evening.

But when I pull the car up, I see the neighbours standing outside our garden and I hear some yelling and screaming. I get out and, bugger me, it's Shirl. She's on top of Trudy, headbutting her, bashing her face in, thumping her in the stomach and God knows what else.

"For Chrissake!" I yell at the neighbours. "Don't just stand there!"

But they do. They stand there. I don't blame 'em. It's a mistake to get between two scrapping women. The thing is, though, most women don't know how to fight properly. They slap each other and pull hair but that's about all they do.

It's not what I'd call fighting. They're like two blind cats spitting at each other in the dark. Now, when two blokes fight, they get down to it. They're in there, doing the business. But women? Slap, slap, slap. That's all. Men fight to hurt the other bloke. Women, it's about getting rid of their own anger, not doing the other one over.

Greg, our friendly neighbour, sidles up to me. "This is all your fault, Frank," he says again. He's like a record stuck in a groove.

"Come with me," I say.

"What?"

"Come with me."

"No."

"I'm not gonna hurt you. Come with me."

I take him in the house, get two buckets, fill them with cold water. I give one to him. "Carry this."

We go back into the front garden, where Trudy's pulling Shirl's hair and slapping her round the face.

Aiming carefully, I throw my bucket of water over Trudy. She screams her head off and backs off Shirl like a

248

cat caught on an electrified fence.

"Give me that," I say to Greg. He hands me the other bucket. I slosh it over Shirl.

The neighbours give me a loud round of applause and a cheer. "Now," I shout at them, "fuck off, why doncha? And you," I shout right into Shirl's face, "go home. I don't wanna see you here again."

I turn to Trudy, who's trying to smooth out her lovely black hair and bawling her eyes out. She's got blood all over her face. Not a pretty sight. "Let's get you inside and clean you up."

When we're indoors and I'm sorting her out, it's not as bad as it looks, it never is.

Trudy says, "I'm phoning the police."

"Don't do that, hon," I call as I go upstairs for her hairbrush and mirror.

"It was unprovoked," she shouts. "I did nothing. She comes round here – "

"What was it all about?"

"I'm bloody phoning the police, I tell you."

"We've had enough kerfuffle for one night," I say, coming back into the kitchen and handing her the stuff.

"Ha!" she snorts. "You just don't want the Old Bill round here, do ya, sniffing about."

"Nothing to do with that," I say – 'though it is – "They'll put it down to a domestic and do sod all. They never do with domestics."

"This wasn't no domestic," she squawks. "This was an out-and-out physical attack on my person."

"All I'm saying is, calm down and see how you feel in the morning. If you feel the same, then call 'em in."

As she's concentrating on brushing her hair by now, she doesn't say a word.

"One thing's for certain," I say.

"And what's that, O Wise One?"

"We're gonna have to move," I say. "We can't carry on like this."

"I'm starving," she says, putting the brush and mirror

down. "Where's that Chinese and the wine?"

I've forgotten all about it. I go out to the car. It's still there, on the front seat. Stone cold, of course. We chill the Chardonnay for a while, warm the takeaway up in Trudy's new microwave and watch *Quantum Leap*. Tonight, Sam's a cop in New York. Afterwards, Trudy's calmed down so we go to bed and make a night of it.

Next day, she's decided not to bother with the Old Bill.

"I'll go down the council and see about moving," she says.

"Trudy," I say, "I've bin thinking."

"Does that mean you're taking the rest of the day off?"

"How's about us moving to Yarmouth?"

"Yarmouth?" she says, astonished.

"Why not? You, me, Nancy and Molly. It's really nice there. I know a lot o' people. And my mum and dad are there. You can get a transfer to another betting-shop. It'll be good. How about it?"

When she comes home from work, she says, "All right, let's do it."

"I'll go down to Yarmouth, find us a place."

I ring my dad.

"Dad," I say, "I'm moving back to Yarmouth. Can you put me up for a few nights?"

"There's always a room here for you, son," he says.

"Yeah, but I gotta find a place for me, Trudy and her girls."

"Who?"

"Trudy."

"What happened to Shirl?"

"You don't wanna know."

There's an intake of breath and then he says, "Frank, I can't keep up with you. First, it's Linda, then it's Shirl, now it's Trudy. When are you going to settle down, eh?"

"I am settled down," I tell him. "I've got a family now. Responsibilities."

"And what about Eve?"

"She's staying with Shirl."

"If you say so, son," he sighs. "When can we expect you?"

With my contacts, it ain't difficult finding a house. Trudy's boss fixes her transfer and so now, all we gotta do is get her furniture and stuff shifted. I ain't got anything to shift, have I, it's all in the house me and Shirl set up and I don't want it. I'm not going begging to Shirl and I ain't having Eve go without.

My mum does what she always does. She helps us out. She lends Trudy five hundred for removal expenses. Trudy says she got a tax rebate coming soon. She'll pay her back out of that. She has to work her notice at the betting-shop and we have to arrange new schools for Nancy and Molly but once all that's done, we're on our way.

She and the girls like the place I've found and all of us spend the next week setting up home. Nancy and Molly love living at the seaside, I'm with my old crowd again and Trudy's pleased with a fresh start.

"This is great," I say, as she places the last china ornament on a shelf over the stereo unit. I pick up the last remaining cardboard box ready to fold and stack in the dustbin.

"Yeah," she says. "Maybe Shirl did us a favour."

After about a month, though, things are not right with me. I feel guilty. I'm loving being with Trudy and the girls, don't get me wrong, but what about Eve, my own little girl? She's nine, like Nancy and Molly, and I can't see why they should be having all the fun while she's stuck on that crap estate up in Coventry. They'd all get on so well with each other. I'm convinced of it.

"I can't do this," I say to Trudy. "It ain't right."

"What you talking about?"

"I gotta bring Eve down here. It's not fair."

"Fair?" she says, wandering over to the stereo unit. "What's fair got to do with anything? I'll tell you what's not fair. This poxy stereo unit and you playing nothing but Elton fucking John all day and every day. I'm sick of it."

She picks up the stereo unit, hoists it up to her

shoulders and smashes it straight on to the floor. Pieces go everywhere. One bit jumps right across the room and hits me on the leg. I don't move. She stands among the mess she's created, looks down and then up at me. "So no more Elton John. Is that clear?"

I scrunch my way over to her. "So this is the real Trudy, is it?" I say. "Now I'm seeing what you're really like."

"I'm sick to the teeth of 'Healing fucking Hands'," she shouts. "How many times do you have to play it, for Chrissake?"

"I set you up in a lovely home," I shout back. "I treat Nancy and Molly like they're my own and you won't welcome my little girl into our family. You're jealous, that's what it is."

And with that, I get out the house, go to the pub and have a few beers – well, more than a few. I wander along Yarmouth front, get to my Uncle Vic's hot dog stand and say hello. I call on Mum and Dad – but they're out. I go to the Singing Spoon caff for a burger and chips.

It's ten at night before I get back home. Everywhere's dark. I put the key in the front door and go in. It don't sound right. Echoes like an empty house. I switch the hall light on. It *is* an empty house.

She's only gone and taken everything. There's not a stick of furniture, not a carpet or mat, not a curtain or precious ornament. Even the smashed up stereo has been cleared up. Everything in the kitchen has gone. I can't even make a cup of tea or pour a glass of water. I don't know how she did this so quick or so soon.

But she did. There's no way you can pick up the phone and get a removal van at your door the minute you need one. No fucking way. She planned it. She staged our row. She must've done, the scheming, conniving bitch.

I wander around the place, listening to my footsteps going upstairs. She's left my clothes, my shaving-gear and toothbrush. No toothpaste. When I flush the toilet, it sounds through the house. The clatter of my shoes when I come downstairs is like a Shire Horse clopping over cobbles. I ain't even got a bed to sleep on or a cushion for my head.

It's only then I see a piece of paper pinned on the inside of the front door. Wouldn't't've seen it coming in. The only place to pin anything, I suppose, is on the inside of the front door. As I pull at it, the drawing-pin pings off somewhere. I don't bother to look for it.

It's a note. In Trudy's scrawl. She never could write properly. "Your mum's not getting her money back. I'm not paying nothing back to her. Fuck her. And fuck you."

I look at my watch. Well gone eleven. Too late to get a room in a B&B. I think about calling Mum to see about a bed. But don't. I slump down against a corner in the living-room and doze on and off through the night. Bloody uncomfortable, I tell ya, them floorboards.

Finally, it's morning. I'm cold, hungry and my neck, legs and arms are stiff. I'd have a shower but I ain't got a towel to dry myself. As I pee, I look in the bathroom mirror. What a sight. I try to tidy my hair. She's had the good grace to leave a roll of toilet paper so I do the business, have a shave, clean my teeth with hot water, swill water over my face and dry myself with my hanky.

I look in the mirror again. "What you gonna do?"

First off, I'm gonna get the money Trudy owes Mum. She's got no bloody right to run off without paying her debts. 'Specially to my mum. She can do what the hell she likes but she don't get away without giving back the five ton she owes Mum. If she does that, then I'll walk away. That's it. Get the dosh, give it Mum and go from there. What else can I do? I'm not having my mum out of pocket 'cos o' some crafty ungrateful cow.

I look at my watch. Few minutes past seven. I'll get some breakfast and be waiting at the betting-shop at half eight when Trudy'll be there to open up.

I go back to the Singing Spoon and have a good fry-up — two eggs, fried bread, bacon, mushrooms, grilled tomatoes, black pudding, slice of bread. And a mug of builder's tea.

I get to the betting-shop in good time and wait in the bus shelter. It ain't long before I hear her coming along the street. I'd know them footsteps anywhere. It's her all right.

When she gets to the bus shelter, I jump out. "Oi, you!"

"Oh!" she gasps. "It's you!"

"Who did you think it would be?" I grunt, grabbing her round her neck and pushing her up against the wall of the shelter. "Des O'fuckin' Connor?"

"Let me go!" she yelps.

But I've got hold of her so tight, her eyes pop out like two blue ping-pong balls. "Yeah, you didn't expect me, did you, you bitch."

"Frank, I – I – "

"You owe my mum five ton," I tell her, "and you're gonna pay it back, d'ya hear?"

"I haven't got it," she splutters.

"And this note," I say, pulling it out my pocket. "You know what you can do with that."

I screw it into a little ball and shove it in her mouth. It ain't there for long. She spits it out. Right into my face.

"You're nothing but a low life," she screams. "I've met dead maggots better than you. You think you're the big I Am, don't ya? Well, you ain't. You're a shitty shitty scumbag!"

She tries to push me away but I pin her up against the wall. "What have I ever done to you?" I mutter in her ear.

"If you don't know, I'm not telling you." She spits in my face.

With the hand that isn't holding her, I feel in my pocket and pull out what looks like a twelve gauge shotgun cartridge. 'Cept it ain't. I press the handle and out comes a four-inch blade. I'm only gonna frighten the silly slag. That's all. Only frighten her. She's gotta see I mean business.

She screams and grabs my hand. I try to pull away but she's yelling and shouting like I'm gonna stab her or something. And I'm not. I'm only frightening her. But she

254

won't have it. She don't understand. I pull the knife away to press the handle and put the blade back in.

But she won't let me. I'm pulling, she's pulling and the blade catches her in the chest. She lets out a shriek loud enough to raise a dozen zombies hiding in Lowestoft cemetery. It's only a tiny nick. I haven't stabbed her or anything like that. I didn't even clip her. She was struggling with the knife, she clipped herself. No big deal. I can't even see any blood, just a small tear in her blouse. I push her to the ground, flip the blade back in the handle and walk off.

I've had it with her. I had it with Linda. I had it with Shirl. I thought me and Trudy had a good thing going and now, 'cos she can't get her own way, she's the same as them. Linda throws herself on my car, Shirl stabs me in the leg, Trudy smashes up furniture, empties the house and accidentally tears her blouse with my knife.

What is it about me that attracts mad raving female psychos? I'm better off on my own, I tell ya. At least, then, I can get some peace and quiet.

I make my way down to the sea front to Uncle Vic.

"Hallo, Frank," he says. He's opening up his hot dog stand. He looks at me. "What's the matter?"

"I've just had a fight with Trudy. She pulled this – " I tell him about the stereo, Elton John, the empty house and what happened in the bus shelter. In the end, I'm some old biddy blubbing her eyes out at a funeral.

"You're joking," he says.

"Oh, there's nothing wrong with her," I say. "I didn't stab her or anything."

"Thank Christ for that. What you gonna do?"

"What can I do?" I say. "Just try to forget the whole thing."

After a couple of fags, he says he's gotta get on, so I cross the road on to the pavement alongside the beach when I notice a copper running towards me. Uh-ho, here we go. He stops, dashes back to his car, gets in, drives up next to me and jumps out.

"Frank Peters?" he says.

"What?"

"You're under arrest for attempted murder."

"What?"

"You're under arrest for attempted murder."

"You must be off your fuckin' head."

"Get in the car."

He takes me to the station and, like the copper said, they charge me with attempted murder and put me in a cell while they find a brief. After about half an hour, the door clicks open and the plain clothes who interviewed me comes in.

He says, "Do you know how bad Trudy is?"

"You're not allowed to do this," I say.

"I can do what I like."

"No, you can't," I tell him. "You're not allowed to come in here and talk to me. If you wanna talk to me, take me up to the interview room."

"You stabbed her."

"Don't be stupid."

"She's on the hospital theatre table," he says. "They're operating on her. They can't stop the blood."

He stands there for a minute, watching me. I keep quiet. The way he's talking, I'm thinking now I'm not so sure whether the knife went in her or not. If it did, I'm done for.

"Well?" he says. "Aren't you going to say something?"

"Yes," I say. "You're not allowed in here. I'm gonna put in a formal complaint about you."

He looks at me, turns round and goes out. A few hours later, my brief tells me that, although the dressing is a small plaster on her chest, they're doing me for attempted murder. I mean, a small plaster like you'd use if you cut your finger with a piece of paper! That's not attempted murder. If they have to charge me with anything, it should be GBH.

I'm hauled up to a special court where the plain clothes gives evidence for remanding me in custody. I'm slung into Norwich Prison and I'm there for nearly a year. God knows why. I don't understand how it can take lawyers a year to prepare a piddling little case like this for trial. What are they doing? Eventually, at long last, they get round to it and I'm shipped off to Norwich Crown Court for trial.

In his summing up, the judge, sitting up there in his red robes and long wig, wants to know why I'm charged with attempted murder. "Doesn't warrant it," he says. "It doesn't even call for wounding with intent. From the events leading up to the incident and the other facts of the case, Peters did nothing other than get involved in a heated argument which resulted in a minor domestic accident."

Quite right, m'lud. Couldn't've put it better myself. Give that man some puff.

The jury finds me not guilty of attempted murder but guilty of wounding. I get three years. That's all right. For a kick-off, attempted murder would've bin fifteen. But three! I've already done a year on remand. That leaves two. I'll be out in a year. Well pleased with that.

* * * * *

Next door to me and my cell is Herbie, who's in for GBH. We've become good mates. And then there's this other bloke, the next cell along, who we've sussed out is a nonce.

One day, Herbie, me and one of the SOs is talking and I say, "So what's he done?"

"Yeah," Herbie says. "When can we get our hands on this fucker?"

"Peters," the SO says, "that man has just finished a nine-year sentence and he's getting out Monday. He's vowed to do what he's done all over again. And there's nothing we can do."

"So what's he do?"

"I'm not telling you," he says. "It's done with."

"Not 'til he gets out is it done with," Herbie says. "What's he do?"

"Whatever is the worst thing a man can do to a seven-year-old boy without leaving him for dead, that's what he did. That's all I'm saying."

"Why," I say, "don't you open his door and leave him to me and Herbie and the others. We'll sort him out." I remember what happened in the showers in Aylesbury with Mr Lawson all them years ago. I reckon we can do with some o' that here.

The SO says, "I would love to. I would dearly, dearly love to do that but we can't."

"Course we can."

"Not these days, Peters," he says. "We can't just let people bash nonces up whenever they feel like it."

"Course you can."

But that's that. Without the SO's co-operation, there's nothing we can do. After he's gone away, Herbie and me look at each other.

"We're getting old, mate," he says.

"No, we're not!" I say. "I'm only – oh!"

"What?"

"I just remembered. It's my birthday today. I'm – "

"You ain't old, Frank," Herbie says. "You're fucking senile."

" – thirty-eight."

"Happy birthday."

"Yeah," I say. "Mum always baked me a cake." I stand there, for the moment very alone. "Time was when a good doing over up a back alley was all the justice anybody got. Now we gotta be nice to 'em. Now we gotta *understand* 'em. Did I ever tell you about that time in Aylesbury – "

"Only about three hundred times," he says. "C'm' on, I'll make you a birthday cuppa. Take my arm, old man."

* * * * *

A few weeks later, I've run out of tea-bags and I'm dying for a cuppa. One'll last me a few cups so I stroll along to see who's there to lend me one. Ed's usually about, usually got one to spare.

"Ed?" I call out. "You there?"

Ed Sarson is a dangerous individual. In for a fifteen. Bank job, bashed the manager's head in and made off with about a quarter of a million. Not that it did him any good. One of his gang grassed him up over that and a few other jobs, besides. So now, he hates everyone, including himself, and don't waste no time taking his revenge out on anyone who even so much as squints in his direction.

He's a big bloke, a lumberjack on his day off. Hair everywhere, could single-handedly supply a wig factory. Loves air-guitarring to heavy metal bands with names like Birth Control, Death SS, Suicidal Tendencies and – this one always makes me laugh – Pink Fairies. Though I suppose, as they come from Ladbroke Grove, they must have something going for 'em.

But me and Ed get on. He knows I'm never gonna threaten him. He can rest easy with me. More to the point, he likes his puff and I supply him. It's that sort of business relationship that trumps everything else. He knows if he comes on at me, he's well and truly fucked.

"Ed," I say, going into his cell, "got a tea-bag I can borrow?"

Well, what a sight.

Ed's in his black jeans, no shirt, showing off his tattoos, standing over his bed. The bedding and mattress are piled on the floor up the other end of the cell.

On the metal frame, 'cos our beds are metal, is a young lad. His wrists are strapped to the top and his bare ankles to the bottom. His face is so white you can see his skull and tears are streaming down his face.

Two long wires come off the bed with razor blades tied at the ends. It's an old trick. You put the razors in the light socket on the side of the wall, slide 'em along the switches and they pick the electricity up so you can run your radio, make a cup of tea or whatever you wanna do. In this case, electrocute a young lad you've previously strapped to your bed.

259

"What you doing, Ed?" I say. I look down at the lad. "Hello, Gary. You all right?"

"Hello, Frank," Gary gasps. "I'm fine. How about y'self?"

"That won't work, Ed," I say.

"'Course it will," Ed says, picking up the ends ready to push into the light socket.

"No, it won't," I say. "For a kick-off, Gary's clothes'll protect him. For it to work best, you've gotta get him naked – "

"Yeah, well," he says, hanging on to the wires, "I can do that."

"Second, you gotta do it like Charlie Richardson did it," I tell him, holding on to his arm. "Ed, if you don't study your history, you're bound to get it wrong. You have to attach the terminals to his tits and bits."

"I can do that, too."

"You also need a bath of cold water to put him in before you switch the current on," I tell him. "And you ain't got a bath of cold water, have ya? That's where you're doing it all wrong. You ain't got a bath of cold water. No good without a bath of cold water, I'm tellin' ya. You gotta have your cold water."

"I can get some."

"How?" I say. "Think about it, Ed. What you're doing here ain't practical. Anyway, what's Gary done?"

"He grassed me up, didn't he?"

I look down at the lad, still strapped to the bed frame. "How old are you?"

"Twenty-one."

"Ed," I say, "he ain't old enough to know anything worth grassin' up about. What's he got on you? No, don't tell me, I don't wanna know. All I can say is, he ain't no grass."

"He fuckin' is," Ed says. "Once I get hold of a cold bath, I'm gonna waste him, he's goin' out."

"Gary ain't no grass," I say. "I mean, look at him. Do you want to get life for doin' over a scrawny specimen like

260

that? Look, Ed, I'll tell you what I'll do. And gimme them, for fuck's sake." I snatch the wires off him. "Leave it out, as a favour to me, and I'll give you a quarter ounce of puff."

Ed stares at Gary, who's now stopped snivelling and started sniffing hard to pull back the snot running out of his nose.

"What d'ya say?"

"Quarter of an ounce?" he says.

"Quarter of an ounce. So happens I've got it on me." I pull it out and let him see it.

He stares long and hard. Finally, he takes a deep breath. "All right, Frank. But just for you, mind. But you keep that toe rag away from me, do you hear, keep him away or I'll – "

I hand it over, untie Gary, get him off the bed frame and tidy him up.

"Back to your cell, Gary," I say, pushing him out. "Go and have a lie-down. I'll be along in a minute."

"What did you want?" Ed says when he's gone.

"What?"

"What did you come here for?"

"Oh yeah," I say. I have to think for a second. "Tea bag. Have you got a tea bag?"

While he's finding the tea bag, I undo the wires. Then we put his bed back together and I leave him sitting on it ready to enjoy his puff.

When I get to Gary's cell, he's down to his Y-fronts washing himself all over like someone scrubbing the devil out of his soul. I was right. He is a scrawny specimen.

"The bastard!" he hisses when he sees me. "I'll have him, I swear, I'll have him!"

"Keep away from him, Gary," I say. "I've seen Ed cave a black guy's head in and slap him in the hospital wing. He's not to be fucked about with."

"Look, Frank," he says, dripping wet, turning to me. "He got my sister up the duff and now he does this. Once I'm cleaned up, I'm off to see the screws."

"I told him you're not a grass, mate, and now you're gonna do this."

"I didn't grass him up," he mutters, wiping himself down. "I just told him he's gotta take responsibility for what he's done. She's fifteen, for fuck's sake!"

"But now you're gonna grass him up for what he did to you – "

"Too right I am, mate," he mutters, pulling on his Levis, zipping himself up.

"So you *are* a grass."

"Call me what you fuckin' well like," he says, pulling his tee-shirt on. "He can't go around treatin' people like that."

It's an ill wind. The Governor transfers Gary to Lincoln, calls what I did "an outstanding act of bravery" and takes twenty-eight days off my sentence.

* * * * *

Ken says to me one day – Ken Watson's an old con who's been in Norwich for about seven years – "When I get bored, I get me a stint in the hospital."

"Oh yeah?" I say. "Why's that, then?"

"You lay on your bed and watch telly all day."

"Sounds a good number. How do I get there?"

"Tell the doc," he says, "you're gonna top yourself and, no messin' about, they'll take you straight to hospital."

"No kidding?"

"No kidding," he says. "I do it all the time. It's like taking a holiday."

So next time Dr Valavanis comes round, I say, "I feel suicidal."

"Oh!" he says. "Oh, oh, oh, oh, oh! What do you feel like doing?"

"I feel like cutting my throat."

"Well, we can't have that," he says. "I'll get you into the hospital where we can sort you out."

Great stuff. I get my toothbrush, a change of clothes

and a couple of books. Then the minibus transports me over to the hospital wing where Doc is waiting for me.

"I'll show you where everything is," he says.

He takes me to the dorms. Eight to a dorm, a telly at the end of each bed. Lovely.

"Yeah," I say. "A few days here'll fix me up."

"Oh no, Peters," the doc says. "Not here. You're going upstairs with our other mental cases."

"Whaddya mean, upstairs with your other mental cases? I ain't no psycho!"

"Maybe, maybe not," he says. "We don't know, do we? Suicidal tendencies come from mental disorders. This dorm is for our physical disorders. Upstairs is for our psychiatrics. We've got to find out what's troubling you."

"But Ken Watson told me – "

"And how is Ken?" Dr Valavanis says. "We haven't seen him for a while."

" – he sits on his bed all day and watches telly."

"Ken's nearly seventy-five," he says. "Every so often, we let him come here to help out. Good therapy for him. And, of course, we can always do with some extra help. Sometimes, I think it's the only thing that keeps the poor chap going. Please give him my regards when you next see him. But it's you I'm concerned about, Peters. You. We can't have a good-looking, physically fit fellow – "

"How do you know I'm physically fit?" I yelp. "I might have – " I search about for something – "osteoporosis."

"Anyone can see you're fit," he says. "Look at you! Muscles so crowded together they haven't got room to breathe. No, Peters, if you're suffering from suicidal ideation, we've got to get to the root of the disturbance. It's upstairs for you."

Up we go. It's like where I've come from. Cells wherever you look. Dr Valavanis introduces me to the senior ward nurse, some gorilla who makes Desperate Dan look anorexic, then he goes off and Desperate Dan takes me to my cell.

"When you've settled in," he says, "come along to the

263

recreation room and I'll introduce you to the rest of the gang." When he speaks, he's like Nick Berry singing "Heartbeat". It's beautiful. Just goes to show, don't it.

So I walk into this great big room with the biggest telly you've ever seen and I sit down. But I can't see the screen 'cos some guy's holding the telly, his arms are spread out round it so no-one else can get near.

"That's Fraser," someone says in my ear.

I turn and take a gander.

A young lad, can't be more than nineteen, in black jeans and white tee-shirt with a James Dean haircut, has sat himself next to me. He's so close he's nearly on my lap. "I'm Jason," he says, holding out his hand.

"Frank," I say, shaking.

"Nice to meet you, Frank," he says. "Ain't often we get a better class of person in here. He," he says, pointing to the telly hugger, "hears voices. Is convinced they're coming out the box. He reckons – he reckons if he wraps himself around it – he reckons if he wraps himself around it, he can stop 'em from escaping from the box and burrowing into his head."

"That's nice."

"Yeah," he says, edging up even closer, if that's possible. "Do you know what?"

"No, go on."

"You're probably the only sane fucker in here," he says. "They're all off their heads."

"Oh yeah?"

"Yeah," he says. "'Cept me, o' course."

"Oh, understood, understood."

We sit there for a good five minutes, saying nothing, watching Fraser doing fuck all except hug *The All New Popeye Show*.

Jason then jumps up and says, "Glad we had this little chat, Dad, but because you're such a dirty old sod coming on to me like that, I've got to take a shower." He walks away, pulling off his tee-shirt and undoing his jeans. By the time he gets to the door, he's stark naked, leaving his clothes wherever he's dropped them.

A couple more days in and I've talked to every patient, 'cos that's what they call them here. Patients. Except a bald middle-aged bloke who does nothing but stand in the middle of the recreation area. Sometimes, for a change, he sits on the floor up a corner hugging his knees, staring, never blinking, for hours on end. Don't say a dicky-bird. Soils his clothes, gives off a stink like I've never come across before, God knows what he's eating, and the attendants take him away, clean him up and bring him back. Then they wait for it to happen all over again.

Then, for no reason I've been able to work out, he'll burst into song. It'll be some o' that Italian opera like them Three Tenor geezers come out with. What a terrific voice! He sings like an angel. But in the middle of the song, he'll stop and go back into himself.

After a few days, I reckon if I'm gonna be here, I might as well make myself useful. I speak a bit more to some of them, to get an idea why they're here. I go back to *Archbold*, look up a few things. When I'm on top of everything, I sit down and advise 'em where they're going wrong with the law, how to handle their briefs, that sort of thing.

They're all grateful to me, of course, and soon, everyone – except the bald middle-aged bloke, 'cos there's no getting through to him – is calling their briefs in for consultations.

Dr Valavanis calls me in. "To see how you're getting on," he says. "Still having suicidal ideation?"

"What?"

"Still thinking about killing yourself?" he says.

"Oh, you know," I say. "Comes and goes. Never too far away from my thoughts."

"Are you experiencing feelings of hopelessness?"

"Isn't everyone?"

"How are you sleeping?"

"Like a top, mate, like a top."

"Are you eating well?"

"When I can find food worth eating."

"Are you depressed?"

"Wouldn't you be, stuck in this place?" I say. "You're all right. You can get in your car and go home at the end of the day."

"Do you have panic attacks?"

"No."

He takes a deep breath, shakes his head, opens a file and reads it for a bit. "I see you're keeping yourself busy." He puts the file down and stares at me for a few seconds. "Think you're Perry Mason, do you?"

"Eh?"

"Haven't you appointed yourself legal representative to quite a few patients?"

"I'm advising a few on their situation."

"Peters, it's clear to me you're no more suicidal than I am." He closes the file. "I'm sending you back to the block. And next time you think you can land the soft option by coming in here, I'll introduce you to the few we don't allow in the recreation area. Then you'll get some idea of what suicide, depression and panic are really about. Go back to your cell, gather up your things and an officer will escort you to where you belong."

I stand up.

"And," he says, shuffling his papers about like he's angry, "don't waste my time again."

* * * * *

When I'm a couple of months away from release, they let me out on a weekend's home leave. Shirl puts me up – we're back together now – and she and Eve and me have a good time, shopping, eating out, going for a long walk in the countryside. Eve's pleased to see me, and Shirl and me get on really well.

So when it comes to Monday morning, time for me to make my way back to Norwich – you know, I can't be arsed.

266

"Shirl," I say, "I'm going on the run."

She groans. "Remember what ah said when ye got back frae Snaresbrook? Nae sooner oot and back to yer auld ways."

Chapter 13. Blakenhurst

"Well, that's what I'm gonna do."

"You, on the run?" Shirl snorts. "Yer aff yer heed! You couldnae survive a Sunday picnic in Tannochbrae." She brushes the hair out of her eyes. "If yer gonna play silly buggers, you're nae doin' it here."

"Course I ain't, you silly tart," I tell her. "Staying' at home ain't being on the run, is it? I've got mates. They'll put me up."

"Och," she says, getting up from the table, "and spend the rest of yer life hidin', never seein' me, never seein' Eve. Och, Frank! Yer two months frae release. Did yer ma drop you on yer heed when you were born?"

"Denny Blacklock'll look after me. He'll fix me up with a place in Spain. I'll live out there."

"No, he will nae."

"Yes, he will."

"No, Frank, he will nae," she says. "The polis got him for drunk drivin', dangerous drivin', drug peddlin', God knows what else. He's in gaol."

"Nobody told me."

"Well, I'm tellin' ye noo."

She wanders into the hall. I follow her.

"There's always – "

"No, there isnae," she says before I can finish. "They got his lad, Richard – "

"Ryan."

"Richard, Ryan, who gi's a toss? He's inside. And afore ye go through yer list, the Old Bill picked 'em all up, all yon mob, so ye can forget the lot of 'em." She's putting on her coat, picking up her bag, opening the front door. "Want anything?"

"What?"

"Shops, you want anything?"

"A couple o' bottles, maybe."

"You're nae gonna run far if you're pissed oot yer

heed, eh?" she says and closes the door.

I call a couple of mates. Shirl's right. Denny Blacklock, Ryan, Teddy, Jags and the rest of 'em are inside. I give Sean Boughton a ring. We ain't spoke since the trial at Snaresbrook. Seems his bird's away for a week visiting her mother in Cleethorpes so he can let me kip on his sofa 'til she gets back. Then I gotta be outa there.

It's better than nothing. At least while I'm there, I can sort something out.

Yeah, well, let me tell you. This going on the run lark ain't all it's cracked up to be. Not if you stay in the same town. My advice to anyone going on the run is get out the area or have a mate who can give you somewhere to lay low.

Now, if this had been Denny, he'd've found me somewhere out the area but Sean, where he lives is the only place he's got, so I'm stuck indoors except at night and all Sean wants to do at night is watch telly, eat pizzas from some shithole down the road and drink himself into a deep sleep with crap beer.

And as for having to be out within the week 'cos his bird's coming back from her mum's, I'm going crazy after four days. At least inside, you get to move about a bit, talk to people, do things. Here, all I've got is Sean, his two-up two-down, pizza, beer and fucking *Coronation Street*. Ten times worse than being in yer actual prison. I'm better off in Norwich.

So the day Sean's bird is coming home, I thank him for his hospitality, make my way to Bedworth police station and hand myself in. I'm put in a cell until they get the wheels to take me back to Norwich.

Only they don't. They take me to Blakenhurst in Worcestershire, which is in the opposite direction from Norwich.

It's different from any other prison I've been in. With Aylesbury, Springhill, the Scrubs, Block 98 and the rest of 'em, it's "Do this, Peters", "Yes, Mr Fellowes", "Do that, Peters", "Fuck you, Mr Florizel". But here –

When I walk into Reception, the SO at the desk says, "Good morning, Frank. I'm Cal, your Reception Officer for today. If you need anything or have any questions, please don't hesitate to ask."

"Yer what?"

He's got a little badge on his shirt. "Callum."

"I call you Cal?"

"Yes, please," he says. "And I call you Frank."

He sits me down – everywhere else I had to stand – he pours me a coffee, we fill in the forms. When we've finished, he says, "Here" – handing over a card – "is a full phone card. Use it anytime to call your family."

I take it. He's right. It *is* a full phone card.

He leans back. "This is a privatised gaol, Frank. We believe in treating our customers – " – *customers*! – "like civilised human beings who have made a mistake or two. Everyone is capable of improvement and rehabilitation."

"Even me."

"Even you, Frank." He sips his coffee. "Everything here is brand new or fully refurbished. Treat everything and everyone with respect and we'll treat you the same."

"Oh yeah," I say. "Right." Like I believe it.

He puts his pen down and waves over a PO. "Robbie will take you to your accommodation."

A young blond lad, doesn't look as if he's started shaving, strolls over. "This way, Frank."

As we walk through the wings and past the A Wing railings – privatised or not, this place is set out like all the others – landings, stairs, row on row of cells – someone's ranting his head off. He stops and shouts out, "Gaa, bloody hell! Frank! Hey, Frank! Over here!"

It's Marky, one of the few English blokes apart from myself from the estate.

"Marky!" I shout back. "How're doin'?"

"Do you know him?" Robbie says.

"Yeah."

"We're frightened to death of him," Robbie says. "We don't know what to do with him."

"'S easy," I tell him. "We're mates. Put him in my cell."

Robbie shows me to my cell. Laid out like all the other cells I've bin in only this one is shiny bright and brand spanking new. I settle in and then I'm taken to meet the Governor. Only he ain't called the Governor – General Manager or some such stuff.

"Welcome to Blakenhurst, Frank," he says, shaking my hand. He sits down. He offers me a seat but I stand. Sitting don't seem right. He's the Governor, whatever he calls himself. Cons stand in front of governors, they don't lounge around passing the time of day.

"I see you were awarded twenty-eight days in Norwich for your act of outstanding bravery," he says, reading from a file in front of him.

"That's right."

"But then you blotted your copybook and failed to return after a weekend home visit."

"That's right."

"Which means, I'm afraid," he says, still reading the file, "you forfeit those twenty-eight days." He looks up and smiles. "Sorry."

"'S how it goes, innit?"

"Yes, Frank," he says. "As you say. That's how it goes. So you'll spend three months with us and let's hope that will be an end to your relationship with Her Majesty's Prison Service."

When I get to my cell, Marky's there. He's moved his stuff in and lying on the bottom bed in his blue and white striped boxers and white vest. "Reckon that's only fair, Frank," he says, getting up and shaking my hand. "You got me this move so you get the top."

"You're looking good," I say, scanning him up and down. He's about the same age as me, a mop of jet black hair, good muscle tone, pecs bulging out his vest, strong legs. Stubble on his chin which he obviously tends to with great care. "Work out, do ya?"

"Every day," he says. "They've got a great gym 'ere.

271

You?"

"Every day."

"Great. We're gonna make a great team. What you doin' here?"

I tell him my story. Then he tells me his. For about the fifteenth time, he got into a fight with some yobbos in a pub. Only this time, he smashes a glass over one o' their heads and cracks his skull. "One time too many, Frank," he says. "My own fault. I gotta learn to control my temper."

"You need some anger management."

"Yeah," he says. "The doc's looking into it, see what he can do for me."

"So that's why that sprog of a PO's afraid of you, is it?"

"I wouldn't touch him," Marky says. "It's just sometimes, shut up in this place, I have to let it out, you know what I mean?"

"Look, mate," I say, "we're here together now, we'll work out all day every day in the gym and we'll have a nice little thing going on. How about it, eh?"

We shake hands, then hug, smile a lot and laugh a little bit.

"Great to see you, Frank," he says.

"And you, mate, and you. Let's have a cup o' tea."

It don't take long for us to establish a routine. Marky's wife smuggles an ounce of puff in for him every week, so most days we're in the gym and most nights we're in our cell, listening to music and puffing.

As for how Blakenhurst is run, the screws ain't got a clue.

One morning, Shane, one of the POs for our floor, walks into our cell, leaves the door wide open.

"Oi!" I say. "What have I told you about walking into a cell like that?"

"Sorry, Frank," he says. "Do you want me to knock first?"

"It ain't nothin' to do with knockin'," I say. "You got

every right to come in here whenever you like. Come here."

I motion him over to the door. Marky's on his bed, watching.

"Look," I say. "You haven't put the lock down, have you, you brainless twerp. You put the lock down so I can't kick the door shut and keep you prisoner, you silly bastard."

"Sorry, Frank," Shane mumbles, putting the lock down.

"Where did they find you?" I bark. "And where are our newspapers? Why haven't you got our newspapers?"

"They're outside, Frank."

"What good are they out there? How do you expect Marky and me to read 'em with our morning cuppa if they're out there?"

He trots out and brings 'em back.

"That's more like it," I say. Marky's got his fist over his mouth, stifling his sniggering.

It's the same with the food. As we walk along the line, it's "I saved this for you, Frank," and "Have this one, Marky, it's the best in today." We're given little cakes, chocolate pieces and fancy gateaux they've put aside for us. So after dinner, Marky and me go back to our cell and have a little party with whatever's on offer. We really appreciate what they do for us. And they really appreciate the quarter of an ounce of puff we slip 'em every week. Make no mistake. It's business deals like this that make the world go round.

* * * * *

One morning, after I've been there about a month, Marky's taking a shower, I'm in my white Y-fronts in our cell, having a wash, and Mr Cotterill comes in.

He says, "I need a favour."

Mr Cotterill – it's never first names with him, not like Cal and Shane and the rest of 'em – he's the only PO in Blakenhurst everybody don't like, inmates and officers alike. Probably the Governor as well, if anyone bothered to ask.

Mr Cotterill's always smartly dressed and struts about as if he owns the place. Which he don't, of course. Reminds me a bit of Mr McKay in *Porridge*, the way he talks and carries on. "Yes, Mr Cotterill", "No, Mr Cotterill", the officers go. "Okay," or "All right, whatever" is the most the cons give him to his face and "Tosspot" or "Fucking idiot" when he ain't within earshot.

The reason nobody likes him is he's well known for getting prisoners hurt and using other prisoners to do the hurting for him. Even in the short time I've been here, I've seen two blokes beaten up 'cos they called him "Tosspot" and "Stupid wanker" when they thought he wasn't listening and he was.

Yeah, so, he says, "I need a favour."

"And good morning to you, too," I say. I carry on. I ain't gonna give him the satisfaction of letting him think he's important enough for me to stop what I'm doing.

"There's two young lads down on 2 Landing and they're driving me mad – "

"How's that then?" I say, splashing water over my head and face.

"They don't respect me," he says, "and I won't have it."

"What do they do?"

"Whenever I give them an order, they laugh at me."

"And?" I say, getting a towel and drying myself.

"And," he says, "I want 'em hurt."

"Who are they?"

"Houseman and Barton."

"What?" I say, putting my towel neatly on the rack. "Gavin and Stu? Them? That pair? They're only lads. They can't be more than twenty. They're youngsters, they don't know how to behave proper, that's all."

"They've got to be taught a lesson," he says. "They have to understand who's running this place. It'll stand 'em in good stead for the future. Will you and Marky do it?"

I reach for my socks, sit on the bed and pull them on. "And how are we gonna do that?"

He comes forward a couple of steps, stands in front of me. "I'll bring balaclavas in and baseball bats. I'll make sure I'm the only officer on the wing and then you can bash 'em up at your own leisure."

I stand up, reach for my shirt. He steps back.

"And what are Marky and me gonna get out of it?" I say, doing up the buttons. "We ain't doing this for nothing, are we?"

"You'll get full privileges for a week – "

"A fortnight."

"Ten days."

"A fortnight."

He scratches his neck. "A fortnight."

"I'll have to talk to Marky." I pull my trousers on, do 'em up. "I can't speak for him."

"Understood," he says. "Understood."

I sit back on the bed and pick up my trainers. "I'll let you know."

Off he goes.

I don't move. Did I hear what I think I heard? It's one thing to know this sort of thing goes on, it's another to get involved. I thought it was us prisoners who were supposed to be in the wrong but here, it's the prison officers who are bent. That's not how it's done. You can't have a system like that. What's the point of law and order if them who are supposed to keep the order are more bent than them who've broken the law? It ain't right. It ain't fucking right, I tell ya.

I'm still sitting on the bed with one trainer in my hand when Marky comes in, clean and smelling like some hard-nosed brass looking for a trick.

"You ain't fuckin' gonna believe what just happened," I say before he's even had a chance to put his kit down.

"No?" he says. "Go on."

"That Cotterill screw wants you and me to clobber

275

Gavin and Stu down on 2 Landing with baseball bats."

He puts his kit down and stares at me. "You're kiddin' me."

"No, I'm not."

As I move along to give him room, he sits down and I tell him all about it. When I've finished, he's shaking his head and his mouth's stuck wide open like a ventriloquist's dummy that's lost its voice.

"What we gonna do, Marky? Cotterill's getting people hurt in here. You and me both know that ain't right."

"No, it ain't," he says, jumping off the bed. "Too right it ain't. Let's fucking screw the fucking screw."

Next morning, when Cotterill's wandering about, I call him in. Marky's sitting up the corner, pretending to read the paper.

"Mr Cotterill," I say, "I told Marky what you said but best if you tell him yourself just to make sure I didn't get nothing wrong."

Cotterill nods in his direction. "I want Houseman and Barton, you know those two wankers on the 2, bashed up with baseball bats. I'll bring the bats and balaclavas in."

"Go on," Marky says.

"I'll make sure," Cotterill says, "I'm the only screw on the wing so I'll open 'em up and you can knock the stuffing out of 'em."

"Go on."

"I want 'em hurt, hurt bad."

"Go on."

"And in exchange I'll give you and Peters here two weeks' full privileges. Is it a deal?"

Marky slowly folds his paper like he's got all the time in the world – you gotta admire his cool – places it on his lap, looks at Cotterill, then at me. Then he says, "We ain't gonna do it, mate. So fuck off."

And that's what Cotterill does. He fucks off.

We don't say a dicky bird. We wait a good five minutes. Then I close the cell door real quietly. Marky gets up off his chair, goes down on his hands and knees and, from under the bed, pulls out his Magnavox AW 7790 AM/FM Dual Cassette ghetto blaster. He switches it off. He rewinds the tape and presses Play.

"Mr Cotterill, I told Marky what you said but best if you tell him yourself just to make sure I didn't get nothing wrong."

He rewinds again and pulls a tape out of his pocket, pops it in the other deck, presses a few more buttons and in fifteen minutes, we've got a copy. He gets a tape from his other pocket, does the same again and before you know it, we've got a second copy.

"Right," I say, "you hide the original, I'll hide one of the copies – "

" – and we don't tell each other where we've hidden them," Marky says. "Then – " – handing me my copy – "Part 3 of *The Shocking Case of the Fucked Screw*."

What with one thing and another, it takes us a few hours to stash the tapes, so it's not 'til the next day we catch Alan Wentworth, one of the Senior Officers – one of the good guys.

"You got a minute?" I call from the cell door.

"What is it, Frank?" he says, walking over.

When he's close up, I say, "Would you mind coming in for a minute? Marky and I have something to tell you."

He steps in. "Marky," he says, nodding.

Marky's sitting next to the table and the ghetto blaster.

Closing the door, I say, "One of your screws is bent."

"What do you mean?" he says.

"I suggest you listen to this." I nod to Marky. He presses Play.

"Mr Cotterill, I told Marky what you said but best if you tell him yourself – "

I'm watching Alan while he listens. At first, he's interested, then he's shocked and finally, he has to steady himself against the table.

"Oh my word," he says. "Turn it off. I've heard enough." He stares at the ghetto blaster for a while, then says, "Can I take the tape with me?"

"It goes nowhere without us," Marky says.

"And don't try nicking it," I add, "'cos it's a copy – "

" – and the original is safely hidden away," Marky finishes.

"Mmm," Alan says. "Quite right. I'd do the same. Anyway, I'm going to see the Governor."

Marky and me hang around in our cell for about half an hour and when it's obvious nothing's gonna happen, we go out and get on with our work. An hour later, Alan finds me and says, "Get the tape. The Governor wants to see you."

When we get to the Governor's office, Marky's already there, sitting outside.

"Wait here," Alan says as he goes in.

Marky and me don't say a word. Ten minutes later, the door opens and Alan beckons us in.

Mr Tunstall's sitting behind his desk, cleaning his specs. He's not very happy. I don't blame him. Neither would I be. A tape-recorder's planted in the dead centre with the loudspeakers facing him. As soon as he sees us, he puts his specs on and holds out his hand.

I don't say nothing. I hand over the tape. He puts it in the deck. He presses Play.

"Mr Cotterill, I told Marky what you said – "

When it's finished, he takes it out, lays it on the desk and stares at it like it's a turd next door's cat has crapped over a birthday cake his mum's decorated for him. Finally, he leans back, looks up at Marky and me.

"What do you want?" he says. "Name it."

"Name it?" I say, realising he'll give us anything so his bright, shiny privatised prison don't get a bad name.

"Well," Marky says, "to be quite honest, I could do with an open prison."

I can't believe it. Marky's trading over something like this! I thought he was better than that. Looking straight at him, not the Governor, not Alan, I say, "I don't want nothing."

"Frank," Marky says, "there must be something."

"No."

"No?"

"No."

"Mmm." Marky rubs his chin a few times, glances over at Alan who's standing by the window, back at me and then says, "Mr Tunstall, there's only one thing we want. We want the Old Bill brought in."

Tunstall stands up, slow, like, and, just as slow, picks the tape up and puts it in his jacket pocket. "You two," he says, "are nothing but a couple of demented twats. You do know that, don't you? You come in here and tell me how to run my prison – "

"I'd rather be a demented twat," I say, "than what you got in here. I tell ya, mate – "

"Don't you call me 'mate'," Tunstall says. "I'm not your mate."

"I tell ya, *mate*," I say, jabbing my finger at him, "you got a fucking mental case walking around that landing and if you don't call the Old Bill in, someone else will. It's as simple as that."

Now Tunstall's sweating. He takes his specs off, puts them back on, falls back into his chair. Finally, he waves at Alan, then Marky and me and points to the door. Alan comes forward to take us out.

"Make no mistake – " I say.

"Yes, all right, Frank," Alan says, pushing me towards the door. "That's enough. You've had your say."

"We won't trade with you," I shout as I'm edged out. "We want the Old Bill brought in."

"Come on, Frank," Marky says. "We're done."

Alan takes us back to our cell. "Stay here. You're to have no contact with anyone else."

Marky says, "We'll miss our dinner."

"It'll be brought to you," Alan says, shutting and locking the door.

Half an hour later, Jerry, one of the cons, and a PO we don't know bring us dinner.

"Good on yer," Jerry says. "All the boys are behind ya."

"Get a move on!" the PO barks.

Jerry winks and does a thumbs up.

The cell door shuts, the key turns.

"How do they know?" Marky says, picking his fork up and stabbing a beautiful Cumberland sausage filled with coarsely chopped pork, black pepper, herbs and spices. "We ain't told nobody what's going down."

"We don't have to," I say, diving into a heap of fluffy mashed potatoes, julienne carrots and onion gravy.

We spend the rest of the day reading magazines, dozing, talking about what's gonna happen next, doing press-ups. When nothing does happen, we finally bunk down and sleep the best night's sleep we've had in ages.

But next morning, after Jerry and yet another PO we've never seen before have served us a breakfast of orange juice, scrambled eggs, mushrooms, bacon and baked beans, toast and marmalade and a pot of tea each –

"Frank," Marky says, "we ain't never had food this good before. If this is what we get when we grass up, maybe we should do it more often."

–the cell door clangs open and Alan Wentworth is there. I've not seen him look so serious. Ever.

"Come on," he says.

We leave our breakfast and go to the Governor's office. Alan takes us in and leaves, closing the door behind him. There's two coppers. No-one else. Not even the Governor. Neither's sitting behind the desk. They've arranged four chairs around a little table up the other end of the room and they're sitting in two of them. They see us and stand.

One of 'em's a big bloke, must weigh seventeen stone if he weighs an ounce. He's got a forest of black hair on his bonce and his cheeks hang down like a bloodhound's. He's wearing a dark blue suit which, if it was mine, I'd've had pressed before I left the house. He's holding his hand out.

"Mr Peters?" he says as we grip and shake. His voice is deep, way deep. "I'm Detective Chief Superintendent Tom Beatty." He lets go and shakes Marky's hand. "Mr

White?"

"Mr Beatty."

"This," the Chief Super says, turning to the other bloke, "is Detective Chief Inspector John Hawks."

He's bald, thin, his grey pin-striped suit pressed and creased to within an inch of its life. No, he ain't bald. His head is polished and shining. It's as if someone's dipped it in a light solution of warm water and a small amount of washing up liquid, then taken a cotton cloth or sponge and scrubbed it gently. Like I clean snooker balls. That's how polished and shining his loaf of bread is. Like the pink.

"Coffee, gentlemen?" Beatty says. We nod. He doesn't look at Hawks. "John, would you mind?"

While John's busy not minding pouring us coffee and handing it out, Beatty says, "I hear from Mr Tunstall we have a little problem. Will you tell me about it?"

Marky and me look at each other. We're not sure. I mean, I know we wanted the Old Bill brought in but now they're here –

"Look, Mr Beatty," I say, "we're in a funny position. We're taking one of their own down and if anything goes wrong, me and Marky are gonna, how shall I put it – "
And I stop.

He doesn't smile. "'Bashed to fuck' sums it up, I think, don't you, John?"

John chuckles. "On the nail, sir."

Beatty leans forward. "Mr Peters, Mr White, you won't get bashed to fuck. Or to anywhere else, come to that. Let me assure you, we've warned everyone. There is no possibility any violence will come to you in this or any other prison. Shall we listen to the tape?"

Hawks dives under the coffee table and pulls out the same tape recorder the Governor used. The tape's already in. He presses Play.

"Mr Cotterill, I told Marky – "

When it finishes, Beatty nods at Hawks, who opens the door and calls Alan in.

"Mr Wentworth," Beatty says, "will you kindly

accompany us back to Mr Peters' and Mr White's cell and then take Detective Chief Inspector Hawks and me to wherever Cotterill's hiding. You got your handcuffs?"

Three weeks later – they don't hang about, not like they did with me over Snaresbrook – Cotterill's hauled up at Hereford Crown Court and Marky and me are shipped over as witnesses.

After I've given my evidence, the judge says, "Why did you do what you did?"

I give it to him straight. "Whether you're a villain or whether you ain't, you can't have certain people walking the streets. Nonces or whoever. You've got to have the law and this guy overstepped the line. You got youngsters in there doing a bit o' porridge, frightened to be inside, and this lunatic is sending people in to bash 'em up. He had to be stopped."

Cotterill gets eighteen months.

Chapter 14. Southend-on-Sea

"Shirl," I say a couple of weeks after Blakenhurst, "I'm gonna go straight."

"Och, aye?" she says, opening another bottle of wine.

"I want you, Eve and me to live in Yarmouth. I'll get a proper job and we'll live like a normal family."

"Yeah," she says, glugging away like the vineyards in Spain are holding a bankrupt sale, "and ah'm Bonnie Prince Charlie."

"No," I say. "I mean it. Let's make a fresh start. I've got a mate, Gary Hibbertson his name is, he runs one of the piers there. I'll get a job with him."

It's a week before she agrees.

I give Gary a call. "Give us a job, mate. I need a bit o' work."

"Anything for you, Frank," he says. "So happens I have got a vacancy. Putting the deckchairs out, keeping the place clean and tidy, that sort of thing. It's not managerial, not what you were used to with Ted Hardwick, I know, or anything like that, but it *is* a job and I need someone I can trust."

"I'll take it," I tell him. "Let me sort out somewhere to live and I'll be in touch."

'Cos I know my way around Yarmouth, getting a place is easy. Mum and Dad are pleased to see us – well, Eve, more than me and Shirl – and within a couple of months we're settled in, Eve's in a good school and Shirl gets a job. I'm not earning big money but I don't care. If everyone's happy, so am I.

* * * * *

Three months on, I'm already cheesed off with the miserable money I get paid for the hours I put in. 'Cos it's summer, I'm at it twelve hours a day, seven days a week. Gary says we have to make the most of it 'cos between

October and April, there ain't no punters, no work, no wages, no business. It's all right for him, sitting in his office, adding up his profits. But for me and the others, it's slog slog slog all day long for pay that wouldn't cover what I used to spend on a night out.

Gary says August Bank Holiday Monday is the busiest day of the year so it'll be fourteen hours, count 'em, of me picking up litter, emptying bins, clearing up where kids have been sick and then there's the condoms – who shags on Yarmouth Pier on August Bank Holiday Monday? And the hot dogs, the dog ends, the dog shit. There was a time I loved dogs. Not now.

"Frank! Over here!"

I look round. Hundreds of people are milling about. How am I supposed to see who's shouting my name?

"Frank! Frank Peters!"

I look round again. A hand's waving from the other side of the pier. I stand still when I see a figure weaving its way through the crowds.

Bloody hell, it's Melv. I ain't seen Melv for, must be six years. He's the guy who used to supply me merchandise when I ran Coventry and Nuneaton. He's the guy I met round the back of Euston and sold me the two kilos that ended up with me being arrested at Coventry Station.

He ain't changed a bit. Still the same slob he was then. Hair all over the place, Iron Maiden tee-shirt, jeans – I swear they're the same jeans he was wearing when we last met. He must be more than forty if he's a day and he still dresses like an obese juvenile headbanger.

"What are you doing here?" he says.

"Workin'," I tell him.

He edges me up a corner, behind some one-armed bandits.

"What d'ya mean 'working'?" he says.

"I'm goin' straight, enn I?"

"Don't make me laugh," he says. "You, go straight? And I'm your Aunt Fanny."

"'S true as I'm standin' 'ere."

He lowers his voice to a whisper. "Look, Frank, this town is wide open. How about it? It'll be like the old days. I'll supply and you do the business."

"I dunno, Melv. I'm out of all that now."

I watch the holiday-makers walking by. Just then, in a screaming fit, a squirt of a snot-nosed kid throws his ice cream on the floor, splatting the stuff all over the place. His slag of a mum shouts at him, clips him one and drags him away, leaving his mess for someone else to clear up. That someone else is me. All for three pound fifty pence a fucking hour.

"You're on."

* * * * *

We take Yarmouth over. Within twelve months, Melv and me have it all sewn up. Shirl and me get a beautiful town house. Oak beams running through it, on the outside and all the rest of it. Who gives a toss about Broxbourne now?

"Funny," I tell her when we move in, "how you don't complain about where the money comes from when I get you a house like this."

"Shut yer gob," she says.

I invest in the pub across the road and I get something I've always wanted: a 1964 Wurlitzer 2800 jukebox. Now I can play a hundred 45s. That's two hundred songs from the 'fifties and 'sixties with a wonderful, super big sound. The cabinet is perfect. It's the original, o' course. None o' your stuck-on imitation. Costs me a grand, including restoration. Worth every penny.

Shirl has all the clothes she wants. Tellies in the kitchen, lounge, our bedroom, Eve's bedroom. I buy Eve a piano, find her a music teacher and soon she's taking lessons. I get myself a silver Audi V8 Quattro.

Everything's good. For the first time in I don't know how long, I'm enjoying myself.

* * * * *

One of the geezers who works for me is a dealer in Yarmouth trying to develop his business. For the short time I've known him, I've found I can rely on him. Always got his eye open for an opportunity, always keen to make a deal, however big or small. "No job too small," he smirks like he's starting up a one-man plumbing business with a white van. The thing I like most about him is he's clean. Don't use the shit himself.

He's thin, five ten, got black frizzy hair and a mean pencil moustache. Wears black button-up shirts. Always got a cheroot in his mouth. Like a Mexican bandit. All he needs is the titfer. But he ain't Mexican. He's from Wales. That's why we call him Jonah. And he ain't a bandit. He's a dealer. He's Jonah the Card. "Card" for short.

I ask Melv if he wants to meet him.

"If he's good enough for you," he says, "he's good enough for me. He's your man, not mine."

This is how I work it. I buy the goods from Melv and ship them up to Yarmouth. I tell Card and the five other geezers in my team the day's prices. They distribute and sell. They return the unsold goods and takings to me, I give 'em their cut and keep the profits for myself. The more they sell, the bigger their cut, the more profit for me. Below a certain sales level, commission only.

As I'm running everything on strictly business lines, at the end of the second year, when everything's snuggled in nicely, I bring in sick pay and paid holidays. I don't do health stamps or tax, of course.

At the same time, I offer Card the position of my deputy. He's proved himself to be trustworthy, got a good head on him and I need days off just like everybody else.

"Thanks, mate," he says, shaking my hand.

"Stop calling me 'mate'," I tell him. "It's Frank or Boss, it ain't 'mate'."

"Sorry, mate."

"As I said," I say, "I ain't your mate. I never was. I'm your boss. Understand?"

"Yes, mate."

"Good," I say. "I ain't had a holiday since all this kicked off, so once you've learnt the ropes and got the hang of everything, I'll have a week off. Spend some time with Shirl and Eve."

I take him through the books, give him the spare set of keys to the lock-up and after a couple of months, I'm ready to let him operate on his own. I tell him to call me any time, day or night, if he gets a problem.

Shirl, Eve and me don't go away. Not a lot of point when we already live at the seaside. I ring Card every day to make sure everything's tickety-boo. It is. Anyway, that's what he says and who am I to argue? If I can't trust Card, who can I trust?

"Show me the books," I say when I get back.

We spend the next hour going through the figures. Everything looks okay.

"Any problems with the team?"

Card shakes his head. "Nah. Good as gold."

"Right," I say, looking at my watch. Half two. I get up. "I'm taking Eve to her piano lesson at four. Having dinner with Melv tonight – "

"Oh?" Card laughs. "Am I invited?"

"Dunno, mate," I say, picking up my jacket. "If you are, you'll already know about it."

Card shakes his head again. "So I ain't, then."

"So you ain't," I say, putting my jacket on, straightening my tie. "Right! I'm popping home for an hour with the missus. See ya tomorrow."

"See ya, mate."

Melv rang me this morning. He wants a word. Booked a table somewhere in Ipswich, about the same travelling for each of us, for seven thirty. I'll leave home about six, that'll give me enough time.

I hardly recognise Melv. He's smartened himself up. Gone are the tee-shirt and jeans. Best suit and tie. Hair cut and styled, no more the permanent seven-day stubble. The real deal. The cool business dude.

"Look at you," I say, as we shake hands.

"Yeah," he says. "I thought it was about time I acted the part. You don't get nowhere dressed like a slob with stains down your shirt."

For starters, Melv selects mackerel with salami, avocado, cucumber, crab cake, pine nut and black olives. I go for a chicken ravioli with sweet corn, leek, smoked prune, asparagus in a cep consommé.

We dive in. Delicious. I've seen the prices. It bloody well ought to be.

"How's Shirl?" Melv says. "Haven't seen her for a while. Getting on all right, is she?"

"Oh yeah. We're sorted. I got her a nice little job – "

"What's she doing?"

"Secretary to an estate agent."

"Very nice."

"We've got a lovely house. Eve's doing well at school. Piano lessons and everything. Lots o' friends. Loves living at the seaside. Yeah. All good."

Melv chews on the last of his crab cake as I finish off the consommé.

The waiter brings the main course. Halibut with smoked eel, red cabbage and a baby gem lettuce, flavoured with Worcestershire sauce for Melv. Sea bream accompanied by pearl barley paella, spinach, fennel and samphire with an olive and caper bon bon for me.

"And Simon?" I say, between mouthfuls. "Everything all right?"

"Oh yes," Melv says. "We're very happy. My make-over was his idea."

"He was right. You're a different man. Unrecognisable."

"That's what everyone says."

For dessert, we share an apple tart tatin with vanilla ice cream, elderflower, calvados jelly, and toffee doughnut. A perfect end to a perfect meal.

As we take our time over coffee, Melv lights up a Sobranie, me a Dunhill, We lean back in our seats, grinning at each other, owning the world.

"Great meal," I say. "Excellent wine. Thanks a bunch… Melv, it's always great to see you. I don't have to tell you that. But why are we here?"

"Rod Overland's retired."

"Aah," I say.

"Yeah… So how about it?"

"Interesting," I nod, drawing on my fag, feeling very wise. "Retired, eh?"

"Yes."

I look up. "Who the fuck's Rod Overland?"

"He runs Southend… Well, he did."

"Did?"

"Essex Police are sponsoring his accommodation at their Brixton estate."

"Unfortunate."

"For him, maybe," Melv says. "But not for us. How'd you like to take over Southend? You've done a good job in Yarmouth, you've now got Ticket – "

"Card."

" – whoever – running things for you. Why not move down to Southend and take over the business there? Then maybe once a week, for the time being at any rate, monitor Card until we're confident he can run Yarmouth without your valuable input?"

"So what's the set-up in Southend now?"

"Everything's still in place," Melv says, lighting another Sobranie. "Just needs someone to head it up."

* * * * *

"Cannae stay in one place for more 'n five minutes, can ye?" Shirl barks at me when I tell her we're moving.

"I go where the money is," I tell her.

"This lovely hoose," she says.

"I'll get you another."

"And *ma* job? Ah love ma job."

"I'll get you another."

"And Eve?"

"She'll get used to it. She always does."

"That's nae the point!" she gasps. "She shouldnae have tae. She's very happy here."

But Card *is* happy.

"It's a great opportunity for you," I tell him.

"Thanks."

"Don't let me down."

"I won't. Thanks."

"Until you get on your feet, I'll come up every Friday and look things over. You can always ring me, any time, day or night."

"Thanks."

"And you can stop thanking me. You've earned it."

"Thanks."

Shirl, Eve and me move down to Southend into a comfortable flat. Shirl gets a job in a florist's, which she loves the minute she starts, we find Eve a good school and soon everything's rolling along very nicely indeed, thank you very much.

Soon, it's clear to me that Rod Overland has let the business slip, his men didn't think much of him and he wasn't getting the best prices for the merchandise. It takes a couple of months to sort it out.

Meanwhile, I'm going up to Yarmouth once a week to spend a day with Card, check things out, make sure he's keeping up to scratch, searching out new business opportunities, looking after his team. They tell me he's all right. So everything's going fine.

One day, I'm up in Yarmouth, scanning the ledger.

"What's this, Card?"

"What's what, Frank?"

"Saturday, you show a quarter of a kilo going out, none coming back in."

"Yeah."

"But the return's five hundred less than it should be."

"Can't be."

"Just here," I say. "Sunday's the same." I scan the rest

of the week. "The same Monday, Tuesday, Wednesday and yesterday." I tot up the figures. "You're three thousand short for the week." I look him in the eye. "What's going on?"

"Nothing's going on," Card says, stroking his moustache, fiddling with his shirt.

I stare at him, say nothing, wait. Something's going off and I wanna know what it is. If I keep quiet, he'll give it up. He sits there, sweat starting to creep on to his forehead. He don't say a word. I don't say a word. I've got all day. He ain't.

"If you don't tell me, Card," I say, "I'll think the worst."

He lights a cheroot, takes a drag, watches the smoke disappear. "I'm operating a little side line."

"You're fiddling the books."

"I'm stacking up my pension fund."

"You're selling Melv short."

"I'm using a double-entry system."

"Okay." I let out a huge sigh. "Whatever you say." I stand up. "It's clear you don't need me no longer." I put on my jacket. "So this is the last Friday I'll be up. You're on your own from now on."

"Thanks for everything, Frank," he says, also standing up. "I couldn't a done it without ya."

He stretches out his hand for me to shake. I ignore it.

"I've known Melv a long time," I say, going to the door. "He's a great guy, one of the best." I turn. "But if you fuck him about – "

"I'm not. Honest."

" – he'll find out," I tell him. "Don't fuck him about. He'll send his boys down and blow your brains out."

A month or so later, Card calls me. "Boss – "

Boss?

" – I need your help."

"Wassup?"

"They paid me a visit," he says. "You gotta help me put it right."

"What happened?"

"They found out, didn't they?"

"I dunno. Did they?"

"Someone grassed."

"It weren't me," I tell him.

"Course it weren't you. But how did they find out?"

"Dunno, mate," I say. "But I told you, didn't I? I told you. What they do?"

"They broke one o' my legs and one o' my arms. I'm in hospital and the Old Bill's sniffing about. You gotta help me, Boss."

"Tough shit, *mate.*"

* * * * *

"Get out!"

"At least let me get dressed first."

"Your choice," I say. "Either get out now or stay and get dressed while I smash your face in. What's it to be?"

He scrambles off the bed, picks up his clothes and stumbles out. Feet thump downstairs, then silence and, a few minutes later, the front door opens and slams shut. A motor door opens, closes, an engine starts up and the motor speeds off.

Shirl says, "That was – "

"I don't give a fuck who he is!" I shout. "And cover yourself up, for Chrissake."

She doesn't. Instead, she leans over to the bedside cabinet, takes a sip of wine and lights up a Rothmans.

"Of all places, Shirl," I say. "*Our bed.*"

"Aye, ah may as well use it," she says between drags. "*We* never dae."

"After all I've done for you."

"Nae for me, Frank. For yerself, ye mean."

"You've never had to ask for nothing. What have I ever done to you?"

She snorts, "Sod all. Aye, that's the problem. You smother me wi' things, money, drugs, time inside and

292

never, nae once, have ye ever said – " She stops. Now the stupid tart's blubbing.

"How long has this been going on?" I say.

She thinks blubbing's gonna solve things. Well, it won't. That's what women do when they can't get their own way. Blub, cry, flood the place with crocodile tears. By now, you'd think we'd be used to it but we fall for it every time. But not this time.

"Him?" she managed to get out. "That was our first time."

"And before him?"

"Why have ye – "

"How many before him?"

" – never said – "

"How many?"

" – you loved me?"

"You don't know, do ya?"

* * * * *

Eve's gone away for the weekend on a course for piano-players. I spend that night dossing on the settee downstairs. Next morning, Saturday, I'm up early, out the house before Shirl's awake, take a long walk, get breakfast at one o' them cafés along the Esplanade, carry on walking.

I'm gonna leave her, of course. I knew that as soon as I woke up. We've been through all this before. When we was in Coventry. But this time, it's different. This time, it's for good.

After all I've done for her. Dragged her out of that swamp of an estate. Gave her a lovely home, a beautiful daughter. Kept her well provided for. The bint never had to want for anything.

And what does she do? Stabs me in the leg, disrespects me whenever she can, sleeps around, a whore in a French knocking-shop, not giving a toss whether I know about it or not. I see that now. I'm angry I never saw it before.

293

But I've never been one for getting emotional about things and I'm not gonna start now. Practical, Peters, you've always been good at practical. So do what you have to do. Eve is the important person now, it's her you've gotta provide for. She's all that matters. You don't matter. Shirl don't matter a flea's sneeze. Only Eve matters.

Eve, my beautiful, beautiful daughter.

I stop and look around. I've walked all the way to Westcliff.

I pull out my phone. "Melv, I have to see you... No, mate, I'll drive down now, if that's all right. See you in a couple of hours."

I get a taxi home, don't go into the house, get straight into the motor and soon I'm at Melv's. I tell him I'm leaving the business, nothing he can do about it, it's over, everything is over. Without Shirl, without Eve, I'm finished, exhausted, done, all in, no point to anything any more. He takes me for a drink and tries to talk me out of it. But it's no use. Ever since I met Shirl, everything I've ever done has been for her and Eve.

"The worst thing about it," I say, "what hurts the most, Melv, is the bloke I caught her with was half my age. A boy."

"C'm' on, Frank," he says. "You'll get back together again. Give it time."

"You shoulda seen him, Melv. Built like a Russian gymnast." I stare into my beer. "Like I used to be. And look at me now."

"You're not that bad," he says. "For your age."

"Yeah... That sums it up, don't it? For my age. She's chucked me on the scrapheap, Melv."

I finish off my pint. "If that's how she wants it, then stuff her." I stand up and hold out my hand. "Thanks for everything, Melv." We shake. "Really appreciate it. I'll ring you Monday. Arrange a time to bring the books and merchandise down."

Back in Southend, I book into a B&B. It's not much but

it'll do until I find somewhere permanent. I spend the evening in the local boozer. The Robin Hood.

Sunday, I ring a few mates, see if they know of anywhere, walk around town trying to make plans – failing – spend the afternoon and evening in the Robin Hood, get back to the B&B pissed out my head, fall on the bed, wake up Monday morning.

No-one's home. Shirl's at work, Eve's at school. I shower, put on some clean clothes, pack a couple of suitcases with as many clothes as'll go in. I drive to the lock-up for Melv's merchandise and the books.

Next, the bank. I draw out every penny. Four grand. I thought I had more than that. No idea where it's gone. Must a spent it. Close the account. All the direct debits, everything, cancelled. Of course, they want to know why I'm doing it so I tell 'em I'm going abroad and not coming back. They start jabbering about how I can transfer my account to a bank where I'm going but... You know what? I can't be arsed. I walk out while they're still yacking. Fuck the lot of 'em.

On the way back to the motor, I pop into Tesco for a six-pack and a handful of them plastic carrier bags.

"Frank?"

I turn around, look about.

"Frank Peters?"

At the end of the aisle is a middle-aged bloke, my age, a mop of black hair, jeans, white tee-shirt, empty carrier bag in one hand, empty wire basket in the other. He comes towards me.

"It *is* Frank Peters, innit?"

"Yeah?"

"Don't you recognise me?" he says. "Charlie Milliken. John Warner's School? Remember?"

I look him up and down. "Course I remember," I laugh. "We broke into the tuck shop." I look him up and down again. "You were tall then. You're not tall now. What happened?"

"I stopped growing," he shrugs. "Everyone else caught

up."

We shake hands.

"So how come," I say, reaching for a six-pack, "you're in Southend? What you up to?"

"How about," he says, "we go for a drink? Talk over old times."

Turns out Charlie came home one day and found his wife in bed with a bloke half his age.

"What is it with women?" he says. "Why can't they be happy with what they got?"

"Tell me about it. So you're on your own now?"

"Yeah," he says. "And I don't like it, Frank."

"Charlie," I say, "you could be talking about me."

He tells me about wheeling and dealing with dodgy goods and ending up in Pentonville on a one.

"Now I'm getting by, Frank. That's about all." He takes a long drink. "That's about all... But what about you? What you bin up to?"

I tell him about Shirl and Eve, about what happened over the weekend, the bloke half my age, closing down my business – I don't go into details – and how I'm looking for a place to live. "So if you know of anywhere. "

"Funny you should say that," he says. "As it happens, I do. Mr Tring, he's my landlord, he's got a real big house he's divided up into flats, well, rooms, more like, you know the sort o' thing. I know he's got one left he's trying to fill. Shall I give him a call?"

A couple of hours later, we're round there with Mr Tring and I've paid a deposit and a month's rent in advance. I move in straightaway. It ain't much. A bed, a table, two chairs and the rest of it, but it's a room, it's mine and I'm safe. That's all I'm after at the moment. Safe and on my own.

When at last I *am* on my own, I sort out the cash. Three and a half grand to Shirl to look after Eve, the other five ton for me. I don't need much and Eve's the most important person in my life from now own. She gets everything I can give her. I write a letter to Shirl, another to Eve, put them and the notes in one of the Tesco bags.

Then I call Melv and fix a time tomorrow for me to deliver the books and merchandise. I don't keep any back. Melv knows how much is coming to him and I don't diddle him. No point. Look what happened to Card. Besides, Melv's been good to me and I never know if I'm gonna need him again.

I go to the B&B, get my stuff, check out. Then to Shirl's, shove the bag, the letters and my front-door key through the letter-box. I drive off before she's got time to work out who's there. Back to my new room to unpack my gear, set myself up. By now, it's getting on for eight in the evening and I'm hungry and thirsty so go to the Robin Hood for pie, chips and a couple or three or so pints.

Next night, after seeing Melv, I'm back in the Robin Hood.

I spend the night and next day sleeping the last few days off, then back on the beer.

Next day, Charlie calls round to see how I'm getting on so we go to the pub and talk about our school days until we can't talk no more and he's so pissed at the end of it he can't get home so he crashes in my room. The next day, we do it all over again. And the next. And the next.

And the next.

"You know what?" he says, after a week. "We can't go on like this."

"No, we can't."

"No," he says. "That chair's bloody uncomfortable. I've got a flat. You're coming home with me. I've got a spare room. You can share my flat. 'S easier to get pissed and crash out there. The pub's nearer. You can help with the bills."

We pack up my stuff and I move in. There's still two weeks' rent left on the room but Mr Tring says he's keeping the deposit as well because I'm moving in with Charlie. I don't understand that and neither does Charlie but I don't argue 'cos here I am, sharing a flat with an old mate, neither of us giving a fuck about anything except getting plastered.

* * * * *

When you're paying rent, paying bills, buying food, shoving coins into the laundrette, spending twelve to fifteen quid a night on the sauce, the money don't go far. So sometimes Charlie and me go round to other blokes' places to drink. We take some cans but the more people who turn up, the more beer there is to get my hands on.

The first two or three times we do this, it's only blokes dossing about, throwing back the beer and talking about, well, whatever it is blokes talk about when they doss about boozing. Always, afterwards, I can't remember nothing.

One time, though, we're in some flat, God knows where, when some woman wanders in.

"Is this where a lady can get a good time?" she sings, waving a bottle of vodka in the air. Some lady.

"Come and sit with me," someone drawls, "and we'll party."

She picks her way through lolling legs, cans, bottles and wandering hands and throws herself on to his lap.

She's gotta be in her forties, with frizzy black hair and wearing a black dress and black necklace she must've got from a charity shop. She looks like the owner of a Spanish tapas bar. She unscrews the top off the vodka bottle, grabs a glass off the coffee-table and pours, throws it back.

"Ooh!" she drools. "That's better." She pours another. "And what's your name, honey?" she whispers to the fella she's sitting on.

"Jude."

"Oh!" she squeals. "That's my name."

"What? Jude?" he says, suddenly alarmed. "You ain't a bloke, are ya?"

"No," she giggles. "Don't be daft!" She shakes her boobs. "Do you think these are fake? No, Jude. I'm Judy. Give us a kiss." She slaps her lips on his and gives his mouth a good seeing to.

On and off, they're at it for the best part of an hour. The rest of us carry on as if they're not there. We drink a lot, smoke a lot. Someone hands some puff around. Don't talk much, though. Why should we? We're here to drink and get zonked off our heads.

By four in the morning, we're out of booze, the fella passing around the puff is flat out face down on the kitchen floor, Jude and Judy have disappeared somewhere and everyone else is dossing about wherever they can find somewhere to settle. One bloke thinks another bloke is an armchair and is perched on top of him, snoring away like a puffin' billy. Before long, I'm curled up in an armchair, fast asleep.

It's getting on for eleven when I wake. I'm busting for a pee. My mouth's like a rhinoceros's arse. Some of last night's party animals are moving about in slow motion. Others are still crashed out. The bloke who was perched on the other is now splayed face-up across the floor, his shirt covering his head, his trousers soaked. I go to the bathroom. Some guy's asleep in the bath with the shower on, drenching him. I think about switching it off but, as he don't seemed bothered, I leave it.

After I've pissed away the night, I go into the kitchen. It's a battlefield of empty bottles, broken glasses, used mugs, half-eaten pizzas. The blocked sink is a sea of red, green and yellow vomit. The fella who passed around the puff is still flat out face down on the floor.

I stand in the doorway and look around. Is what I see me? A washed-up alky who keeps company with the likes of this? Tarts who'll fuck anything that's got a pulse. Piss-soaked bodies who can't control their functions or their clothes. More bodies who can't tell the difference between a human being and a piece of furniture, between a bath and a bed, keeping dry and a running shower. Kitchens that make the insides of a pig's stomach look like a gourmet meal. Is this what I've become?

It takes me about fifteen minutes to get my jacket. Once I've found it, that is. And no wonder. Charlie, fast asleep in his Y-fronts on the bed, no sign of his clothes anywhere, is lying on it. I have to roll the fat lummox over before I can get to it. But every time I push him to one side, he rolls back, dribbling down his chin, trapping my hands. In the end, who gives a fuck, I push him so hard he rolls off the bed, lands with an almighty thump on the floor. "Clap hands, here comes Charlie," he shouts in his sleep.

I get out, make my way to The Lovin' Spoonful, a café a couple of streets away. I go there a lot. What's good about it is they don't mind how long you stay, even if you buy only one cuppa – and the staff are friendly. They talk to you, take an interest. It's a good name, The Lovin' Spoonful, 'cos that's what it is. Melody and Sandy are on duty today.

Sandy comes over. "You look like you need a strong black coffee."

I don't look up. "Please."

She goes and gets it. "You all right?"

"Yeah… Course I am… Not really, no. Oh, God." I bury my face in my hands. I think I'm gonna cry. Me, a grown man, about to blub his eyes out in front of a woman. I don't do that. And I don't do it in public.

"What's wrong, Frank?" she says, sitting down opposite me. "Tell me."

I look at her. Although I've seen her many times before, and talked to her, this is the first time I've looked at her proper.

She's not my type at all. I've always gone for birds taller than me, with hair draping over their shoulders and clothes you'd only find in a high-end boutique. This one's different. About my age. About my height, so on the short side. Cropped auburn hair, jeans, plain blue shirt, a blue tabard with "The Lovin' Spoonful" across it.

We spend the afternoon talking. Sometimes she gets up and serves other customers. But she always comes back and sits with me again.

For me, nobody else is in the place. It's just Sandy and me. I talk and talk like I've never talked before. Once I start, I can't stop. Sandy listens like nobody's ever listened to me before. When I think about it, nobody ever has. Why has nobody ever listened to me? That's all I've ever wanted. Someone to listen to me. Ain't that all anyone ever wants?

I tell her about the important people in my life. Dad. Harry Whetstone. Grandpa Wilf. Steve Bartram and his brothers who beat me up. Bobby Crick. Evan Phillips... Tim and the judo classes.

Nobody bothers us. Nobody comes near.

Finally, she reaches out and squeezes my hands, ever so gentle.

I let her see me shed a few tears. And I'm not ashamed.

* * * * *

Sandy and me meet a couple of times after that. I've really taken to her and I think she has to me. She's lovely. It's nothing regular. I've got more important things on my mind. The five ton I kept back from giving to Shirl for Eve don't last long once I've paid a couple of months' rent and got some food in.

I reckon the only way to get beer is to nick it. I've thieved a lot in my life but I've never walked into a shop, picked a case of beer up and walked out without paying. Never stooped to shop-lifting.

Now I'm stooping.

I don't go in the same shop two days running. With at least sixty shops in Southend selling booze, I count 'em, I can by my reckoning do one a day for two months without going in the same place twice. O' course, some of 'em are a long way from home, so even if I don't use them, I can still go in each one only once a month. I walk into a shop, pick up a case of beer, put it on my shoulder and walk out without a dickey-bird.

Easy.

When I fancy a change, I nick one o' them boxes of sherry with taps at the bottom. They can hold up to eight pints. If I'm careful, they last as much as a day.

One day, Charlie and me have a row about me not paying my share of the bills so off I go again, nick some beer and go down to Southend sea front. I loll about on a hill overlooking the casino, knocking it back, chain-smoking my way through a new pack of twenty.

Some drinkers come out of a bar.

One of 'em says, "Do you wanna come back with us for a few drinks?"

I follow them wherever they go, into some house, God knows where, throw down my throat whatever they're having, then another house, nick some when we get short, sleep wherever I am at the time.

I get back to the flat.

Charlie says, "Where you bin?"

"No idea."

"You've been gone three weeks."

"Oh yeah?"

"Who've you been with?"

"No idea."

"Sandy's looking for you."

"Fuck off."

* * * * *

"What do you think you're doing?"

"If you don't fuck off, I'll break your fucking jaw. Now fuck off."

"You're stealing beer from my shop!"

"And what you gonna do about it?"

"I'm calling the police, that's what I'm gonna do about it."

* * * * *

"Francis Wilfred Peters, you have pleaded guilty to shoplifting, common assault and being drunk and disorderly in a public place. You are sentenced to six months' imprisonment."

* * * * *

"Look at you."

I open my eyes and stare up. Sandy's standing over me, hands on hips. She ain't pleased.

"Just look at you," she says.

"Leave me alone," I slur, saliva and sick dribbling down my chin.

"Frank," she says, "it's eight in the morning and you're shaking. C'm' on."

She crouches down, grabs my arm and pulls me up. I can hardly stand. She props me up against the wall and, while she's picking up a plastic carrier bag, I start to slide down.

"Oh no, you don't," she says, pushing me back up. She opens a can of beer. "Drink this." She pulls my head back and pours the stuff down my throat. "There y'are, that'll stop the shakes."

I have a good glug. "I need to pee."

"Over there, in the corner," she says, pointing to a pile of old newspapers, empty cans, mouldy half-eaten pizzas and a dead rat.

After I've finished, she says, "What you doin' here?"

I shake my head.

"This is a squat, Frank. It's for drug addicts and homeless drunks. You're worth better than this."

"I'm not," I say. "This is where I belong."

"Bollocks."

I'm shocked. It's the first time I've heard Sandy swear. "What did you say?"

"I said, 'Bollocks'," she snaps. "No-one belongs in this filth. Didn't they teach you anything in Chelmsford Prison?"

"Only that, when I'm not inside, I'm a worthless pile of shit." I look at her. "Do you know, while I was in there, I saved a man's life?"

303

"And out here, you can't even find a safe place to sleep. I'm taking you down to the sea front for a meal. It's about time I sorted you out."

I stare at her long and hard. "Why are you doin' this?"

* * * * *

After that, when Sandy isn't at work, she don't let me out of her sight. She thinks I'm worth saving. She's the only one who does. A chronic alcoholic with a prison record as long as your arm? I wouldn't bother. She does.

She comes round on her way to work at seven in the morning and finds I've crashed out in an armchair instead of going to bed and have already been drinking two hours. When she gets home at five o'clock, she comes round, Charlie lets her in and finds me asleep in front of *Blue Peter*.

"Leave me alone, why don't ya?"

But she doesn't.

This goes on for a couple of months.

In the end, I say, "You ain't gonna let go, are ya?"

"No."

"We can't go on like this."

She smiles. "You mean you can't go on like this."

"How about we get a place together?"

"For a start, Frank," she says, "we ain't go no money."

In my book, that's a yes. Then it hits me. She likes me. She actually likes me. She likes me for me, not for what I can give her or do for her, not for who I know or who knows me. But for me. Despite everything, she likes this sad, drunk shoplifter. Why didn't I see it before?

"If I get some money," I say, "then how about it?"

"On one condition."

I knew it. I knew there'd be a catch. There always is.

"Come on, then," I sigh. "What?"

"We go to the doctor's," she says, "and get you into rehab."

So that's what we do.

304

Mr Tring's got an empty flat a couple of streets away from where me and Charlie are living. He says I can give that address to the Social if they help out with the deposit, some furniture, bedding and the rest of it. The Social coughs up nearly two grand and we move in.

Sandy comes with me to the doctor's and he gets me into a month's rehab. All the weirdos and crackpots in there show me what I've become, which makes it easier for me to dry out.

When I get home, I realise where Sandy and me are living is a dump. I ring round a few mates and, just when I'm giving up, Roy, a bloke who used to go around with my dad, says he's got a town house in Rochford that's standing empty.

"I'd rather let it at a discount," he says, "than watch it fall apart. It's been empty for at least two years."

"I'll look after it," I tell him.

"Too right you will," he says. "You'll treat it like it's Buckingham Palace."

"Course I will," I say. "You know me."

"No, I don't," he says. "But I know your dad. That's good enough for me."

* * * * *

A couple of months after we've moved in, I get a call from Judy Munrow.

"How'd you get my number?" I say. I'd decided to lie low for a while. I don't want the world and his wife knowing where I am.

"Tomorrow night's party party party time," Judy sings down the phone. "I want you and Sandy to come along and say goodbye."

"What?" I say. "We're not splittin' up."

"Not you, you berk," she cackles. "Me! I'm off to Spain in a couple of weeks. I'm holding a bon voyage party to say goodbye to all my nearest and dearest friends."

I've only met the woman once and she puts me down as one of her nearest and dearest. How does she treat those who are actually her nearest and dearest?

Anyway, as me and Sandy have had it hard over the last year, I reckon it'll be nice to have a night out, meet a few people.

We have a lovely time.

Judy's very keen to get to know me. "I've heard all about you," she chuckles.

"Very nice," I say. "Good for you."

The best bit is when Sandy and me are driving home.

She says, "I'm really proud of you, Frank. You didn't argue, you didn't threaten anyone, you didn't lose it. Best of all, you kept off the booze."

And you know what, she's right.

"You did that," I tell her, "not me."

What a lady.

* * * * *

A couple of months later, while Sandy's out getting the weekly shop, my phone rings.

"*¡Hola!*"

"What?"

"*¡Hola!*"

"Who is this?"

"Frank! It's me!" a woman's voice screeches right into my lughole. "Judy!"

"Judy who?"

"Judy Munrow, you *idiota*," she chortles.

"Oh, Judy!" I laugh. "How're you settling in?"

"*Muy bien, muy bien* indeed, *gracias*," she says. "Yourself?"

"Muddling along," I say, finishing off a can, belching, opening another. "You know how it is."

"Listen to me, Frank Peters," she says. "I want you to come over to Spain. There's business out here for cocaine and whatever. I'll introduce you to some people I've met.

Then you can sort something out about having it shipped to London."

"Nah," I tell her. "I don't do that now."

"Don't be daft. Anyway, from what I hear, you're struggling. You need the dough."

"Where d'you hear that?" I say. "Who's bin talking?"

"There's thousands to be made," she says.

"I dunno."

"Come over. Have a look. We'll set up in business together."

"Why don't you do it on your own?"

"I haven't got the London connections," she says. "You have."

"I'm not sure."

"Frank, this is right up your street."

"Sandy wouldn't like it."

"Who's Sandy?"

"You remember Sandy. She's my – "

"Oops, gotta go. Rodrigo's here. Call you in a couple of days. *Hasta la vista,* baby."

Chapter 15. Spain

I've looked at a map. Murcia. South-east Spain. Judy's villa's near the country club and it's bloody amazing. I've never seen anything like it. You come off the street straight into a garden full of palm trees and, here we are in the middle of June, sun blazing down, and flowers are bursting out all over the place. Reds, blues, oranges, purples, yellows. Can't move for 'em. Don't ask me what they are. I ain't got a clue. Buttercups and daisies, that's my lot.

She takes me into the bungalow. Not the sort of bungalow you find in Gravesend, Hornchurch, anywhere like that. This ain't a bungalow like I know bungalows. Well, it ain't a bungalow, is it? It's a villa.

We go through a small hallway into the living-room, which is the size of the ground floor of where Sandy and me live. You could put our place into this living-room and lose it, it's that big. Three big brown leather sofas, four brown leather armchairs, tables, flowers, dishes of fruit. Oil paintings on the walls. The works.

The fitted kitchen, just as big. Two sinks, dishwasher, two fridges, three freezers. Who needs three freezers? What can you do with three freezers that you can't do with one?

Three bedrooms with double beds and built-in wardrobes you could get single beds in.

The bathroom's got a bath the size of a small swimming-pool, the shower you can get a football team in, still have room for the ref and his linesmen and, if it's Romford playing at home, the crowd as well.

Every room has white walls, floors with brown tiles and rugs, shutters on the windows.

Steps outside lead up to a knock-out roof garden and down to a swimming-pool as big as the living-room and the kitchen.

This girl's doing all right for herself. She's got it

together. Got the connections. Does know what she's talkin' about, after all. I mean, look at the place. I thought she was talking a load of old bollocks about the drugs. Just goes to show, don't it?

"Great place you got here, Judy," I say, falling on to one of the sofas, making myself comfy.

"It is nice, isn't it?" she says, smiling as she flumps down next to me. She pulls herself up close.

"Let's get one thing clear, shall we," I say, "before we go on."

"And what's that, honeybunch?"

"I'm here on business," I tell her, drawing away. "I've got Sandy back home and we're doing all right. I'm not playing away while I'm out here. This is business. That's all. Business. Understood?"

She laughs. Like she don't mean it, though. The sort o' laughing someone laughs when they know they've got it wrong and they're trying to pretend they haven't. "Yes, yes, yes. Of course, sweetheart. Business." She gets up and brushes herself down. "Of course."

"As long as we've got that settled."

"Business." She coughs. "Right! Shall we go?"

"Go? Where?"

"Home, of course," she says. "Where did you think?"

"But – "

"But what?"

"I thought – "

"You think I live here?" *Now* she laughs like she means it. "Christ, no. You think I can afford a place like this? You think I've got a million quid to throw away? You think I'd get you over here if I had that sort of money?"

"So what we doing here?"

"This belongs – " she says, waving her hands in the air.

"How come you've got a key?"

" – to some senile bloke me and Johnny are thinking of doing over. The oil paintings are originals. Look at 'em! Must be worth a fortune. And he's got a safe stashed full o' banknotes and his dead wife's jewellery."

309

"And who's Johnny when he's at home?"

"My son," she trills. "And that's exactly where he is this very moment. At home. Waiting for us. Didn't I tell you?"

"No," I snap, getting up. "You didn't."

"Oh." She sounds disappointed. 'Though I'm sure she ain't one bit of it. "I'm sure I did. Yes, well, anyway. Johnny's my partner in crime. We do absolutely everything together."

"Everything?"

She giggles. "Almost everything."

Judy's place, on the outskirts of Murcia, is a broken down shack. That's the only word for it. Shack. The front door's scratched and the paint's peeling off. The windows are so black you can't see through them. The curtains are scraps of material she must've got off a rubbish tip somewhere. The furniture – I wouldn't dump it in that doss house I was staying in when I met Sandy.

And if all that weren't bad enough, eleven barking and yelping dogs are wandering around the place free-rein as if they've booked into a mutts' holiday camp. The last time I saw so many dogs like this together was when I worked at Sean Underwood's scrapyard. But Magnum and Candy were under control, they did what I said. This load of scruffy, smelly, slobbering, underfed mongrels are out of control.

"Fuck these dogs running about," I say.

"Nah, nah, nah," she sings. "They're all right."

"Believe me," I tell her. "I know dogs. One attacks, they all attack. Where's Johnny?"

"Out for the day," she says, tickling one of the dog's ears.

"You said he'd be here."

"I'll show you to your room."

"No, thanks," I say. "I'll find somewhere."

There's a *pension* at the end of the street. It ain't the Ritz but it's cheap, clean and light and they provide food. It'll do me. I'm only here for a few days and it's better than bunking down in Judy's shithole of a place and catching mangy fleas.

That evening, my first in Spain, we go to a bar. Johnny turns up from somewhere, dressed as if he's slept in his car. He's about twenty-eight, stocky, short auburn hair, wears a silver neck chain and a shirt someone's made from a deckchair that's on the run from Dartmoor.

"Nah, then." He snarls like a bronchitic bloodhound – maybe it's him that's escaped from Dartmoor and the shirt tagged along. "Nah then, I've fixed us up to meet The Man tomorrow." He pulls on his fag and squints his eyes at me. "*El Hombre*."

"Paul Newman, is he?" I say.

"Course he ain't Paul fuckin' Newman," he sneers. "Are you some sort of clown? We meet at noon."

"Oh! So it's Gary Cooper."

Johnny looks away and then back at me. "Jesus H Christ. No, it ain't fuckin' Gary fuckin' Cooper, either. I'll pick you up at ten."

"Two hours? Where we going?"

"Come on, boys!" Judy calls from the other side. "Stop talking shop. We're supposed to be celebrating."

"Celebrating what?" I ask as she comes over.

She chinks her empty glass against mine. "Our new partnership, of course."

"Yeah, well," I say, "let's see what tomorrow brings, shall we, before we start toasting to anything."

"And again," she says, handing her glass to Johnny without looking at him. "This time tomorrow, we'll be in the money. D'ya wanna see my tits?"

"No, thanks."

"There!" she says, smiling broadly, throwing her head back and lifting her sweater up, her tits flopping out. "Get a load o' that!"

She does a twirl so everyone in the bar can see. A big cheer and a round of applause erupt. Someone shouts, "Wahey!" Someone else, "Nice one, Judy!" Someone else sings "I've got a luvverly bunch of coconuts." As quick as

311

the hubbub rises, it dies and everyone goes back to what they were doing.

They're not even good tits. They're a couple of punctured off-colour footballs. A woman her age shouldn't be doing this. She should have more self-respect. You wouldn't catch my Sandy doing that.

"Judy," I shout, "behave yourself, will ya?"

"Oh, Frankie baby," she laughs, punching me in the gut, "don't be such a prude. It's all good fun, ain't it, Johnny?"

"'Ere," he says, handing her a glass of cheap white wine, pulling her sweater down.

True to his word, ten next morning, Johnny's outside the *pension*.

We leave Murcia pretty quick and then it's straight out into the wilderness. First, it's trees. Then it's a tree. Then it's no trees. Then it's flat scrubland with tumbleweed. Any minute, I expect Clint Eastwood and his smokin' cheroot to come out from behind a giant cactus, guns drawn, ready to mow us down.

'Cept there ain't no giant cactus. Not even a little cactus. We speed through villages whose names I don't know and, even if I do, don't know how to pronounce. Cats lyin' about. Women in black dresses stumblin' around with baskets full o' fruit and veg. Old men sittin' on wooden seats, starin' into the air, smokin' pipes, watchin' us zoom past.

Even though it's, what, gone eleven o'clock, it's hot. "Hot" ain't the word. Blistering. I loosen my shirt, take a glug from my bottle of water.

Johnny's a good, careful driver, knows his way. It takes exactly two hours. For all of that time, he don't say a word. Neither do I. There's not much to say. When you're driving across – a desert, I s'pose you'd call it – you don't feel like talking.

It's August, 2002. Next month, I'll be 49 years old. I'm with some bloke I met yesterday, driving across a Spanish sierra, goin' to see if I'm gonna buy merchandise from another bloke who probably don't even speak English and *then* go into partnership with an over-the-hill tart who flashes her tits at a bar full of drunks.

I'm humming the music from *The Good, the Bad and the Ugly*.

Duddle-uddle-uuuh wah-wah-wah –

Okay, so we're not in Italy. Or Mexico. We're in Spain. But it's the same thing as far as I'm concerned.

Duddle-uddle-uuuh –

We come to another village. Looks to me like all the others we've bin through. White houses, red roof tiles, front porches, lazy cats, yellow sun, nothin' movin'.

Johnny slows down.

"Are we here?" I say.

"Down the high street a bit," he says.

High street. *There's only one street.* To have a "high street", you gotta have other streets. But there's no other streets. Just the one. "The High Street."

Johnny stops the car and points to a sign. "See?"

Calle Sancho Panza.

"Is that the Spanish for 'high street'?" I ask him.

"Does it look like it?" he sneers.

"I dunno, do I? How do I know?"

"It's Spanish for 'Sancho Panza Street'."

"Why's it called that?"

"Because," he sneers again, like I'm an idiot, "we're in La Mancha."

I've no idea what he's talkin' about. I don't ask. He's got me marked as a turnip. No point giving him more ammo.

We coast along the high street – or not the high street, along Sancho whatever it is – until we reach a guy sitting on a chair outside a white-walled bungalow. This is definitely a bungalow. Not a villa.

He's wearing a blue cap, a blue-and-white check shirt and jeans. Open sandals on his feet. And he's holding a rifle across his chest. Like you do.

Johnny pulls up and gets out. "Wait here."

He goes over, they chat for a minute or so and then Johnny waves me over.

We go in.

It's dark in here. Like they haven't got any lights they can switch on. Maybe they don't want anyone from the road seeing what they've got. After a few seconds of getting used to it, I see a room at the back with a door made of iron bars, like them jails you see in old westerns with the giant metal square keyhole at the side. I go up to it and squint through.

Stacks, I mean *stacks*, of cocaine, puff, heroin and whatever else are packed everywhere. In the middle, sitting on a chair is another guy with another rifle, a bullet belt strapped over his shoulder and round his chest and, on his head, one of those enormous black hats. He looks like a Mexican bandit, straight out of them B films we used to see at Saturday morning pictures. He can't be for real.

But he is. He reaches over, picks up a small poly bag and, smiling, passes it through the bars. I say, "*Muchas gracias.*" I've learnt that much since I've been here.

I take the bag, open it, try the sample. It's the real stuff, all right. Probably some of the best cocaine I've ever come across.

Then he's jabbering away, sixteen to the dozen, in Spanish. I've no idea what he's on about. I look at Johnny.

"He's giving you the prices."

"Oh yeah," I say. "Right."

The fella who brought us in hands me a sheet of paper.

"Price list," Johnny says. "Delivery charges, lead times."

"Oh yeah. Course," I say. "*Muchas gracias.*"

"Any questions?" Johnny says.

I'm trying to read the price list but it's impossible in this dark. "No. I've got what I want. Tell him I'll, er… Ask him how I get in touch with him to do a deal."

Johnny and the two men are jabbering away again. Seems to me they get very excited, voices raised, fingers and hands waving all over the place, the guy behind the bars stands up, stamps his feet. And as suddenly as they started, they stop, smile at me and nod a lot. The guy behind the bars hands me a scrap of paper.

"That's their number," Johnny says. "They change it every month. If you don't use it within the month, you'll have to come here and start again."

I nod and smile, though I've no idea if they can see my face in the dark, put the price list and the phone number in my pocket, get out into the sunlight and light a fag. Johnny stays for another excited chat and then comes out with the guy who showed us in.

"Come on," he says to me. "Let's go."

We get into the car, he starts it up, leans out the window and shouts "*¡Adios!*"

The fella waves back. "*¡Adios!*" He steps forward, comes round to my side. "*Hasta la vista.*" And then something else.

Johnny says, "He says he hopes to see you again."

"Oh yeah," I say, nodding. "*Muchas gracias.*"

"You say," Johnny says, "*Y espero verte de nuevo.*"

I look at the guy. "What he said."

Driving back, Johnny and me don't say a word.

I study the price list. Which is written in English. Which means, I'm supposing, those guys back there spoke English all along. Which also means I don't know if I can trust them enough to do a deal.

Besides, I can't set this up all on my own. I'll have to get back to England, get in touch with Melv, see if he's interested in coming in with me. My mind's going through all the arrangements we'd have to make. I mean, it's not as if where we've just been is on the coast. It's slap bang in the middle of nowhere.

After a while, I stare at the scrap of paper with the phone number. Untraceable mobile, of course. They probably change the phone as well as the number every month. I know I would.

"Everything all right?" Johnny says.

"Yeah," I say.

"We'll go out tonight," he says. "Have a good meal, a few drinks."

"Yeah. Sounds good."

Judy, Johnny and me go to the bar we went to last night. "Keep your tits in, Ma," Johnny says as we're going in.

"Sometimes," Judy says, "you're no fun at all."

Johnny orders a massive paella for all of us. Chicken, tiger prawns, chorizo, red peppers, onion, peas, ham, tomatoes, mussels with garlic bread and white wine.

On the way home, Judy says, "I know, Johnny. Let's show Frank that house."

"What house?"

"You know," she says.

He does a sharp U-turn, cars tooting at him, he takes no notice, and speeds off in the opposite direction. Takes a few dives around back streets and then slows down until he reaches a villa set back behind a small garden.

It's like all the other houses and villas in Murcia. White. Path weaving through a nice garden – if you like gardens. Me, I can take 'em or leave 'em. A few plants and flowers in pots dotted about in pebbles and gravel. The villa's not as big as the one we visited when I first got here a couple of days ago, the one Judy tried to pass off as her own.

"There," Judy says.

"There what?"

"That's the place."

"Judy," I say, "what you goin' on about?"

"That," she says as if I'm supposed to know, "is where Sebastian Galliano lives."

"Who is Sebastian Galliano?"

She lights a cigarette, hands it to Johnny, lights another, takes a long drag. She don't offer me one.

"When I can get it, I do a bit of interpreting. Sebastian's a lovely bloke and all that, but he's nicking work off of me. He's undercutting me. He's slagging me off to customers. He's a no good fucking bastard. I hate

316

him. So, Frank, I want you to do me a favour."

"What's that?"

"I want you," she says, "to burn this – this – this *shack* down."

"For a minute there," I say, "I thought you said, 'Burn it down'."

"Well, maybe not burn it down," she says. "A petrol bomb would do the job."

I'm sitting in the back of this car, my mouth's dropped wide open.

"Well," she says, "what about it?"

I light a fag. Take a long drag. Make her wait. "Turn it in, Judy, you can't go around doin' stuff like that."

"Come on, Johnny," she says, as if I've not spoken. "What you waiting for? Let's go home."

When we get back to *their* shack, I get out the car and turn to walk to the *pension*.

But Judy grabs my arm and pulls me towards the door. "Come on, Frank. Nightcap time."

Already, that pack of dogs of hers are barking their heads off, Johnny's unlocking the front door and, before I know it, she's shoved me in. She lets me go, switches on the lights, opens the patio doors and the dogs rush out into the garden, jumpin' up and down as if they've never been in a garden before. Johnny's gone to the bathroom.

"What'll it be?" she says, going to the drinks.

"Beer," I say, sitting down, lighting up.

"So," she says, handing me a can, "are we in business?"

"It depends on my connections in London," I say.

"They'll be all right with it."

"They might be," I say. "They might not. It ain't my decision. There's a lot to work out." I reel off a list: overheads, labour, transportation, shipping costs, packaging, distribution, profit margins, pay-offs.

By now, Johnny's back in the room and he's listening to what I'm saying. "He's right, Ma. We gotta let Frank do his job. He knows what he's doin'."

A couple of the dogs rush into the room.

"'Allo, Buster, wotcha, Rusty," Judy says, tickling their ears. "What you got there?"

Buster's got a slice of steak in his mouth and he's growling and shaking it like he's caught a rabbit and he's killing it. Rusty's crouched down on the floor, slobberin' and chewin' away at something else.

"Looks like a bit of liver," I say, smiling. It's always nice to see a mutt eatin' grub, doin' dog things.

She takes a bit of meat from Rusty's mouth and inspects it. "No... I think it's kidney."

"Ha! Ha!" I laugh. "You got a steak and kidney pie tree in your garden?"

"Course not," Judy says. "That's Archie."

"Pet rabbit?" I ask.

"Archie ain't a rabbit," she says.

"Well," Johnny chuckles, "could've bin. He did have whiskers and big floppy ears."

"And his prick was just as hard to find!" Judy guffaws, spilling her wine.

"So who's Archie?" I ask.

"*Was*, Frank, *was*," she says. "Archie was my husband."

"And my old man," Johnny chimes in.

I shift about in my chair. I look at Judy. I look at Johnny. I give a little laugh. Sounds nervous so I draw on my fag. "Um... What d'ya mean?"

Judy shakes her head. "I don't know how I can make it clearer, Frank. Archie was my husband. But he ain't no more. I'm a widow. I thought you knew."

"Well, I knew you didn't have a fella," I say. "But I didn't know he was dead."

"I killed him," she says.

"*We* killed him," Johnny adds.

"You mean, *you* killed him."

"*We* killed him."

"No, we didn't. You did."

"We did."

"Judy!" I yell from what feels like another planet.

318

"What the fuck are you two talkin' about?"

"The slob had been on *another* bender," she says, rolling her eyes like she's bored of telling the same story for the ninety-ninth time. "He'd been gone for three weeks and when he came home, he was pissed. I mean, *pissed*! You could smell it a bloody mile off. When he came in, I was as mad as hell. I was shouting at him, calling him everything under the sun and he took it. Laughing his head off. He could hardly stand.

"And I lost it, Frank, I lost it. I thumped him and I thumped him some more. Soon I was punching the fuck out of him. I couldn't stop. He fell over and was lying on the floor – "

Johnny takes over. "I came out of my bedroom to see what was going on and, well, how shall I put it… I joined in. I jumped up and down on his knee-caps – "

"Didn't Archie put up a fight?" I asked, hypnotised by what I was hearing. I mean, I've heard some stuff in my time. Even done it. I gave my fair share to that boy in the showers in Aylesbury. But he was a kiddy-fiddler. He weren't a drunk on a three-week bender. For Chrissake, I went on a three-week bender, didn't I? But Sandy rescued me. She didn't punch my eyes in. She didn't jump on my knees. Sandy rescued me.

"Oh no," Johnny says, "course he didn't."

"Couldn't," Judy says. "I was holdin' him down so Johnny could have a good go at him."

"You weren't holdin' him down, Ma," Johnny says. "You were stranglin' him."

"To begin with, yeah," she says, "I was. But I wasn't strong enough to finish him off. So I got a cushion – that one you're sitting on, Frank."

I lean forward and pull out from behind me a large orange cushion. It's got a picture of a sunflower on it. I hold it up.

"That's the one," Johnny says. "Good cushion, that."

"You suffocated him with this?" I say.

"In the end, yeah," Judy says, looking into her empty

wineglass, wiping an eye. "Had no choice. Poor sod."

We stare at the cushion in silence. Like it's a Kalashnikov or something.

I'm holding a murder weapon in my hands.

Judging by the state of it, it hasn't been cleaned since. Like everything in this place. It's covered in hairs – probably dog hairs, or even Archie's – and, when I look closely, there's a few bite marks as well. Again, could be from the dogs or Archie.

I feel like I'm holding the actual body. I sniff it from a safe distance. Smells dirty, unclean. That's 'cos it is. If that'd bin me, I'd've washed it, or better, got rid of it. I mean, it's a murder weapon, for Chrissake. You don't leave a murder weapon lying around the place, waiting for the Old Bill to find it, do some tests and arrest you.

They don't care, that's the top and bottom of it. They do not bloody care.

Rusty gets up from chewing whichever part of Archie he's got, strolls over and sniffs the cushion. But he's not very interested. He licks his lips and walks off into the garden. Buster leaves his steak and follows him.

I'm still holding the cushion. I don't know what to do with it. I mean, I can't put it back behind me, can I? I can't sit on it. I can't put it next to me – it'd be like cosying up to it. I don't want it near me.

I get up. "Mind if I get a drink?" I don't want one. I wanna throw up.

"Help yourself," Johnny says.

"They were selling them cushions off cheap, weren't they?" Judy says.

"You're right, Ma. They were. Six euros."

"I thought it was five."

"Could a bin," Johnny says. "To be honest, I can't remember." He gives a little laugh and lights up. "'S always the same, innit? It's only when you do something like this, you find out how hard it is. One thing to snuff a body out. Somethin' else to get rid of it once the body's been snuffed."

"What a night that was," Judy says like she's fondly remembering a wild beach party with friends she hasn't seen for a few years and everyone gets sozzled and has sex with whoever's up for it and then they go to an all-night café for an egg, bacon, tomato and mushroom fry-up.

"What did you do?" I ask, pouring a beer, finding another chair, lighting a fag.

"Well," Judy says, taking a deep breath, "first thing I did was make a cup of tea. It's thirsty work. Until you actually do it, you don't appreciate how much effort you have to put into it. The killin', I mean" – she laughs – "not makin' the cup of tea." She laughs again. "Then" – another deep breath – "we stripped him, of course, and dragged him into the garden – "

" – and chopped him up."

"'Though," Judy says, "you did the chopping. I did the cleaning… Oh, Frank, there was blood everywhere. You should have seen it! The dogs helped a little bit but I think the booze in Archie's blood put them off. O' course, not only the blood but the shit and piss. What a stink! Do you remember, Johnny?"

"Course I remember, Ma! It was only three months ago, for Chrissake. Do you think I'd forget something like cutting my dad into pieces and burying him in the garden?"

"Didn't take long, though."

"Nah," Johnny says. "Shoulda dug a deeper hole. The dogs wouldn't a got at him so easy, then."

They don't speak for a while.

I don't utter a word. Not a fucking word. What can I say? I don't wanna be there. I don't feel I can get up and go. I don't wanna know any more. I can't tell 'em to shut up. I'm not a big bloke. Never have been. Never bin a problem before. But now, right at this very minute, I know, between 'em, they could do to me what they already done to Archie.

"Anyway," Judy says at last, "we didn't bury *all* of him in the garden, did we?"

"No, you're right," Johnny sighs.

Judy turns to me. "We tried barbecuing him. But the dogs didn't like it." She shrugs. "Again, I think it was the booze that did it. If they had've, we'd've cooked the whole lot." She shrugs again. "Would a saved us a wodge in dog food. Then all we'd've had to do was get rid of the bones. That would've bin easy enough. But there you go." She looks away, through the doors on to the garden. "So now he's out there."

Johnny gets another drink, hands one to Judy and looks at me, raises his eyebrows.

"Not for me, thanks," I say. I make a big show of looking at my watch. "Is that the time?" I jump up, hoping I don't sound too keen to get out of there. "Gotta go! Plane to catch in the mornin'."

"But you ain't got a flight booked," Judy says, not moving.

"That's okay," I say. "I'll get the next available seat."

"Johnny'll drive you to the airport, won't you, Johnny?"

"Course."

"I'm gonna be up early," I say. "In fact," I add, making another show of looking at my watch, "it's so late now, probably not worth going to bed. I might go the airport as soon as it's light." I make my way to the door. "Pack, you know, get a taxi. No, it's all right, Johnny. It's bin a long day, all that driving – "

Three or four dogs come in. Not the ones from before. Different ones.

"Well," Judy says, getting up, "if you're sure... "

"I'm sure," I say, opening the door. "I'll be in touch. See ya, Johnny."

"See ya, mate."

As I close the door, I hear them talking. I don't hang around to listen. I just wanna be as far away from them as possible. By the time I've walked back to the *pension* and packed my gear, it's nearly five o'clock, the sun's starting to come up. So I ask the woman who runs the place, in my own fumbling way, to get me a taxi.

I'm in England by noon and home two or three hours later. Thank Christ for that. I've decided not to bother Melv with Judy's proposition. I don't care a fuck how good the drugs are or what money we can make out of it. I don't want anything more to do with that woman. She walks into some old guy's villa to steal his paintings. She asks me to petrol-bomb some other guy. She gets her husband and – and –

No, I don't want anything to do with that slag, that slut, that tart, that murderer, that… that –

I tell Sandy things didn't work out. I tell her nothing else. I don't want her involved. The less she knows, the better.

"Good," she says. "It's for the best."

A week later, Judy's on the phone.

"Haven't heard from you yet, Frank. Is the deal in place?"

"Not yet," I say. "Still arranging meetings. Takes time."

"Well, hurry up. Can't sit around here all day waiting for you to pull your finger out."

"I'll let you know when it's sorted."

As I say, I don't do a thing about it.

A week after that, here she is, on the phone again.

"I'm fed up of waiting. Why is it taking so fucking long?"

"It ain't, Judy. I can't rush these people. They're very busy."

"Gimme their fucking numbers. I'll give 'em very fucking busy."

"It don't work like that," I tell her. "You've gotta be patient."

"Look, Frank," she says. "If you don't get this sorted, I'll come over there and punch your fucking lights out. You're not gonna fuck me about. Get a fucking move on."

A week after *that*, she calls again, going off on one.

"No!" I shout down the line. "Stop callin' me! I don't

323

want no more to do with it, Judy, or you."

"Hah!" she bawls in my ear. "I'll tell you when you don't want no more to do with it. I fucking decide, not you." She slams down the phone.

Next day, she rings again. When I see her number come up, I let it ring until she gives up.

Day after, the same.

After four more days of this, every day, I've had enough. It's obvious she's completely lost the plot. And she means what she said about doing me in.

"Sandy," I say, "I've gotta stop her."

"All I want," Sandy says, "is a nice, quiet life with the man I love. Do what you have to."

This bloke I've known for years, Roger Insall, works for the *Sunday People*. In fact, now I think about it, I've known Roger most of my life. We met as schoolkids at the Thomas Ellwood School and grew up together. He wasn't one of my gang and he didn't go around with us. While I was training to be a safe-cracker, he was training to be a reporter on the local rag, the *Hoddesdon and Broxbourne Mercury*. Whenever me and the boys were up in court, he'd be writing up the cases. It didn't take him long to get on to the nationals and then the Sundays, first the *News of the World* and now the *Sunday People*.

Now he's one of their top reporters. Spends of a lot of his time working undercover, going after paedos, criminals, bent coppers. That sort of thing.

It was Roger who, eight years ago, exposed the so-called Bishop of Medway, Roger Gleaves, as a paedophile who raped two fourteen-year-old boys. My old schoolmate was a key witness in the case and got Gleaves put away for fifteen years.

A couple of years ago, Roger exposed Warwick Spinks in the *Sunday People* for kidnapping and trafficking young boys and selling them as sex slaves.

Last year, he posed as a hitman to catch Shelley Molyneux, a woman from Essex who was planning to murder her husband for his money. Roger wrote it up in the *Sunday People*, she was arrested, he gave evidence and she got five years.

But wherever Roger goes and whatever he does, wherever I go and whatever I do, we always keep in touch. Mostly by phone, I have to say, 'cos we're in different places, doing different things, but, all the same, we don't lose our connection.

So I give him a call.

"Roger, I've got a bit of a problem. I need your help. You'll have to come down."

He comes down. 'Cos he knows, if I'm involved with something and I tell him about it, there's a story for him.

"What's going on?" he says, sitting in my front room, sipping a cuppa.

I haven't seen him for a few years but he ain't changed. My height, perma-tanned, dripping with a gold medallion and bracelets, teddy boy quiff.

It's good – no, it's a relief – to see him.

I tell him all about Judy. The drugs, the murder, how she and Johnny chopped Archie up and how she was threatening me. "She's gotta be stopped, you know."

"We'll stop her."

Just then, my mobile rings. Bloody 'ell, it's her, ain't it. This time, I answer it. "I can't talk now," I say. I wave Roger over. We hunch over the phone so he can hear. Thinking quick, I say, "Judy, I'm in a meeting with my people right now talking deals. I'll have to call you back."

"Make sure you fucking do," she hollers. "'Cos if you fucking don't, I'll fucking come over there and fucking hack your fucking brains out and fucking gouge your fucking heart out and fucking feed you to the fucking ducks in fucking Regent's Park. Got that?"

I put down the phone and stare at Roger, who's shaking his head like he don't believe what he heard.

"She's off her head," I tell him. "She's gotta be stopped."

"Leave it to me, Frank," he says. "Make us another pot o' tea, eh, while I make a few calls."

It takes me five minutes to make another brew but Roger's on the phone for about an hour, first to someone called Mark, then someone called Cubby. All this time, I'm lighting him fags and pouring him cups of tea that he lets go cold, then throws back in one gulp. Then he's back to Mark, then back to Cubby.

At last, he switches off his phone and drinks some more tea. "Where's your bathroom?"

When he comes out, he says, "What we'll do, we'll fly over and we'll have her. Cubby and me'll pose as your – "

"Cubby?"

"My photographer. We'll be your London dealers. Once you've – "

"So who's Mark?"

"My editor. As I say, Frank, once you've introduced Cubby and me to her, leave it to us. We'll do the rest. I'll book the flights and hotel. You, me and Cubby'll talk while we're waiting at the airport."

Four days later, we're in a really nice hotel in Murcia. At the time agreed, Judy and Johnny come into Reception, we find some seats up a corner, I introduce everybody, we shake hands and sit down.

"Right," says Roger, "let's get down to business. We ain't here for a holiday. Now Frank here is the go-between. We're the men with the spondoolicks, not him. We've got to be sure you're the genuine article. So what we're going to do is this. We've booked a couple of meeting-rooms and you, Johnny, are going in one room with Cubby to go over things while you, Judy, are going in another room with me and we do the same."

"Why's that then?" Johnny says.

"Look, son," Roger says, "if you can get the stuff like you say you can, we've got to be sure it's all kosher. We don't deal with amateurs, we're serious businessmen. We like to know who we're dealing with. If we're going into business with you, we – "

"Yeah, yeah," Judy says. "Understood. What's Frank gonna be doing?"

"He can do what the fuck he likes," Roger says.

So I say, "I'll get something to eat."

Roger looks at me and says, "Well, fuck off then. I'll call you when we're done."

Pretending to be miffed over how he speaks to me, I get up, leave the hotel and find a lovely place to eat.

I start with a delicious octopus and shrimp salad, washed down with a Brut Nature Cava. Then it's roasted rack of lamb done in the Murcian style – whatever that means, but that's what it says on the menu – with vegetables and a tasty white wine from Rueda Verdejo, some region in Spain. For sweet, I have tiramisu with rum cream. And then coffee, chocolates and a couple of smokes. 78 euros the lot, all in. Not bad, eh?

Half an hour after I've left the restaurant and had a mosey about, my mobile rings. It's Roger. "We're done. Get yourself here."

When I get back to the hotel, the four of 'em are sitting where I left 'em.

Roger says to me, "She's told us everything, so has he." He unzips his holdall, pulls out a tape-recorder, re-winds a few seconds and switches it on.

Oh, don't worry about that. He's fucking all chopped up, no-one will ever find him. Don't worry. He's in little bits.

It's Judy's voice.

Then Cubby pulls up his holdall, dives in and holds up his video camera. "Gotcha!" he says to Johnny. Then he gets out a still camera, aims it at the two of 'em and snaps a couple of pictures.

"What's going on?" Judy says, not moving.

"Listen, you silly cow," Roger says. "We're from the *Sunday People*. You're exposed. It'll be in next Sunday's paper. Then you'll be nicked." He stands up, turns to Cubby and me and says, "C'm' on, let's go."

Cubby and me get up. We don't even look round. We pick up our bags, jump into a taxi, go straight to the airport and fly back home.

327

Sure enough, five days later, it's on the front page of the *Sunday People*. Roger hands over his files to the cops who contact the Spanish Old Bill. They arrest Judy and Johnny. Johnny gets three months for assault. Judy gets fifteen years for murder and desecrating a dead body.

That's sick, that is.

Chapter 16. France

"You see, Melv," I say, "it's like this."

"What's up, Frank?"

I'm sitting in Melv's office. Last time we met he was in a smart suit. And now he's got an office, for God's sake. We're smoking a couple of joints. Haven't seen him for a few months and I thought he'd forgotten all about me but no, here we are.

"Look Melv," I say, "I need some money, like *fast*. I'm stoney broke."

"I thought," he says, "you'd found fame and fortune with some minge in Portugal."

"Spain."

"Beautiful country," he says, drawing on his spliff.

I tell him all about Judy Munrow. "You might've read about it in the papers."

"Was that you?" he gasps. "You were the unidentified lover boy?"

"'Cept I wasn't her lover boy. There was nothin' goin' on between us. It was a strictly business relationship."

"Of course it was," he laughs. "If you say so." He laughs again. "'Well, from what you say, it was probably for the best."

"It was not a good time, Melv," I tell him. "Not a good time at all... But the thing is, the thing is, I was depending on that to bankroll me, to set myself up with some kinda pension, you know? Didn't work out. So much it didn't work out, I ain't got a pot to piss in."

"Is that so, Frank? Is that so?"

"Yeah, that is so," I say. I decide to go for it. There's no point in beating about the fucking bush, is there? "Look, Melv, I don't mind fuckin' off to Belgium, pickin' cocaine up and bringin' it back if the price is right."

"Commission only."

I take a gulp.

"I'm not putting you on my payroll, Frank," Melv says.

"You've got too much form. You're too well known. Not good for business. Commission only."

Not what I'd hoped for. Still, beggars can't be choosers. I nod. "Okay."

Despite what Melv's just said, he offers a good rate. We shake on it and he promises to be in touch in a few days' time.

True to his word, he calls later in the week with the collection details and I'm off. It's a doddle, really, 'cos the blokes in Belgium are there waiting with the package at the pick-up point and I'm back in London within a few hours. Melv pays me my commission so, after a dozen trips, less petrol, I'm raking in some good earners.

After two or three months, Melv's got me going to Holland and France as well as Belgium. I'm doing a couple of trips every week. I tell him I'll do more if he wants.

"The fuzz'll get suspicious if you do any more," he says. "Twice a week's fine."

I know what he means. I get the ferry, go over, buy loads of booze and bundle it in the back of my estate. Then, on the way back to the ferry, I make a short detour, pick up the kilo of coke and pack it under the bonnet. It's packed well in, like I'm keeping the engine warm. When I get to the border, the gendarmes see the boxes piled up in the back and they wave me through.

If I do that seven days a week, they're gonna get suspicious. As it's often the same gendarmes who wave me through, I get to recognise them. And if I recognise *them*, they're gonna recognise me, aren't they, and it ain't gonna take 'em too long to figure that no-one buys that much booze 'cos he likes to party. As I say, they're gonna get suspicious.

So Melv's right. Twice a week's fine. If the weather's good, it's a nice day out. If it isn't, then I think of the money.

I ask Sandy if she wants to come along for the ride but she's having no part of it.

"Bad enough what you're doin'," she says, "without gettin' me involved."

* * * * *

It's a scorching day in July and I've parked the motor in the hovercraft car park at Calais, ready to go back to Dover. I've decided to take the hover 'cos there's queues and queues of holiday makers, screaming kids and God knows who else going the same way and it's always best to mix in with civvies if you can. Chances of getting noticed aren't so great that way.

It's gonna be another two hours, I reckon, before anything moves so I sit there for a while and light up a joint. Get halfway through it when I need a piss. Can't get my todger out there and then so I leave the other half of the joint smoking in the ashtray, get out, lock up and stroll across to the toilets.

When I come out, I sit on a bench, take in a few rays, breath in some fresh air, or what passes for fresh air in a car park like this, what with petrol fumes, diesel fumes, people smoking wherever they like, Christ knows what else. My eyes start drooping, my heads nods. I fan my shirt about, pull out my hanky, wipe my face. It's hot.

It is so fucking hot.

A dog barks.

How the hell has it got the strength to bark in this heat? If I were a dog, I'd lie down in the shade and be quiet. I wouldn't bark my bollocks off.

On and on it goes, making enough noise to wake a dead pharaoh in an undiscovered tomb.

I open my eyes and see it jumping up at a motor. The mutt is fucking enormous. Although it's a German Shepherd, from here it looks bigger than Smiffy, that Doberman that went berserk in Sean Underwood's scrap metal yard all them years ago.

At the same time as all the barking and yapping, his handler, a gendarme who obviously plays rugger in his spare time, is shouting at the top of his voice to anyone who'll listen, *"De quelle voiture? De quelle voiture?"*

For fuck's sake, it's my *voiture*, ain't it? It's my bleedin' motor the animal is jumping up at.

Okay, all right, Frank, let's meet this head on. Keep calm, don't let 'em see you in the least anxious or worried about what's going on. You know, make it appear like you're innocent.

So I stroll over, casual like. "What's going on? This is my motor."

"Pull it over there," the gendarme says in a perfect English public school accent. "Pull it over there."

He points to a separate parking bay, calms the hound down and talks into his walkie-talkie. All at the same time. I can tell he's done this before.

As I'm driving over and parking, seven French coppers wearing shades and navy blue berets, all of 'em carrying guns, appear from nowhere, like they've materialised from the USS Enterprise, Captain Kirk following close behind.

I get out and stand back. They get the dog in the motor, in the back of the motor, every bloody where in the motor. Then it's barking again, this time even louder than before. This time, it wakes the Valley of the Kings, mummified pharaohs are wandering around, complaining they've been disturbed from three thousand years' sleep.

The cops move round to the bonnet.

I start to sweat, hoping it don't show. I play it cool. I go over to look at the dog. But I stand well clear. To be honest, it's a beautiful thing even if it's bigger than the Hound of the Baskervilles.

"What's its name?" I say to the mountain handler.

"Lucy."

"*Lucy?*"

"What is wrong with Lucy?"

"Nothing," I say. "Lucy… Yeah. Lucy is good. Thought it'd be Hulk or Hunk or Smiffy – "

"*Smiffy?*"

Two of the cops with the shades are busy emptying the

rear end of the estate, piling the crates of beer on the tarmac, pulling up the floor where the spare tyre and jack are kept. Another two are rummaging about in the inside.

One of 'em jumps out. "Ah-ha!" He's holding something up in the air.

Lucy, her handler and me walk over and take a look. It's the half-smoked joint I left in the ashtray.

"Is this yours?"

"Yeah, it's mine," I say. "It's a joint. Fuck me, you can't nick me for smoking a joint."

They've wasted the best part of an hour searching my motor and all they come up with is a half-smoked joint. All of 'em except Lucy and her gendarme walk away without another word, leaving *me* to load the booze back into the boot.

When I've done that, Lucy's gendarme says, "Come with me."

We go into the toilet block, he flushes the joint away, takes me back to my motor and says, "Go. You can go."

I don't say a word. I get in, drive on to the ferry and I'm away with the two kilos still stashed under the bonnet. I can't believe it. I thought I was done, I thought I was on my way to a French prison. When I get to Dover a couple of hours later and I'm waved through without so much as a nod, I know I'm safe.

And that's that. Well, it is this time. Frank, I tell myself, watch it. Be careful.

The thing is, though, it's worth the risk.

A kilo of coke is worth £350 when it leaves Colombia. Street values in London price that same kilo at fifty grand. I'm bringing in two kilos a time. Melv pays me 5% a kilo of the street value. So for every trip I make, I gather in five grand less travel costs, which are nothing, really, when you think about it. *And* I get to keep the booze.

As I say, I do two trips a week. That's ten grand a week for driving over, buying a few crates of beer and collecting the merchandise. I reckon that's bloody good. Doin' all right. Worth the chocolate biscuit.

But then, just shows, dunnit, you shouldn't take your luck for granted. Just when you think things are goin' your way, Fate steps in and gives you a bash on the nut up a blind alley. Shoulda read the signs, matey, shoulda read the signs.

'Cos, a couple o' weeks later, I'm coming back into Dover and they spin the motor, they really spin the motor and I'm thinking, bloody hell, what's goin' on here, then?

"Next time," he says, "we'll fucking go right over this."

Shoulda listened.

There is a next time.

Always is, always a bleedin' next time.

Next time, this particular day, my instructions say the merchandise is hidden in an underpass along the D127 outside Calais. I get there all right enough. No probs. I park in a little lay-by on the opposite side of the road, in front of two battered Transit vans. Their windows are blacked out.

Now, I don't care what anyone else tells ya, that's the Old Bill – or *les keufs*, as our French cousins have it. I know it is. I can smell the Old Bill a mile off. They've got their cameras in there. They're filming me. I know they are.

What do I do? What the fuck do I do?

I light a fag. That's what I do. I sit there, smoking a fag, having a think. Do I drive off without the parcel? If I do, that's not only that gone for a burton but everything else as well. That's everything finished. Finito. Kaput. Do I drive away and come back later? No point. They'll still be there. Not an option.

Do I get out, get the drugs and drive off?

What's the worst that can happen?

Oh, what the hell. Fuck it.

I get out and walk over the road.

There's a lot of old vegetation and weeds, Christ knows what else, a supermarket trolley, piles of stinkin' dog shit, used condoms, used needles, other rubbish. But there it is, a box of booze, waiting for me to take it away.

I pick it up, put it on my shoulder, walk back to my motor, put it in with the rest of the booze, drive off and get the ferry.

No-one stops me.

When I get into Dover, I'm queuing right at the very back and I sit there, seein' 'em head straight for me.

"You," the Customs bloke says, "front of the queue. You're being searched."

They direct me past all the others, into a parking bay. As soon as I've stopped and before I can even switch the engine off and get out, they've opened the boot and they're in. They know exactly which box to open. Fourteen boxes I've got on board and they go straight to it. One of 'em opens it.

"It's on!" he shouts so the whole of bloody Dover and the rest of bleedin' Kent can hear. "It's on!"

He keeps on shouting it. "It's on! It's on! It's on!" He pulls the cocaine out and holds it up.

Strike me, he's off again. "It's on! It's on! It's on!"

I mean, how many times does he have to say it? Ain't once enough?

The Customs officer who's standing next to me says, "You're nicked, son. You are well and truly fucking nicked."

They take me back to Dover nick, lock me up 'til my solicitor gets here.

"Frank, you got a choice," he says. "If you go not guilty, you'll get a nine or ten. But you can't do that, can you?"

"Not really," I say. "They got me, didn't they?"

"If you go guilty, here and now, you'll draw a six. Simple as that. What's it to be?"

The way I figure it is, I'm in Dover and the court for Dover is Canterbury. Canterbury, believe it or not, sees drugs cases day in, day out, 'cos everybody nicked at Dover for drugs goes straight to Canterbury. Plus you get the people who actually live in Canterbury going to Canterbury court as well. So drugs ain't unusual for them on the bench.

If I go guilty and save the court time, they knock a third off the sentence. Fuck me, Moses, I don't want a nine stuck up my bollocks. So if they give me a six and I behave myself, I'm out in three with probation for the other three.

So I go guilty. My solicitor said I've got a choice. Well, I haven't, have I?

That's what you get for wanting money fast. I wanted it fast and that was my mistake.

I'm put on remand – don't get bail on a charge like that – and taken off to Elmley Prison on the Isle of Sheppey.

Sandy, bless her, is heartbroken. But she don't let me down. She visits me every week without fail, come rain or shine. She tries to smile all the time she's with me but, now and then... you know.

"I've got your dressing-gown and pyjamas by our bed, Frank," she says, "ready for when you come home."

Seven months later, they haul me up to Canterbury Crown Court where, sure enough, I get a six and I'm shipped off to Maidstone Prison.

After about eighteen months there, I'm on the gardens, wandering around watering all the grass, and a screw comes up to me and says, "Come on, Frank, put that watering-can down. You're moving."

"What dya mean?" I say. "I've got a fucking visit this afternoon."

"Tough," he says. "You're moving. Grab your belongings, you're moving. Like right now."

They move the whole wing out. God knows how many police buses and God knows what, Black Marias, whatever you call 'em, they've got, but they're loading every prisoner on. Nobody's got any idea where they're going. I don't know and they don't tell us. They don't tell us nothing.

Turns out, the reason for the mass evacuation is because the wing has developed Legionnaire's Disease in the water system, in the showers. So they have to evacuate everybody.

We're in this coach for I don't know how long. We end up in Dovegate. That's Derbyshire. Fuck me, I ain't gonna get no visits up here.

But the next day, I kid you not, Sandy's here, visiting me.

And from there, I get put in the worst poxiest place you can imagine. Belmarsh. It's got a prison in there within another prison. Belmarsh is the only prison you don't fuck around in. You don't backchat the screws 'cos they run that gaff and woe betide you if you think any different 'cos they won't have no backchat and they won't take no fuckin' around either.

The thing is they're dealing with some serious fuckers in there. They're dealing with bombers, fuckin' terrorists, fuck knows what. So they gotta be like that.

The days of the true villain in a prison – people like me – have gone. That's all in the past. Dinosaurs, the lot of us. Now, terrorists, rapists, paedos, psychos, fuckin' God knows what else are in there. Different ballgame. It really is.

After three months in Belmarsh, I put in to be re-categorised. I know I stand a good chance 'cos they want Belmarsh free for them other nutters.

The SO calls me down and says, "Peters, you got D Cat. You're going to Standford Hill."

That's the Isle of Sheppey.

Lovely!

It's summer. Open prisons are fantastic in the summer. Not so clever in the winter, o' course. But it ain't winter yet. It's summer. And once I'm back on the island, I don't want for nothin'.

I meet up with Ned, a mate of mine who's finishing off a twenty. Lovely, lovely bloke. But he's done too much bird because, when he gets out, he gets himself nicked again. He's done way too much bird. Can't live without it. Don't know what else to do.

After a while, I'm allowed home for four days at a time

– Friday, Saturday, Sunday, Monday. Which makes me keep my nose clean. 'Cos if they know I fuck about with drugs, I lose everything and I'm shoved right back to where I started.

I don't wanna do that. Not now I've got Sandy.

So I keep my nose clean.

Chapter 17. Home

2006, I get the six.

2009, I'm out on three years' supervision.

When I get out, Sandy's waiting in the car with her son. I walk through the Standford Hill turnstile gate and we go home.

It's lovely. Sandy's got us a new bungalow, 'cos of the neighbours at the old one, and, when we get there, it's clean and shining and she cooks us a terrific meal.

We sit and talk.

I tell 'em I'm not going to clown around any more. I just want to settle down, behave, and be normal. Be fuckin' normal, for Chrissake. Stop coming up with fuckin' stupid ideas of how to make money.

'Cos there's no way I'm gonna hurt Sandy or leave her on her own again. I would never do that. Not now.

Plus, my beautiful, beautiful little grand-daughter. I absolutely adore her, can't be away from her. Not like I was away for my children. Last week, I took her to Winter Wonderland and it was absolute magic. Her little face lit up when we were in there. It was a great night, it really was. But that's what life's about now.

* * * * *

I never had a family life. I didn't know what being part of a family was all about. But Sandy shared her family with me and made me feel part of her family and it's been unbelievable. I've calmed down a bit but it's been hard work, because for so many years I was footloose and fancy free, drinking, drugs, whatever. That was my life – that, and thieving, o' course. And to come into a family that's completely and utterly straight and all the people round you are straight, it's been hard work for me. Really hard. You see, when you're with a villain, you talk your own language. But talking to straight people is very different.

339

Very hard. And I still find it hard.

Sandy turned my life round completely. When she took me on, I had fuck all, nothing, and I didn't have nothing to offer her. But that didn't bother her.

And that is love, true love. It's a tremendous thing.

I owe Sandy and her family everything. They accept me.

So, all I can say is, thanks, Sandy. Without you, I'd be dead.

No two ways about that. I was drinking myself into oblivion, just to shut down. When I was with her to begin with, I didn't think it was gonna work. I thought, "What am I doing here?" But I thought a lot about it and today, I idolise her. I think the world of her.

Believe you me, if you've got Sandy on your side, you've got a fucking good partner. She won't let you down. If she says she'll be there, she's there. If she says she's going to do something for you, she does it. She's that sort of person. She's amazing.

Sandy taught me how to live on the proper side of life, what a family means and what being wrapped around a family means. I never had none of this... none of it. When I met Sandy, I was totally wild, with the booze, the dope – all the lot of it. She calmed me down. She talked to me. Most of all, she listened. To me.

'Cos I've got the best woman in the world, I don't want for anything. The days of looking for the big money are over. And the rest of it. I don't wanna know.

And I certainly don't wanna see any more fuckin' prisons, that's for sure. I'm 63. I've spent fifteen years in prison and twelve years on probation. That means I've spent a quarter of my life locked up. And where did it get me? *Where did it get me?* Nowhere. That's where.

I'm not a villain no more. I don't get involved in anything any more. I don't wanna be. Fuckin' gangsters, fuckin' tearaways and all the rest of it. I've had it.

You see, the trouble is, when you get people like me go up in courts, we don't stand a chance, because they don't talk months with us, they talk years because of our records. I'm not gambling with that. Can't afford it. No way can I gamble any more years away. My life would be fucked and there's no way I'm gonna go through that.

* * * * *

I've had some good times. I've enjoyed myself. I lived life to the full and I took what life threw at me. But would I do it again? I don't know. I honestly don't know.

I think a lot of it has to do with the surroundings you're brought up in. And how you're brought up. I was brought up with pikeys and Borstal boys – nearly all of 'em around us were ex-Borstal boys, pikeys or one thing or another. I think environment plays a big part. If you're going out to work and half the fuckers are nicking this and nicking that, it don't take long for you to think, I'll have some of that. That's how it was. And then you think that's what everyone does. So you carry on like that.

* * * * *

These days, living the quiet life at home, if I've learnt anything, it's this.

Finally and after everything – and a lot more besides – I've found something I never had before.

Something it's taken me this long to understand is the only thing in my life I ever wanted.

Someone who's good and kind and cares about me.

Sandy.

THE END